Regent's Study (
General Editor: Pau

God and the Art of Seeing

Visual Resources for a Journey of Faith

Regent's Study Guides

God and the Art of Seeing

Visual Resources for a Journey of Faith

Richard Kidd
Graham Sparkes

Regent's Park College, Oxford
with
Smyth & Helwys Publishing, Inc.
Macon, Georgia

© 2003
Published by Regent's Park College, Oxford OX1 2LB, UK
in association with Smyth & Helwys Publishing, 6316 Peake Road,
Macon, GA 31210, USA

God and the Art of Seeing: Visual Resources for a Journey of Faith

Library of Congress Cataloging-in-Publication Data

Kidd, Richard, 1950-
God and the art of seeing : visual resources for a journey of faith /
Richard Kidd & Graham Sparkes.
p. cm. (Regent's study guides; 11)
Includes index.
ISBN (USA) 1-57312-413-3
ISBN (UK) 0-9518104-9-9
1. Christianity and art. 2. Painting–Appreciation.
I. Sparkes, Graham, 1955-
II. Title. III. Series.
BR115.A8 K53 2003
246–dc22
2003013212

To all those creative artists who,
at immense personal cost,
have enabled us to see more clearly
God's elusive presence
in the world around us.

Contents

Acknowledgements

Grateful thanks are offered to the Galleries, Museums and Collectors who have given permission for the reproduction of the paintings within this book and on its cover. They are listed in the Gallery Catalogue which follows these Acknowledgements, and all their rights are recognized.

Excerpts from *Words and Images of Edvard Munch* by Bente Torjusen ©1986 Bente Torjusen are printed by kind permission of the publishers, Thames and Hudson, London. Texts by Edvard Munch © Oslo Kommunes Kunstsamlinger.

Excerpts from *Edvard Munch* by Arne Eggum © 1983 J. M. Stenersens Forlag A. S. are printed by kind permission of the publishers, Thames and Hudson, London. Texts by Edvard Munch © Munch Museum, Oslo.

Excerpts from *Munch: His Life and Work* by Reinhold Heller ©1984 John Calmann and Cooper Ltd, London are printed by kind permission of the publishers, the Chicago University Press and John Murray Publishers Ltd, London. Texts by Edvard Munch © Munch Museum, Oslo.

Excerpts from *Munch: The Scream* by Reinhold Heller © 1973 Reinhold Heller are printed by kind permission of the publishers, Allen Lane/ The Penguin Press, London.

An excerpt from the poem 'The Minister' by R. S. Thomas, in *Collected Poems 1945–1990* ©1993 R. S. Thomas is printed by kind permission of the publishers, J. M. Dent, London.

An excerpt from the poem 'The Rowing Endeth' from *The Awful Rowing Towards God* by Anne Sexton ©1975 by Loring Conant, Jr., Executor of the Estate of Anne Sexton. Reprinted by permission of Houghton Mifflin Company. All rights reserved. The poem can also be found in Diane

Preview: Before Entering the Gallery

In the following pages we want you, the reader, to join us on an imaginary tour of an art gallery. It is an unusual gallery since it contains the work of only six artists, and we would like you to think of each chapter as a room dedicated to the work of just one of the artists exhibited. Space is limited. Each room, while containing a number of paintings, is arranged to give prominence to two pictures which have been carefully chosen on account of their potential as a resource for theological reflection.

This book is testimony to a particular experience shared by its authors. We are agreed that both our lives have been immensely enriched by the hours we have spent in galleries. Essentially the experience is one of joy, joy in the presence of visual forms — pictures, sculptures, landscapes, seascapes, cityscapes, and other memorable artefacts. We are saddened, therefore, to find others who seem to know little of this experience. Western Christianity, it seems, has focused so strongly on words, creeds and doctrines, that many Christians have forgotten that the visual image is the primary human experience — we 'look and see' long before we 'speak and hear with understanding'.

We are also agreed that, for us, this joyful experience is of much more than passing significance. Emerging from a good exhibition we feel ourselves to be energized in ways that we cannot distinguish from other moments to which we would attribute 'spiritual' importance, and, over the years, we would recognize many of these moments as notable markers on our 'journeys of faith'.

Perhaps we should make it clear at this point that, if you have come looking in our gallery for pictures depicting well-known 'religious' scenes painted by evidently Christian artists, you will be disappointed. None of our artists makes 'being Christian' a major feature of his or her work; but we are in no doubt that each in some way offers genuinely 'spiritual' insight, which we as Christians need to hear. These really are significant artists and they are continually dealing with themes relevant to our spiritual journeys.

As we have reflected on our own experience, we have come to recognize a profound correspondence between the seeing-skills that can be developed by giving our attention to significant art and those that are essential for the spiritual quest. We conclude that, by letting these two worlds of experience meet and interact, each is greatly deepened and enriched. Our hope is that this book will enable others also to find something of our joy and, especially for those venturing onto new territory, to open up a new resource for their journeys of faith.

Something else we need to make clear at the start of the tour is that neither of us has professional training in art history or art criticism. In all aspects of the world of art, we are no more than enthusiastic and hard-working amateurs. Our training is in theology and by vocation we are Christian ministers. We have needed the encouragement of others to 'go public' with our theological reflections, spanning the boundary between our own and other people's specialisms. We have come to believe, however, that it is important to risk exposure, and we want to encourage others in similar ways. Unless we take some risks of this kind, we all remain isolated in our specialist worlds, and the potential for wonderfully creative links is for ever lost. Non-specialist readers can take comfort that we are rarely tempted to slide into technical language and, when we need to use technical terms, our inclination is to provide brief sketches of the meanings they carry. We are hoping that this book will inspire its readers to do further work of their own along the border between art and theology and, after visiting each room in turn, we offer guidance as to where and how this might be achieved.

Two simple but telling phrases will help to clarify the skills we have found central to our own task, and which we believe are essential in any attempt to bring the worlds of art and theology into creative dialogue. The first, from the disciplines of art itself, is the phrase 'effort of imagination'.[1] The crucial word is 'effort', invariably the price of genuine insight. The effort begins with an artist who, through an imaginative leap, sees the world in a new way and expresses that 'seeing' in a visual form. The effort continues with a viewer who, through a further imaginative leap, finds that the encounter opens other new ways of seeing. Sometimes the viewer sees what the artist also saw, but often this is not the case. As viewers our seeing is shaped by our own context, and becomes significant in further shaping our own future. The two 'efforts of imagination' are in many ways related, but each has a vitality of its own. The point we are making here is that neither of these insights is gained without effort.

Creative theological reflection on works of art will demand an 'effort of imagination' on the part of our readers, and it is well to recognise this as the tour begins.

The second phrase, which surfaces in a variety of disciplines, including theology, is 'effort of attention'. One notable occurrence is in D. H. Lawrence's preface to Harry Crosby's *Chariot of the Sun*, where Lawrence writes: 'The essential quality of poetry is that it makes a new effort of attention and "discovers" a new world within the known world.'[2] What is true of the poet is also true of all serious travellers on the journey of faith. Again the crucial word is 'effort'. Genuine understanding of any 'other' is the fruit of concentrated attention — whether the 'other' is a poem, a painting or a person — and attention of this kind demands effort. In pastoral contexts this phrase is sometimes used to describe the effort that is required to achieve genuine meeting with another person. The principle once grasped, however, is equally applicable to sculptures, pictures and other artefacts. The point is that significant insight, vision, does not arrive 'on a plate'. It requires effort, sometimes an extraordinarily large effort, in order to trigger its release. Pastors and counsellors know how hard it can be to offer this effort of attention to another person and spend many hours seeking to develop the skills they need. A similar effort is needed to give proper attention to a work of art, and this is also a skill that needs practice if it is to develop.

In a book that brings God and art into close proximity, imagination and attention will both be important. Exponents of various spiritual disciplines will not be surprised that attention to 'the Other' demands imagination and effort. Our claim is that all these 'efforts' are closely interconnected and feed each other along the way — so that the 'seeing of art' and the 'art of seeing' become potent resources for the journey of faith.

What, then, is on show in this gallery? The artists — Edvard Munch, Marc Chagall, Stanley Spencer, Georgia O'Keeffe, Jacob Lawrence and Vincent van Gogh — are amongst our favourites. We have chosen three each, and the chapters are in substance the work of one author. The whole book, however, is a collaborative effort and both authors are glad to identify with the ideas and insights expressed in all its chapters. Another of our shared convictions is that theology is an essentially collaborative exercise, and we feel that our work is all the stronger as a result of being done together. Each chapter or room can be visited in its own right, and we see no reason why readers should be advantaged or disadvantaged by the order in which the chapters are tackled. The integrity of the book gathers around the unifying concept of 'journey of faith', and our hope is that reading it will provide an imaginative resource for your own journey.

Notes

[1] The role of imagination is discussed in E. H. Gombrich, *Art and Illusion* (Phaidon, London, 1960), pp. 161ff.

[2] D.H. Lawrence, in Harry Crosby, *Chariot of the Sun* (The Black Sun Press, Paris, 1931), Preface. For this reference to D. H. Lawrence, we are indebted to Geoffrey Lay, 'The Blind Leading the Sighted', *British Journal of Theological Education* 8/2 (1996), p. 21.

1
Edvard Munch: A Fearful Insight

In this first 'room' of the gallery, we focus on the work of the Norwegian artist and printmaker, Edvard Munch (1863–1944). To some readers this may seem an odd choice. In his mature years Munch did not claim for himself any explicit religious commitment and his pictures have little formal Christian content. Because he is best known for his image of *The Scream*, it is easy to assume that his work would offer little more than an anguished cry from the edge of insanity and quickly to dismiss him out of hand and mind. He is, however, extraordinarily well disposed to lead us on a first excursion into the territory where 'art' and the journey of faith visibly meet. This is grounded in his peculiar, indeed fearful, insight into what we now tend to call 'the human condition'.

We start by looking at some pictures which begin to map something of Munch's life and times. Then, map in hand, we seek to explore a wider web of connections which link Munch's art into other intellectual and cultural networks that are still determinative for many of the contexts in which we tread a journey of faith in our own day.

The Frieze of Life
The Frieze of Life — what a wonderful title under which to gather the finest products of a life's work! Munch, it seems, rarely thought of his paintings as isolated artefacts. As early as the 1880s, he was gathering and exhibiting pictures in connected groups. These he displayed as 'friezes': whole walls, densely hung with a mosaic of canvases, their relative positions carefully chosen to lead the eye on a well-planned journey of discovery. This practice continued through much of a lifetime, during which Munch exhibited his gathered works in a great variety of patterns and combinations. Whilst it is true that much remained constant throughout those years, in reality it is now impossible to provide a unique definition of *The Frieze of Life*, just how many pictures it should contain or precisely how they should be displayed. As late as his 75th birthday on 12 December 1938, when Munch posed in his winter studio for the

Norwegian photographer Ragnvald Vaering, he was backed by yet another immense wall with yet another variation on this now familiar theme. It is his struggle to 'tell the story of life' which, for me at least, creates an effective bridge linking his work to what others would more directly recognize as the journey of faith. After we have looked at the pictures and thought more deeply about their wider context, we will return to consider what we can learn from a detailed consideration of the way in which Munch's vision for *The Frieze of Life* actually developed over time.

Melancholy (1891)

There are a great number of pictures associated with *The Frieze of Life* from which we could choose. Munch produced several versions of all his most significant images, often exploring their potential through a variety of different media and styles. For the purpose of this chapter I have chosen two examples, both oil on canvas. The first — the one which he painted later — is a picture titled *Melancholy*, printed here (Plate 1) in a version that Munch painted in 1892 and exhibited at the 1893 Autumn Exhibition.

Immediately we are struck by its stylized form. Already Munch had departed a long way from the naturalistic style of his immediate predecessors, which many had thought to define 'the golden age' in Norwegian art. *Melancholy* offers a recognizable shore-scape, but with none of the near-photographic precision of the accepted tradition. Instead, we are struck by sweeping forms, bold areas of colour, and a strangely disturbing visual perspective. The eye is drawn by a strong feeling of movement along the shoreline: from the massive rocks in the foreground, through the couple and the man with the oars on a distant jetty, to the boat and back to the seemingly incomplete face of the man who, from the margin, strangely occupies centre-stage in this picture. We are almost inevitably drawn to inquire as to whether there might be some kind of narrative to accompany this painting, and we sense that we are invited to engage in reflection at something deeper than surface level.

This was not Munch's first painting in this style. There are clear resonances with an earlier painting called *Evening*, later renamed *Inger on the Beach*, which Munch had exhibited in 1889. Nor was it his first venture into the representation of profound 'life moments'. Our second example will be *The Sick Child*, a picture in not dissimilar style, which Munch had started to paint for the first time around 1885. *Melancholy*, however, was sufficiently striking in its own right for Munch's then tutor, Christian Krohg, to describe it as the first Symbolist or Synthetist painting in Norwegian art. His judgment appeared in an article, prompted by the Autumn Exhibition of 1891, entirely devoted to this one painting — also at that time simply titled *Evening*.

A connection is commonly made with the so-called Synthetist paintings of Paul Gauguin (1848–1903). Gauguin along with others had contributed to the 1889 Brussels Synthetist Exhibition in which they clearly demonstrated their rejection of Impressionism, with its close attention to surface lights, as still too naturalistic; instead, they asserted their belief in 'expression' through painting of ideas, moods and emotions. Gauguin's first Symbolist/Synthetist work was *Vision after the Sermon* of 1888. In it he uses similar areas of colour to those we can see in Munch's *Melancholy*, though even bolder and more evidently separated by heavy black lines. Gauguin's work is Synthetic in as much as it juxtaposes a group of Breton women in traditional costume alongside an abstract representation of the familiar biblical story of Jacob wrestling with the angel (Genesis 32:22-32). It is Symbolist in that the various elements of the picture, each created in its own distinctive style, are not designed to represent 'things as they are' at all; but rather to evoke a particular mood, to point beyond themselves, from the material to a deeper immaterial reality. This is what many of Munch's paintings from *The Frieze of Life* also achieve with such extraordinary success.

So what can we discover about the narrative suggested by the structure of Munch's *Melancholy*? The full title of the earliest known version of this picture, also from 1891, was *Melancholy, Yellow Boat*. The model for the figure in the foreground is known to be Jappe Nilssen, Munch's twenty-one-year-old friend, who had recently been victim to a passionate infatuation with a married woman, Oda Lasson. Oda was the wife of Christian Krohg, the artist already named who had played such a significant role in Munch's own development as a painter. Oda was ten years older than Jappe, and prominent in the so-called 'Bohemian' community of Kristiania where all these artists lived and worked. The scene shows

Jappe, consumed with jealousy, alone on the beach, while Oda and Christian prepare for a trip in a yellow boat on a light Nordic summer's eve. In fact, other versions of the same painting are variously titled *Jappe on the Beach* and, even more tellingly, *Jealousy*.

Further exploration is greatly helped by the fact that Munch left us a wide range of scrapbooks, journals and articles as additional lenses through which to view his original works. Typical of these is the so-called 'Moss Ledger', which it is thought Munch created around 1915, and into which he inserted pages with notes written at various earlier dates. Many of the entries follow his unique method of writing, characterized by the frequent use of dashes — or 'thought lines' as the Norwegian idiom has it. Two texts stand out for special attention in connection with *Melancholy*. The first reads as follows:

> One evening I walked alone by the water —
> it sighed and swished between the stones —
> there were long grey clouds on the horizon —
> it was as if everything had dried out — as if in
> another world — a landscape of death —
> but then there was life over there on the wharf —
> there was a man and a woman — and still another man
> came — with oars on his shoulders — and the boat was
> in place down there — ready to leave —
>
> She looks like her — I felt a sting
> in my breast — was she here now — but I know she is
> far away — and yet and yet those are her movements —
> she used to stand that way — her arms on her hips —
> God — heavenly father — have mercy on me — it must not
> be her —[1]

Suddenly we have crossed a boundary into another world, which stands in synthetic tension alongside the story of Jappe, Oda and Christian. The second paragraph is thought to recall Munch's memories of his own passionate love during his youth for one Millie Thaulow, else-where simply referred to as 'Mrs Heiberg'. Out of the tension there begins to emerge a strange evocation of a mysterious, almost numinous depth, which is the goal of all effective symbolism. A second text reads:

Down here on the beach I seem
to find an image of my-
self— of my life —
        Is it because
it was by the beach
we walked together that day?
        — The singular smell of seaweed
also reminds me of her
        — The strange rocks which mystically
rise above the water and take
the forms of marvellous creatures
which that evening resembled trolls —
        In the dark green
water I see the colours of her
eyes —

Way way out there — the
soft line where air meets
ocean — it is incomprehensible — as
existence — incomprehensible as
death — eternal as longing[2]

Now we begin to recognize more fully the measure to which we are engaging with a picture of unusual depth, in which stories and shore-scapes, colours and even smells, are conspiring together to prise open fresh insight into some of the most profound experiences in a human life.

Let us consider more carefully what is happening in the transition from Naturalist to Symbolist styles. Whereas the Naturalists looked 'out there', to the 'object' of study as the only truly appropriate measure of quality in a picture, the Symbolists look 'in here', into the 'subjective life' of the painter for an additional, even primary contribution to the impact of the whole. We will examine this transition in more detail later in the chapter; for now we note that we are looking at art which, discontent with the mapping of 'things', also sees as its task the mapping of 'mind'.

Let us look again at the picture. The incomplete blankness of Jappe's face transfers our attention to the shore-scape in search of a fuller understanding of the distressed man's mind, which cannot be read from its *sur-face* (literally: 'on the face') expression alone. It never can. The arc of the bay, the rhythmic patterns of light and shade, and the swirl of rock formations in the foreground impress on us his inner turmoil. An almost musical rhythm in the sweep of the strand is echoed along the horizon, created by a distant peninsular. The whole effect is charged by a minor but significant distortion of conventional perspective. There is something uncomfortably odd about the size of the couple in the distance, which gives them a far more prominent presence than the formal mathematics of perspective should demand. This is further reinforced by the whiteness of the woman's dress, and we feel acutely her impact on his troubled mind. In all this, set as he is looking out from the corner of the picture, we also feel Jappe/Munch's own marginality and impotence to change what is happening around him.

What might at first appear to be the simple picture of a man thinking on a beach now becomes a possible focus for deep exploration into the experience of all those who know the agonizing intensity of a broken relationship. Set in its wider context within *The Frieze of Life*, we have a significant contribution to our understanding of the whole human journey from youth, into maturity and ultimately towards life's end.

This takes us back, then, to one of Munch's earlier pictures. In it we now recognize that it is most crucially the exploration of death that is for Munch the central and all-controlling focus for his insight into human life.

The Sick Child (1885–1886)

With the painting of *The Sick Child* (Plate 2) we are touching a truly seminal moment in Munch's formative experience as an artist. Munch tells us that he painted and re-painted the picture we now know as *The Sick Child* some twenty times before he finally exhibited it under the unassuming title *Study*, in Kristiania at the Autumn Exhibition of 1886.

This astonishing 'effort of imagination' leaves us in no doubt about how deeply Munch was gripped by the events that gave rise to this scene. The effort was not without its reward. Munch wrote:

In The Sick Child I broke new ground —
it was a breakthrough in my art —
most of what I later have done
had its birth
in that painting.[3]

These are strong words; but their truth is amply borne out as we explore
this picture's continuing significance for his own and other artists' work.
It became a marker not only along Munch's own developmental journey,
but also in the history of Norwegian and European art more generally.

The immediate and most obvious inspiration for this picture was an
acute recollection of the terminal illness of his sister Sophie, almost ten
years earlier. Her death from tuberculosis at the age of fourteen had been
monumentally formative for Munch's own life, and the shock-waves
emanating from it are still powerfully evident in this picture. In his own
account, however, Munch explains that there are here other deaths present
too: his mother's and what at one time threatened to be his own, recalled
with fear from his experiences as a sickly child. Ironically he survived his
own near-death skirmish with tuberculosis; it was his sister, at the time of
his own illness seemingly the stronger, who was not so fortunate. As commentators in the following century delighted to psychologize on this
painful story, they suggested that it was the particular combination of his
own survival and Sophie's death that racked him so cruelly with guilt. His
own account of the experience of illness reads as if through a haze of
near-hysterical terror: terror that, in turn, he projected onto his dying sister. The whole sequence is embroiled with memories of his father's own
confused and confusing responses. Munch's notes, written later, offer a
damning indictment against some insidious motifs in the Lutheran
Protestantism of his day. The following quotation sheds light on this
experience, and will also be important when we come further to reflect on
Munch's childhood experiences of formal religion. Here Munch writes
himself into the third person, like an actor in a play:

Daddy it is so dark the stuff I am spitting . . .
It is blood Daddy —
He stroked my head — don't be afraid my boy . . .

Turn yourself to the Lord my boy . . .
Then he got a mouthful of blood which he spit into the
Handkerchief — it became dark red in colour — he held it up
in front of him and looked at it — look father and he showed
it to his sister —
She rushed out terrified . . .
. . . he was so afraid
He felt the blood rattle inside the chest — when he
breathed — it felt as if his whole chest was loose — and
as if all the blood would flush out his mouth —
Jesus Christ Jesus Christ
He folded his hands —
Daddy — I am dying — I cannot die — I dare not . . .
Berte lay stretched out on the other bed praying and
crying loudly and around the bed all the others
some red in the face from crying some white . . .
Do you think I will go to heaven if I die —
That I believe my boy — if you believe —
Do you believe in God god's son and the holy spirit —
Yes he answered but he didn't quite know if he did
he believed there was so much strange in the Bible —
which he had thought of now and again —
Fear seized hold of him — In a few minutes he would be
standing in front of God's judgment seat — he would be
condemned forever forever — he would burn in sulphur —
in hell —[4]

Little wonder Munch never succeeded in achieving a fully positive and healthy view of the Christian religion.

Returning to the picture, today it is hard to believe the appalling way it was received when first exhibited. It is reported that on the opening day of the exhibition, people crowded around it, convulsed with laughter. Gustav Wentzel, a young contemporary, is reported to have shouted 'humbug painter' into Munch's face when he first arrived for the exhibition. The press described the work as 'an abortion' and 'fish stew in lobster sauce'. Why ever would an inoffensive picture like this spark such vehement reactions — a picture which, little more than a century later, now has the power to move many of us to tears? What are the cultural changes sufficient to effect such a shift in the way a picture is received?

Munch was painting into a very specific artistic context. As we have seen, the reigning artistic style in Norway was Naturalism; Gustav Wentzel was a leader among the young Naturalist painters and specialized in the creation of almost photographic realism. This style had flourished throughout the first half of the century, and had made its home in Kristiania through a dedicated community of artists, who clearly saw themselves as guardians of an authentic tradition.

Munch's greatest moment of offence, however, was also the occasion of his greatest achievement. In *The Sick Child* Munch was pioneering the journey from Naturalism, beyond Impressionism, towards the as yet largely uncharted territory of Expressionism — that style in which the 'subjective and internal' are as significant as the 'objective and external'. Munch's twenty revisions represent the struggle to put himself — his emotions, his deepest feelings, his own self — into the picture, seamlessly connected into its specific content, a mother and her dying child.

This was a bold, some said arrogant, step; and it seems that Munch took it with uncharacteristic confidence. It is astonishing to think that he had only begun to work in oil as recently as 1880, and that he had not begun to exhibit in Kristiania before 1883. Perhaps it is no coincidence that his revolutionary achievement also coincided with the moment when his self-esteem was considerably boosted by a blossoming in his relationship with 'Mrs Heiberg' — of *Melancholy* fame. The scale of *The Sick Child* was bold in itself — nearly 120 cm. square — almost without precedent in the traditions of Norwegian figurative painting. Munch defended his boldness with clarity and determination. Contrasting his own efforts with those of his contemporaries, he wrote:

> . . . I maintain that hardly a single one of these painters had experienced their motif to the last bitter drop to the extent I had in The Sick Child. That was not only myself sitting there — it was all my dear ones —[5]

> . . . I started as an Impressionist, but during the violent mental and vital convulsions of the Bohème period Impressionism gave me insufficient expression — I had to find an expression for what stirred in my mind —

> I was assisted in this by my acquaintance with Hans Jæger (painting one's own life). The first break with Impressionism was The Sick Child — I was looking for expression (Expressionism).[6]

A new style in Norwegian art had been born. To call it Expressionism is perhaps somewhat anachronistic and suggests Munch's later reading of his own history. What Munch had done in Norway with paint was the visual correlate of what Søren Kierkegaard had done with philosophy, Emile Zola was doing with the novel, and a whole movement in Europe would do under the various guises of Existentialism — in parallel with the growing ascendancy of psychology as the all-embracing paradigm.

How, then, did Munch manage to do all this using only oil on canvas? Part of the answer lies hidden in the twenty revisions. It is thought that the idea of constantly reworking an image was suggested to Munch by reading Emile Zola's novel *L'Oeuvre*, published in the spring of 1886.

> In the novel the result of the constant retouching and overpainting is a formless mass of lines and colours. The artist's intentions and genius are only revealed in various details, which have been miraculously preserved in the senseless and frantic pursuit of perfection.[7]

In the National Gallery in Oslo it is now possible to see a stunning sequence of x-ray images that uncover some of the layers in the process of Munch's creative endeavour. One layer, no longer visible to the naked eye, discloses thin paint running down the canvas, as if the scene were viewed through a film of flowing tears. On the surface, we still see deep scoring with a knife or spatula, which can be read as an expression of his passionate feelings in the presence of his subject. Rarely can an artist have achieved such intensity through the look on a child's face, skilfully focused by shocking red hair against a white pillow.

Munch had begun with the conventional techniques of a naturalistic painter. His models for the sick girl and her attendant were real people: the twelve-year-old Betzy Nielsen and his aunt, Karen Bjølstad. By the time the work was ready for exhibition, however, their images had been repeatedly overlaid, their naturalistic precision had long since been hidden. In their apparently finished form, the figures in this emotional drama were presented to a viewing public scratched and gouged rather than painted. The only indicator that Munch's confidence in his achievement was, at least in measure, tinged with uncertainty was his decision to exhibit the painting under the title *Study* — in recognition of its seemingly unfinished appearance. Today — our 'ways of seeing' gradually modified by a hundred and fifty years of cultural history — few would guess it was anything less than a finished work.

The months following the exhibition were not easy ones for Munch. As if to distance himself from the acuteness of his experience of rejection at the Autumn Exhibition, Munch presented the picture to Christian Krohg, the mentor from whose work he had both learned and rebelled. Soon his relationship with 'Mrs Heiberg' was to collapse, and a whole catalogue of disasters became inseparably associated with his memory of the creation of *The Sick Child*. Shaken, Munch retreated from the cutting edge of radical experimentation and, at least for a while, his position on the forefront of artistic innovation went on hold. It would be several years before his newfound style would begin to flower in new works like *Evening* and *Melancholy*.

Anxiety and death as persistent motifs

As is already clear, anxiety and especially death are prominent motifs in Munch's work. Further examination of his childhood and adolescence continues to reinforce the point. He writes:

> I inherited two of mankind's most dangerous enemies —
> the inheritance of consumption and insanity —
> disease and madness and death were the black angels
> standing by my cradle —
>
> A mother who died early gave me the germ of consumption —
> an overly nervous father — pietistically religious bordering on
> fanaticism — from an old family — gave me the seeds of
> insanity —
>
> From birth — they stood by my side — the angels of
> anxiety — sorrow — death followed me outside when I played —
> followed me in the spring sun — in the beauty of the summer —
> They stood by my side in the evening when I closed my eyes —
> and threatened me with death hell and eternal punishment —

And then it often happened that I woke up in the night —
and stared in wild terror into the room
Am I in Hell —[8]

There is, then, no doubting where the fundamental energy for the famous image of *The Scream* originates. But Munch's own scream, his intense cry of pain, also contains the germ of another possibility, a seed of hope. Munch, with acute self-awareness, recognizes in himself that it is precisely this cauldron of suffering which is, simultaneously, his greatest burden and his unique resource. Of his art, therefore, he writes:

What is art —
Art grows from joy and
sorrow — but mostly
from sorrow —
It grows from man's life —
Is art a description of
     this life this movement —
Shall one depict the different
pleasures — the different
     misfortunes — or shall one
only see the flower — whose
nature substance and vibration
     are determined by
the joy and the pain —

I do not believe in an art which
has not forced its way out through
man's need to open his heart —
all art literature as well as
music must be brought out with
     one's *heart blood* —[9]

The final italics are mine; Munch wrote the words 'heart blood' in red capitals. Here we see most clearly why, for many a fellow traveller, Munch's exploration of the human pilgrimage can become a resource for the journey of faith. He had learned from the pitiful example of his father that the formal words of a religion can easily be reduced to an empty sham, a cover hiding us from the reality of the human condition. Whilst ditching the words — for him, instruments which had inflicted so much personal harm — Munch never jettisoned the quest for, and the desire to express, that deeper relentless hope which strangely anchors the human spirit.

Munch's own illness, the deaths of his sister, his mother and later his father were all devastating and formative for the person he was becoming. As self-consciously he puts himself 'into' his art — the person of the artist never divorced from the object that becomes his focus of attention — time and again these deaths are present. So far we have looked at just two early snapshots from *The Frieze of Life*: *Melancholy* and *The Sick Child*. The titles of others belonging to one or another version of *The Frieze of Life* reinforce the central motifs in Munch's vision: *Anxiety, Consolation, Death in the Sickroom, Jealousy, Separation, The Lonely Ones, The Sin*. None is far from the ever-present exploration of dying and death. At first viewing, it might seem that a particular picture represents something essentially objective and external. *The Lonely Ones*, for example, first painted in oil in 1891 in a version now lost, could represent any one of a thousand couples standing on a deserted shore, gazing out over a tranquil sea. As in *Melancholy*, however, Munch impresses this specific couple with all the intensity of his own experience of betrayal and isolation; we can read our way more deeply into the universal experience of bewildering aloneness, often most alarmingly magnified in the company of others. It is just this sharpness of perception and expression which makes a picture like this one emotionally accessible to such a wide audience.

With the passage of years, Munch reworked all these images many times. By the mid-1890s he was experimenting more and more frequently with various methods of printing. Pictures which had first appeared as oil on canvas could now be seen in a variety of colour-ways, each plumbing fresh depths of his own, and our, inner experience. In time, Munch became a highly skilled printmaker, and artists continue to admire his ingenuity across a wide range of media: intaglio (drypoint, etching and mezzotint), lithograph and woodcut. At one level, this can be seen simply as an impressive exploration of new technical possibilities; Munch broke

fresh ground in almost every area of printmaking. At another level, however, it provided a richly fertile domain for an exploration of his own
inner life. Printmaking gave him the facility for endless revisions —
something we have already seen to be crucial for writing himself 'expressively' into his earliest oil version of *The Sick Child*. In old age the
proliferation of his prints and his continued fascination with experimentation led to this delightfully memorable story from his time as a
printmaker:

> Munch's esteem for his works was, however, always overshadowed by
> his never-ending fascination with new visual effects. Discussing the
> artist's cooking habits, Stenersen relates that: "[Munch's] . . . cooking
> was very simple — for dinner mostly bread and soup, or water, some
> vegetable, and a piece of fish. Not wanting to clean the fish, he would
> cut off the tail and cook that instead of the main part. If he couldn't lay
> his hands on a lid he might cover the pan with a print — once it was The
> Sick Child.
>
> 'Watch out!' someone standing by shouted. 'Don't you realize it is
> The Sick Child you are using?'
>
> 'So what?' he replied calmly. 'It doesn't cost me anything. In fact,
> it'll be interesting to see it steamed.'[10]

It was a version of *The Sick Child* that featured amongst the first of
his drypoint prints of 1894. A little over 10 cm. square, the picture is
much as we know it from the earlier oil, though inverted, and the 'expressive' effect is now largely generated by a complex network of hatchings,
many strong verticals giving a sense of intimacy and relationship between
the characters. Below the familiar image of the grieving mother and the
dying child, however, is a further image, lightly etched, of a spring landscape with a single tree reaching into a cloud-filled sky — perhaps, some
suggest, to symbolize the coming of spring and hope for the invalid child.
This was only the first of many further images of this same scene. Other
etchings, under the slightly variant title *The Sick Girl* were to follow,
increasingly dark; eventually, as in an 1896 version, only the girl's head is
seen glowing pale against her pillow.

Experimentation with colour lithography opened new possibilities.
Munch's friend, Paul Hermann, describes a magical moment concerning

the production of colour prints of *The Sick Girl* whilst visiting Clot's, a famous printmaking shop in Paris:

> I wanted to have some printing done at Clot's when I was told: don't go, Mr Munch's coming has been announced. The lithographic stones with the great head were already lying next to one another, neatly lined up, ready to print. Munch arrives, positions himself before the row, closes his eyes firmly and begins to direct blindly with his finger in the air: 'Go ahead and print . . . gray, green, blue, brown.' Opens his eyes, says to me: 'Come, drink a schnaps . . .' And so the printer printed until Munch came back and gave another blind order: 'Yellow, rose, red . . .' And so on another couple of times . . .[11]

Prelinger comments:

> Intuitively, mystically, the artist created a work of great technical subtlety and sophistication, working with one, three or four stones.[12]

To the casual observer all this might seem random and chaotic, but the resulting images reveal the extraordinary scale of this artist's talent.

Melancholy was among the first colour woodcuts with which Munch experimented, initially in 1896 and again in 1901. Munch invented and developed his own 'puzzle method' of printing. It relies on first cutting his woodblocks into several sections with a jigsaw, a technique which offers itself for endless experimentation with colour combinations. Pieces of the puzzle can be inked in different colours, re-assembled and printed simultaneously with a single pull. The precise shape of the puzzle-pieces has a profound effect on the final image. In *Melancholy*, the fact that the dock and the rowing boat belong with the same puzzle-block as the beach and the pensive figure in the foreground greatly intensifies the sense of connection between the events in the distance and the distress in the mind of the young man in the foreground. Always one of his favourite images, prints of this scene were pulled in a countless number of colour variations. At the turn of a colour, as Prelinger puts it, 'melancholy under a peaceful blue sky could become despair under flaming red heavens.'[13]

There is evident joy in Munch's playful search for a 'right' colour. Whilst there is much use of black and dark shades in the representation of sorrow, we are often surprised by the unexpected effect of a new combination. Munch's own favoured colours for the *Melancholy* motif were orange, blues and pea green, a combination such that 'The tension between the hot and cool hues seems to reflect the conflicting emotions of the slumped figure.'[14] Later, some pulls of the 1901 version extensively use black, 'imparting a literally black and hopeless despondency absent from the more passionate play of colours and emotions in the early rendering.'[15]

All Munch's major motifs were revisited over and over again; some of the most significant were reworked each decade over a span of fifty years. When Munch wrote to his biographer Jens Thiis in 1932 concerning *The Sick Child*, nearly fifty years after painting this image for the first time, he was in no mood to apologize for his acts of repetition:

> Now I have painted a new version of it for the fifth time . . . A painting and a motif that I struggle with for an entire year are not expended in a single picture. If it is of such significance to me, why should I not then paint and vary a motif five times? Just look at what other painters depict over and over again ad infinitum: apples, palm trees, church towers, haystacks.[16]

Art historians sometimes venture to try and name the 'definitive' version of a particular image, but it is unlikely that Munch would agree with such a concept at all. It is not just that one image is better or worse than another, rather that each adds another dimension to the depth of his overall vision. The possibility for willing viewers is to be drawn into the process of experimentation, and with each variation to explore yet another angle on the deep emotions of the inner self — both Munch's and our own.

Munch's experience of religion

We have already seen something of the impact that the religion of Munch's father had on the artist's young life; now we shall further explore Munch's continuing spiritual development, based on a combination of his visual and written legacy. Opinion is divided as to whether, in later life, it is proper to speak of Munch as a 'person of faith' at all. Did the rejection of his father and his father's religion mean a once-and-for-all end to his own religious journey, as some commentators suggest, and the beginning of lasting 'atheism'? Or could it be that, from the depth of his pain, rejection paved the way for another kind of faith experience, an experience that continues to be manifest throughout his artistic work? I am not convinced that it is possible to answer this question definitively either way; but, then, neither am I convinced that it is useful to do so anyway. All I would claim for Munch is that, out of the variety of his painted, printed and written fragments — the only imprint of his life still available to us — it is possible to recognize 'moments', to sense 'resonances', which suggest real engagement with what I am calling the journey of faith. Often the content of these moments is profoundly ambiguous; but I wonder whether the ultimate ambiguity of faith and doubt, forged as it is on the anvil of human suffering, is any greater in Munch's testimony than it is in the story of any other genuinely searching traveller.

I am attracted by a motif taken up by a variety of more recent theological writers who seek to revalue the spiritual significance of 'atheism', so-called. Jürgen Moltmann, for example, does this to considerable effect in his reflections on the contribution which Albert Camus' writings made to the development of his own thinking — at the very core, indeed, of his groundbreaking book, *The Crucified God*.[17] Moltmann makes the point that it is only those who have wrestled towards a more-than-ordinary grasp of 'theism', and its real difficulties in the face of human suffering, who genuinely reach a position where they can credibly call themselves 'a-theist'. Frequently it is the acts of what now we would call deconstruction, by so-called atheists, which pave the way for a serious re-evaluation of just who God is for a particular time. It is important, of course, not to undervalue the integrity of a mind of Camus' calibre agonizing over the question of God, lightly claiming him, for example, the identity of what Karl Rahner used to call an 'anonymous Christian'. The crucial insight is this: that the route towards credible theism is paved with many a-theisms, carefully considered rejections of the 'less-than-gods' to which we all so easily succumb along the way.

Specifically, I think we can see Munch becoming 'a-theist' in relation to his father's peculiar and particular version of theism, which Munch experienced as profoundly destructive for his own and other people's lives. To emerge even relatively guilt-free from such oppressive religion is remarkable in itself. It is little short of a miracle, then, that Munch never fully lost his taste for the divine mystery, that sense deep within which sustained the potential to kindle another kind of theism, all the richer for its testing in a refiner's fire. How far Munch really achieved this for himself we cannot be certain; what we do know is that, as a resource for our own journeys, he can become for us, and others like us, a highly significant 'spiritual' companion.

In the remainder of this section, we focus on three strands from Munch's story that shed further light on his experience of religion. We look again at Munch's understandably negative attitude to the religion of his father; we look in more detail at some of those 'moments' which seem to signal a possibility of hope; and we follow up the hints which emerge concerning Munch's own continuing spirituality, despite and in the midst of his intense struggles.

There can be little doubt that the experience of growing up in Dr Munch's household was massively significant for Munch's formative years. The old man had that peculiar way — not unknown in the behaviour of others whose religion verges on the fanatical — of swinging wildly between almost sentimental intimacy and ruthless strictness, a lethal cocktail which can be both disorientating and destructive for any young life. So, for example, Munch provides his readers with glimpses of a loving Christian father; but more typically he portrays a fearful figure, in whom we see military duty and legalistic obedience dangerously combined with an overpowering religious faith. It will be no surprise to discover that his father never really affirmed his son in his chosen career, as artist. Rarely did Dr Munch miss an opportunity to voice disapproval at his son's commitment to an artist's lifestyle which involved sketching nudes in a life class, and mixing with a host of like-minded 'undesirables'.

All this stands in sharp contrast with Munch's experience of his mother. She was also victim to her partner's fanaticism. It seems, however, that she retained for herself a residue of freedom, out of which she could share creatively with young Edvard. Sadly, her last gesture was far from liberating. Shortly before her death, she addressed her family through a final letter. It read as follows:

> Jesus Christ will make you happy here and in the hereafter; love Him above all things, and do not grieve Him by turning your backs on Him; often I am filled with fear that in Heaven I might not see some of you who are my heart's delight here on earth again, but with faith in the Lord who has promised to hear our prayers, so long as the Lord still grants me life, I shall beseech Him to save your souls. And now, my beloved children, my dear, sweet small ones, I say farewell to you. Your beloved Papa will better teach you the way to Heaven. I shall be waiting for all of you there.[18]

This has the distinctive ring of his father's religion, and it certainly became a resource that enabled Munch's father to strengthen his grip on the family's religious obligations. Munch recalls how this letter was repeatedly used as an emotional lever, the threat of displeasing their departed mother becoming a device to contain her children's behaviour and deepen their guilt. He also recalls from that time significant changes in his father's disposition towards him, clearly connected with the loss of his mother. Before her death, in 'loving father' mode, Dr Munch would set Edvard on his knee and rehearse the Nordic Sagas, uniquely a feature of their Scandinavian inheritance. After her death, however, the Sagas were replaced with tales that emphasized the terrors of eternal damnation, so that the threat of hell provided a constant backdrop for Munch's experience of life.

Munch's memory of being present during the recital of prayers, both at the time of his mother's death, then aged five, and later at the time of Sophie's death, then aged fifteen, became identified for him with deep feelings of isolation and rejection. He was excluded from the rituals of death themselves, as 'too young to understand', and he was drawn into what, even at that age, seemed to him to be crass denials of the true deadliness of these hugely important deaths. Both his father and the priest would lightly speak of these enormous personal losses in terms of victory and spiritual gain. Later, Munch recalled that the image of God, steadily growing within him through that time was, like his own father, vengeful, selfish and incomprehensible — fundamentally unjust and unfair.

The overall effect of this religious torture was, of course, guilt and alienation from any credible understanding of God. There are agonizing phrases in his journal in which Munch can be heard striving to empathize with his father's pain at having a son who could not share his own religious certainties. We know that Munch persisted beyond the death of his mother with regular attendance at church, being confirmed into the Lutheran Church at the age of sixteen. By the mid-1880s, however, the stage at which we begin to see his creative output as an artist, it is hardly surprising to find him beginning to profess his outright denial of God.

Nor is it surprising to find that his father's death in 1889 became the occasion of yet another personal crisis, one that threw him into a sustained period of depression. At the time he was already living an isolated life in a Paris apartment. It is not hard to imagine Munch repeatedly replaying in his mind his father's stern voice: disapproving of his art, his relationship with 'Mrs Heiberg', his wider group of 'Bohemian' friends, all this against a backdrop of hell and condemnation. With a note of heart-rending resignation he wrote: 'What I wanted he failed to understand; what he valued most, I could not understand.'[19] Still only in his mid-twenties, for Munch death had become the single most significant motif in his young life. It became a constant theme in his art, a pivotal focus for personal reflection and, ironically, the essential source of life in his work. At one time Munch wrote of death:

> It is so weird to think that one day you will be totally gone. That you have to be. That the time must come when you can say to yourself, Now you have ten minutes more, and then it will happen. Then you will feel how little by little you become nothing.[20]

That he could sustain, in the midst of such pain, reflection of this quality, expressed through both word and picture, is a mark of his superlative stature as a spiritual companion.

It is, then, out of this ferment of guilt, anxiety and despair that we identify the emergent strands of Munch's mature spirituality. Two threads stand out for particular comment, one primarily intellectual, the other more evidently experiential. Intellectually, we begin to see the makings of a new way of understanding the concept of immortality, an interpretation very remote from the one he rejected as part and parcel with the religion of his father. It draws on a contorted, but effective, mix of scientific and mystical sources: Newton and Darwin fused with a particular brand of mysticism much in tune with the art of the Symbolists. He wrote:

> It is a foolishness to deny the existence of the soul; after all, that a life begins cannot be denied.
>
> It is necessary to believe in immortality, insofar as it can be demonstrated that the atoms of life or the spirit of life must continue to exist after the body's death. But of what does it consist, this characteristic of holding a body together, of causing matter to change and develop, this spirit of life?
>
> Nothing ceases to exist; there is no example of it in nature. The body that dies does not disappear. Its components separate one from the other and are transformed.
>
> The fanatical faith of a single religion such as Christianity resulted in a rejection of faith, resulted in a fanatical faith in the non-existence of God.
>
> . . . All of it was associated with that great wave that spread over the earth: Realism. Things did not exist unless they could be demonstrated, explained arithmetically or physiologically. Painting and literature became whatever could be seen with one's eyes or heard with one's ears. It was the shell of nature.
>
> People were satisfied with the great discoveries they had made. They did not realize that the more discoveries are made, the greater and the more are the mysteries to be solved. Mysticism will always be with us. The more we discover, the more unexplained things there will be.
>
> The new movement, whose advances and fires can be detected everywhere, will express all those things that have been repressed for a generation, everything that mankind will always have in great abundance: mysticism. It will find expression for what now is so refined as to be recognized only in vague inclinations, in experiments of thought. There is an entire mass of things that cannot be explained rationally. There are newborn thoughts that have not yet found form.[21]

On the one hand, then, the law of the conservation of energy and the theory of evolution provide a mechanistic framework within which to grasp an idea of indestructibility; his father's indelible memory, for example, will not leave him. On the other, he rejects the philosophy of Realism — an ideal correlate for a similar highly mechanistic view of the world — in favour of the emerging Symbolist analysis, which clearly recognizes a mystical dimension of depth, no less real than the scientific, but one which the scientific paradigm is powerless to uncover. This is an emphasis we shall find again in other chapters, and notably in the chapter on Georgia O'Keeffe.

A second and more evidently experiential thread in the growing web of his own spiritual identity is well focused in the text which has come to be known as the 'St Cloud Manifesto'. In the pit of despair following the death of his father, Munch experienced one of those 'defining moments', not infrequently a motif in the testimonies of those on a journey of faith. Not that this moment had the power to transform all his future moments; it was not sufficient, for example, to free him from the massive weight of guilt and despair which had already accumulated with the years. It was enough, however, to provide a platform on which to build for his continuing spiritual journey. The story runs like this: whilst staying in the region of St Cloud, Munch took a walk in a local park and, later, he recorded how thoughts began to take shape in his mind:

> For a long time it was cold, then suddenly the weather turned warm and spring-like. I went out on to the hill and enjoyed the gentle air and sun. The sun felt warm, and only occasionally was there a cool breeze that felt as if it came from a burial vault.
>
> The moist soil was steaming. It smelled of rotting leaves. And around me everything was so still. And nonetheless I sensed that there was ferment and life in this steaming soil, in these naked branches. Soon they would blossom and live, and the sun would shine on green leaves and on flowers, and the wind would gently sway them.
>
> To me it seemed as if becoming united with this life would be a rapturous delight, to be one with the earth at all times fermenting, always being warmed by the sun. And living — living!

I would be united with it and from my rotting body plants and trees would sprout. Trees and plants and flowers. And they would be warmed by the sun, and nothing would pass away. That is eternity.

I stopped suddenly. As if from a funerary chapel, freezing cold, a light breeze rose up. And I shuddered, and went home to my room, chilled to the bone.

I felt I should make something — I thought it would be so easy — it would take form under my hands like magic.

Then people would see!

A strong naked arm — a tanned powerful neck — a young woman rests her head on the arching chest.

She closes her eyes and listens with open and quivering lips to the words he whispers into her long flowing hair.

I would like to give it form as I now saw it, but in a blue haze.

These two in that moment when they are not themselves, but only one of the thousands of sexual links tying one generation to another generation.

People should understand the sanctity, the grandeur of it, and would take off their hats as if in church.

I would make a number of such paintings.

No longer would interiors, people who read and women who knit, be painted.

There should be living people who breathe and feel, suffer and love.[22]

Many of us who think of ourselves as being on some kind of spiritual journey will be able to identify with this experience. Our experiences, however, will have their own distinctive content, and it is unlikely that we will be able to express them so eloquently in paint!

It would be wrong to think that Munch's new way of seeing the world necessarily drives the intellectual and the experiential irreconcilably apart. The painting that he imagined in his St Cloud experience is in fact a Symbolist work. Like *The Sick Child*, it begins with the portrayal of real people, a man and a woman; but it cuts through the superficiality of Realism, exploring potentially agonizing personal material in order to expose a mystical depth. An early attempt by Munch to visualize the scene in the St Cloud Manifesto appeared as a simple pen drawing in 1890, but of much greater significance was a dark and mysterious picture from the same year simply titled *Night*.

Unlike his biographer Reinhold Heller, who seems to see Munch as increasingly consolidating an atheistic stance, there are other interpreters of his life and work who read the data very differently. Indeed, they find in Munch's output a growing spiritual, even religious weight. Two examples serve to illustrate how this has been expressed. Bente Torjusen, for example, brings Munch's words and pictures together in a peculiarly creative juxtaposition in his book *Words and Images of Edvard Munch*. He specially notes Munch's indebtedness to the Bible, and suggests that it might well have been a biblical text that inspired the title for his earliest drafts of *The Frieze of Life*, at that time still known as *The Mirror*. The connections to the well-known verse in 1 Corinthians 13 (v. 12: 'for now we see in a mirror dimly') are not hard to see. Torjusen quotes some words that Munch wrote in Paris in the late summer of 1896; they offer an allegorical description of his work, and bear remarkable parallels to the Apostle Paul's whole passage about love:

> I have never loved —
> I have felt the kind of passion
> which moves mountains and transforms people —
> love which tears layers from my heart and drinks blood —
> but to no one have I been able to say —
> Woman it is you whom I love —
> You are my all —
> But how are you then my negative image —
> there where my soul fits in —[23]

Munch as Symbolist can do no more than 'see in a glass darkly',[24] and what he sees has the form of a mirror image. It discloses the negative, the inverse or shadow — an image that Munch frequently uses both visually and verbally for the human soul. In *The Mirror*, the themes of anxiety and death are closely connected with a quest for the missing 'third'; namely love, which forms the title of the final movement in later versions of *The Frieze of Life*.

Another interpreter, Øivind Bjerke, shares Torjusen's conviction that Munch displays continuing spiritual awareness. He points to an evident sense of mystery in Munch's work long after the formal rejection of his father's specific understanding of the Christian faith. In a number of Munch's written fragments Bjerke can find expressions of a kind of pantheism. For example:

> Everything is movement and light: God is in us and we are in God, God is everything. Everything is in us. In us are whole worlds.[25]

> Prayer and religious thought —
> the idea of God, of eternity —
> take us out of ourselves;
> unite us with the universe, with the origins of light, with the origins of life, with the world. It soothes, thus does faith make us strong. It allows us to distance ourselves from the body.[26]

There is in Munch's work, Bjerke argues, the sense of an almost therapeutic mission, often couched in language more reminiscent of the world of religion than the world of art. Bjerke writes:

> The role of the artist that Munch adopted has its historical roots in the idea of the artist as a modern Christ: the artist as chosen one, as a healer. This separation from 'the others' simultaneously caused him to take on the role of victim. He often called attention to the 'wounds' which afflicted him during his life, 'wounds' that condemned him to a life filled with anxiety and loneliness. Negatively seen, one could call this a form of narcissism. But it can also be viewed in a positive light in which the artist's exposure of his sorrows and his joys is exemplary, and he treats himself as a research object.[27]

This interpretation, like Torjusen's, has much to commend it. It does not feel at all surprising to find Munch's life scarred with traces of 'narcissism', just part of a price to be paid for his peculiarly rich insight into the human condition.

The wider intellectual context

In the following pages, Munch's achievement will be located in its wider intellectual context. There are two sections: the first explores more fully the general development of European painting through the period when Munch was most active as a painter; the second, more specifically, sets his output alongside that of his significant Scandinavian predecessor, the theologian and philosopher Søren Kierkegaard. There are, of course, many influential intellectual companions who might have been chosen to focus Munch's achievement in this way. At various points in his own writings, Munch makes special mention of Strindberg, Ibsen and Jæger, and there are others too. Kierkegaard, however, comes especially to mind as one who belongs within the same Scandinavian context, something that Munch himself, in later life, identified as significant.

The story of artistic style, as it unfolded in Europe in the second half of the nineteenth century, is a fascinating one in its own right, and a good place to start this more general exploration. As we have already seen, at the start of this period the Norwegian context into which Munch offered his painting was still firmly in the grip of Naturalism, the style in which mimesis, strict imitation, remains unchallenged as the highest artistic virtue. Naturalism demands of the visual artist very specific skills: extreme clarity of vision, and the very best in hand-eye coordination. Some of the near-photographic results of this movement rightly remain the cause of amazement and intense admiration. In other parts of Europe, however, most notably in France and Germany, acceptable artistic styles were already on the move. Impressionism had flowered, especially in France under the brushes of Van Gogh, Cézanne, Seurat and others. Southern France had become the recognized home of Impressionism; its extraordinary intensity of light and its minimal shadows providing these artists with a unique context for visual innovation. Impressionism, however, is not as different from Naturalism as might first meet the eye and, in some ways, it can even be viewed as an offshoot of its mimetic parent. No longer is it necessary to work with a magnifying lens and a virtually hairless brush; sometimes it looks as if Van Gogh applied his paint with a shovel rather than a brush, and most of the detail is lost in a flare of colour. The focus of attention, however, remains primarily with the object of analysis, the thing 'out there', even if attention is shifted to surface lights and away from precision in shape and shadow. It is true that with Impressionism, the person of the artist begins to be more evidently present; but with the efforts of Munch, and others who effect a transition at the dawn of so-called post-Impressionism, there is the inauguration of something genuinely new. The object 'out there' no longer holds the ring with anything like its former power, and it is the artist, with a personal life and real experiences, who takes a grip on the responsibility for seeing.

There is no clear consensus as to the best technical terms to apply in describing this development. In retrospect, Munch became labelled as the 'father' of Expressionism; but the term did not gain significant acceptance before the second decade of the twentieth century, most famously at the twenty-second exhibition of the Berlin Secession in 1911, by which time Munch himself was no longer a significant pioneer at the forefront of the movement. There is also some confusion about the relationship between what was happening in Scandinavia and a more focused emergence of formal Expressionism in central and southern Europe. Expressionism, full blown, is probably best described as a pre-eminently German phenomenon. It is immensely more significant, for example, that the 1911 Exhibition was held in Germany than it is that the exhibiting artists originated from countries all over Europe.

In terms of their output, the common factor in the work of all these artists is their startling use of colour. With their extraordinary colours, heightened yet further by experimental forms, often stylized and deliberately distorted, the Expressionists seemingly reached inside the objects of their study — be it landscape, still life or portrait. They were, they believed, disclosing something of the depth within themselves, which in turn disclosed something of genuine significance in the objects of their study. In so doing, they offered to the viewing public a stunning new way of 'seeing the world'.

It is not at all inappropriate to speak separately of a Scandinavian version of this movement, Scandinavian Expressionism. It was on show at all the great exhibitions of the early twentieth century, and Munch was by far the most distinguished contributor. As we have already seen, Munch had found in Gauguin a like-mind and like-eye; they were both cutting free from the obsession with photographic detail and bringing together, in a single image, diverse themes and ideas coming both from external sources suggested by the object and from within the person of the artist. As Munch reflected on the process at work in the emergence of this new style, he came to see that, unlike Naturalism's attention to coherence and unity, it is usually tension, contradiction, elusiveness and uncertainty which make Expressionist pictures so intensely expressive. It was, as we have seen, the scratchings on the surface of *The Sick Child* and the use of mysteriously suggestive wood-grains in later prints of *Melancholy*, which form the basis of their power to communicate. It is not that the technical skills of the Naturalist painter are redundant — Munch was a brilliant technician — but these skills are just the starting point for a full expression of the artist's vision. As Munch experimented with colour and form, he was seeking to tell the truth in another way, a fully humanized truth, a truth which reaches to the heart of the human condition. Munch's world is never clear-cut, clean-lined and unambiguous. Typically, it is the opposite of all these historic virtues: muddled, obscure and deeply paradoxical. In particular he was convinced that, by facing full-square the undeniable reality of personal suffering, he could express, for himself and his viewers, a truth which all need to see. It is this more than anything else that makes his work so powerfully expressive, and connects it directly with the real experiences of real people. It is precisely these features that also commend Munch's work to us as so remarkably Kierkegaardian.

Fifty years had passed since the Danish philosopher, Søren Kierkegaard, had explored, in his own highly elusive way, many of the ideas and motifs that we have identified as characteristic of the work of Munch. Whilst it would be unwise to make too much of them, there are some uncanny similarities between their respective childhood experiences, and it would seem odd not to mention them. Kierkegaard was one of only two siblings to survive out of a family of seven children; he also experienced the guilt-creating impact of a strongly religious father, and he was also deeply affected by an early experience of a broken relationship — his 'Mrs Heiberg' going by the name of Regine Olsen.

Even at a cursory level, it is impossible not to recognize a striking similarity between the way in which these two prominent Scandinavians focus their work through the lenses of anxiety and death. There is also a similarity between the ways their respective works were publicly received; both, in time, were dubbed 'fathers' of new movements within the intellectual culture of Europe. Munch is closely associated with the origins of Expressionism, Kierkegaard with Existentialism; both ascriptions are at best half-truths, and can easily mislead. It is certainly true that both these 'artists' stand out from the crowd as creative giants, and that they symbolize important and not unrelated turning points in European culture. Both firmly reject the 'myth of objectivity' and affirm the inseparable unity of subjectivity and objectivity in every creative act. Both, therefore, put themselves deeply and self-consciously (even if, in the case of Kierkegaard, somewhat elusively) into their work. Both prepare the ground for new and different ways of 'seeing the world' — be it in the particularity of Existentialism or, more widely, in the broader movements of 'modern art' in the twentieth century.

In their later lives, both Kierkegaard and Munch also reveal what some have described as a monastic spirit, though this manifests itself in significantly different ways. For Munch it shows itself in domestic simplicity, a kind of self-inflicted austerity; for Kierkegaard, it becomes an all-consuming obsession with self-denial. These, however, are only superficial reasons why it makes sense to bring their lives into some kind of dialogue, and it is to deeper connections we now turn.

Both Kierkegaard and Munch were actively concerned to explore the relationship between aesthetic and religious judgments, and a comparison between their lives would remain fundamentally trivial if it were not for the fact that their strikingly similar experiences and insights drove them to such radically different conclusions. The high degree of similarity between their attention to the great themes of *The Frieze of Life* — anxiety, death and love — make it hard to believe that they could arrive at such a profound disagreement about the relationship between art and religion. Munch, as we have seen, increasingly saw his artistic output as an expression of his own 'spiritual' insight; Kierkegaard reached the conclusion that, when it comes to the spiritual, art is fundamentally misleading and incapable of occupying the qualitatively different space enjoyed by religion.

We must look again at the points where their respective experiences and insights meet. Munch himself in later life, even if a little hesitantly, named some of the connections between their respective insights. In a detailed book on *The Scream*, an obvious focus around which to explore these links, Reinhold Heller identified these connections with particular clarity:

> Later in his life, Munch told one of his patrons that at the time he heard the scream in nature he felt a great fear of open places, found it difficult to cross a street, and felt great dizziness at the slightest height. The experience is one closely akin to Søren Kierkegaard's description of subjective anxiety in his book *The Concept of Anxiety*: "We can compare anxiety to dizziness. He whose eyes look down into a yawning abyss becomes dizzy. But the reason for this is as much in his eyes as it is the abyss itself. For we can easily suppose him not having looked down. Therefore anxiety is the dizziness resulting from freedom." Munch felt a close affinity to the Danish theologian and philosopher. In 1929 he wrote to the Swedish art historian Ragnar Hoppe, then preparing the catalogue for a major Munch exhibition: "I am glad to hear you describe [my work] as exemplary of 'Nordic spiritual life'. People are always trying to shove me down to Germany. But we do after all have Strindberg, Ibsen, Søren Kierkegaard and Hans Jægar up here, and Dostoevsky in Russia. Only during the last year did I become familiar with Kierkegaard, and there certainly are remarkable parallels between him and me. Now I understand why it has so often been said that a similarity exists between his world and mine. Previously, I did not understand this." What is of interest in this statement is Munch's insistent assertion that his art is founded on the experiences of the Scandinavian soul, and his attempt to support this assertion by the guarded reference to Kierkegaard, a reference immediately followed by the denial of any influence. This assumed ignorance must, however, be tempered by letters Munch wrote to friends at the same time relating how, while he was reading through his own diaries, he was also renewing his acquaintance with Søren Kierkegaard's writings. Among the collected works of Kierkegaard to which Munch subscribed in 1920, *The Concept of Anxiety* is one of the few books read, its pages carefully cut so as to avoid the more theoretical theological sections. For both Kierkegaard and Munch, the specific phobia of heights and spaces became symbolic of a greater anxiety, the fear of death.[28]

Munch could see, especially in Kierkegaard's incisive analysis of human anxiety, exactly the same precision of self-awareness that had become the hallmark of his own work. In the same way that Munch enabled his own agony to be present in *The Sick Child* and *Melancholy*, there is no doubting Kierkegaard's personal presence in his description of what, latterly, he called 'the sickness unto death'.

In many of Kierkegaard's writings, there is a controlling theme of paradox,[29] which well describes a message also expressed in Munch's paintings. Even his use of multiple authors invites comparison to Munch's multiple interpretations of familiar images. Both lived their lives around the border between faith and doubt and both affirmed an epistemology, a model for understanding the way that we know the world, based on an inseparable relationship between the knowing subject and object that is known. Why then do they adopt such different stances with respect to religion?

Kierkegaard's approach, it seems, is a direct reaction to what he saw as the excesses of Romanticism, which had reached the limit in its affirmation of the 'knowing subject'. Kierkegaard himself placed the subject in the centre of epistemology, but the passionate interest of the human subject in existence was to be grounded in faith in Christ, in whom the eternal had — paradoxically — come into time.[30] Kierkegaard was against what he thought to be the place of the subject in art, which he perceived to be bound up with a suffering-free, almost sanitized vision of reality in Romanticism. We can all probably recall landscapes painted at the height of the Romantic period that seem to project onto their object an almost Eden-like perfection. Given that this was all Kierkegaard came to expect the art of his day to offer, it is hardly surprising that he left it to religion to provide the truer and harsher vision of reality, one which is rightly shot-through with structured sinfulness and agonizing pain. What in Kierkegaard's view the Romantic image also seems to lack is any way to express the passage of time — the 'dimension' of reality in which suffering most evidently takes place. This is helpfully explored by George Pattison, a Kierkegaard specialist, writing more generally about the phenomenon of 'modern art':

> The theme of art and time overlaps at many points with that of art and suffering. Time, like suffering, breaks up the unity of existence. Existence in time is characterized by dispersion, incompleteness,

change, decay and death. Art, by revealing a world made whole, 'stops the wheel of time' and lifts us out of the dispersion of temporal existence, breaking the barriers between past, present and future imposed by time.[31]

The Naturalist realism of much Romantic art, before the invention of the camera, was seemingly providing freeze-frame snapshots of an essentially pain-free world.

So still we must ask why Munch did not concur with Kierkegaard's analysis? In one sense he did; Munch too felt the weightiness of suffering with exaggerated intensity, and knew that suffering loses meaning unless it is conjoined to a real sense of the passage of time through which it must be endured. The difference was that Munch, as artist, put the suffering, and the passage of time, into his pictures in a way that the Romantics never had. For Kierkegaard there was nothing to illustrate how this might be done; to him it looked as if, even and especially when artists put themselves subjectively into their images, intuitively they did so through rose-tinted spectacles.

What Munch achieved, taking him out of and beyond the limitations of Romantic painting, relied on the same intense awareness of temporal suffering that we associate with the spirit of Kierkegaard, the very awareness he built so expressively into his pictures. It was the reworked layers beneath the surface of *The Sick Child* which transformed a potentially freeze-frame snapshot into something more like the simultaneous projection of slides, capturing intense pain over significant time. In this way Munch and Expressionism reach through and beyond the impasse that constrained Kierkegaard to argue for an unbridgeable gulf between art and religion. Munch distanced himself from the alienating religion of his parents, but fully asserted the reality of the 'spiritual' at the heart of his painting. By so doing, Munch and Expressionism opened new and lasting possibilities for a coherent alliance between art and religion.

Back to *The Frieze of Life*

As already noted, in its earliest versions *The Frieze of Life* had carried the title *The Mirror*, an unusual but significant designation. Using the term this way, a number of things are suggested: the inversion and potential distortion of an image, as well as the way in which an artist, as subject, might become present in the object of reflection.

The general idea of *The Frieze of Life* also provides another mechanism by which to overcome Romanticism's perceived constraint within the abstraction of a suffering-free moment. In *The Frieze of Life* it is possible to hold in creative tension a variety of life-moments which come alive with all the dynamism and wholeness of a human life, simultaneously affirming the reality of human suffering in each of its particular frames.

Heller recalls the way that Lessing's eighteenth-century treatise *Laokoön* had defined a sharp dichotomy between painting and poetry, precisely because of this limitation on a visual image. Lessing had argued that a picture, essentially capturing a snapshot from the extended process of a drama, could not possibly do justice to what a poet can capture through a continuous narrative. Heller explains how he understands Munch to be overcoming this dichotomy in the creation of *The Frieze of Life*:

Each painting, although physically distinct and with a unique motif, would become a spiritual fragment serving to aid in the creation of a greater unit; combined, they were to bring a total statement on human love and death. The effect would be cumulative. Each painting could still be viewed separately, but its full meaning would not be revealed except within the coordination of commentary provided by the remainder of the series. Although he had not done so when he painted them, in 1893 Munch determined that many of his paintings of 1891 and 1892 should be seen only in conjunction with each other, that their interrelated themes should be made manifest within the structure of a serial narrative. In this he assumed some of the power Lessing had relegated to the poet and denied to the painter. Literature's element of time, the revelation of a number of actions following upon each other, became an aspect of Munch's art as the content of each painting added to the content of the preceding one and pointed towards the following one; a plot was created whose totality was greater than the specific content of the paintings creating it.[32]

It is not surprising that Munch showed great reluctance to sell his paintings and let them go; only together, as first he had seen them in his solo exhibition of 1892, could they produce the full effect he desired.

This perspective on Munch's intentions also helps us to understand another of his much quoted sayings: 'I paint, not what I see, but what I saw.'[33] These words are often taken to encapsulate Munch's rejection of Naturalism's supposed exclusion of the painter's subjectivity, for by painting what he 'saw', Munch claims that he or any other artist works themselves expressively into the image. But it also serves to break the tyranny of the temporal moment; by combining in *The Frieze of Life* many earlier moments of seeing, Munch is able, through oil on canvas, to capture a long span of years and an extended narrative of his own internal struggles.

Once conceived, then, it is not surprising that Munch continued to work at the creation of *The Frieze of Life* over many years. It was still appearing in fresh variations as late as 1918 and, as we noted earlier, Munch chose to be photographed in front of a version of *The Frieze of Life* on the occasion of his 75th birthday in 1938 — and now it is significant to note that immediately to his side was a fifth and final painted version of *The Sick Child*.

Connections into the journey of faith

What, then, might we want to take from this experience of exploring Munch's *oeuvre*, his total life output, viewed as a lasting resource for our journey of faith? Two themes come strongly to mind: one primarily theological, the other more pastoral; both, however, have significant practical implications for Christian discipleship.

Theologically, Munch's innovative departure from the received traditions of artistic style also suggests a significant challenge to the received traditions of Christian theology, and pushes us in the direction of fresh insight. At the core is the question how subject and object are related to each other. For Munch this was focused in the relationship between painter and painting; but for the theologian it might draw attention to the relationship between ourselves and the environment we inhabit, or even the relationship between God and the world more generally.

Munch's pictures intimate an underlying conviction that, if true, has profound implications for the way we conceptualize all reality and, consequently, the way we shape our lives in the world. Munch's images testify to a profound integration of subject and object. It might seem to us, for example, as if 'land' is just a thing 'out there', something for us to walk on and exploit at our convenience. In reality it is 'land-scape', where the '-scape' indicates an intimate conjunction between the view and the viewer.

As Christians this reminds us about a fundamental relationship between God and the world with which we should already be familiar. Christianity's distinctive affirmation of incarnation leaves nothing, not even God, disembodied from earthed experience of the world's matter, including its suffering. This insight is deeply transformative of the way we live in and deal with the world. If we ourselves are also truly embedded (incarnated) in the world, not just as external observers but as participants in its deep subject-object structure, how can we justify humanity's tendency to relate to the world as an object for domination, exploitation, and manipulation? Rather, we will want to nurture it, as symbolized in the very act of seeing, until we ourselves participate in the creativity which is making a world and not just 'an environment'.

A proper theological response to Munch's activity as an artist would suggest that we too might make 'experience' the consistent starting point of all our own theological reflection. Such reflection and the theory of knowing (epistemology) implied in it indicate that at the level of being itself (ontology) there is an inseparable subject-object structure to all reality. The starting point for theology, then, is not dependence on an analysis of propositional revelation, of the kind which trapped Munch's father in a prison of guilt and denial; nor is theology's point of departure a philosophical analysis of the language of being, even though this has provided real comfort for an intellectual minority in Europe for much of the twentieth century. Rather, theology begins with actual concrete experiences of life in the world. If this is the case, then 'art' and the 'art of seeing' surface amongst the highest of all possible spiritual resources; the 'see-er', the person of vision, stands out amongst our most significant guides on the journey of faith.

Moving now to pastoral concerns, it is hardly surprising that we find significant resources in Munch's work for strengthening our ability to offer real care to our journeying companions. In the first place, Munch challenges us to ensure that we adopt an appropriate Christian realism. Realism is not used here in that developed philosophical, theological sense, as in 'realist' understandings of God; rather, it is being used in the more earthed sense of facing full-square, and engaging with, the painful experience of real human existence. Some of the tragic consequences of failure to do this were evident in the story of Munch's father. Many of us can testify to the pastoral tragedy that surrounds those who approach death unable to look it full in the face, so that, at the end, death snatches them unprepared from the world. How different are the lives of those who, in life, prepare well for death and, at the end, embrace it intentionally and with hope.

In this post-Freudian era we understand so much more than Munch did in his day about theories which might explain the impact that repressed experiences can have on us: we know more now about unreconciled grief, and losses which are never properly processed and owned. What Munch's *The Frieze of Life* does is to provide us with a catalyst that can help to integrate all our experiences, from birth to death, into a coherent whole. As we allow Munch to escort us into life's most vulnerable moments — be it exposure to the shame we experienced in puberty, or irrational jealousy in the immature pursuit of love, or inconsolable grief in the face of loss — he can help us to re-view these experiences and, with them, recognize ourselves as part of a continuous and coherent narrative. This is an immeasurably valuable resource for the journey of faith.

Munch's commitment to 'tell his story', to put himself on the line, vulnerably as one who is hurt, damaged and broken, is a powerful example for us all. It is the only basis on which to build authentic pastoral empathy with others, and it is the received basis on which God in Christ has already declared unconditional solidarity with us.

Some therapists have already experimented, with measurable success, using some of the images from Munch's *The Frieze of Life* as the focus for healing reflection. By so doing they are literally holding up *The Mirror* to their clients, allowing Munch's own pain to become a resource for the healing of others. In her book *Facing Death: Images, Insights, and*

Interventions, Sandra Bertman records some of the results of her own work with dying people and their loved ones using visual images as a focus for therapy.[34] In particular she reports the powerful impact of Munch's deathbed images on the lives of people in acute stages of grief. From the perspective of health, we might suspect that these emotive images would tip a dying person into fear and despair; Bertman's testimony is that, by offering a framework within which to name what is real, these can become the occasion of healing and a focus for hope.

On three occasions now, I have myself attempted to facilitate shared reflection inspired by a sequence of pictures chosen from Munch's *The Frieze of Life*. Each time the aim has been to enable the group — a local church, a ministers' meeting and a student community — to explore some of their own real hopes and fears and to strengthen them with resources for the journey of faith.

With each of the pictures, I encouraged people to ask three questions. What are the stories suggested to you by this picture, the stories which might lie behind the artist's vision? Are there any points at which these stories connect with your own experience? What resources of scripture would you choose to connect with these stories and the people you meet in the pictures? On each occasion I have been amazed at the insights that are uncovered, frequently by people who come to me afterwards to tell me how they have never seen anything in 'serious' paintings before, but are now resolved to explore them with new interest.

My experiments to date have revolved around three particular images from *The Frieze of Life*: two of them, *Melancholy* and *The Sick Child*, have become the core of this chapter; the third, *The Lonely Ones*, shows two people, a man, probably the artist again, and a young woman standing together before a minimal, but significant shore-scape. It is the intense feeling of separation that usually inspires connections with our own life-stories.

My experience of running these sessions encourages me to believe that pictures like these have enormous potential for genuinely theological reflection on matters of deep human and spiritual concern. I am increasingly confident that they are accessible to a much wider spectrum of the population than could be guessed from the entrance figures into official galleries, and I am keen to continue to explore their therapeutic potential in a wider variety of pastoral contexts.

My suspicion is that *The Frieze of Life*, pastorally so effective at and around the time of death, would be equally useful as a resource for preaching — and, indeed, for teaching more generally. It is only when preachers and teachers act as Munch did, daring to make themselves erable and confront their hearers and learners with the reality of life, including the anxiety they themselves feel in the face of it, that they release the potential that enables real change and growth in others.

At a time when First World societies are rife with depressive illnesses of many kinds, it seems to me that Munch's *The Frieze of Life* comes as a breath of fresh air. At the point when anxiety promises to overwhelm, his images provide us with a seed of hope. That we can tap into the life of someone so perceptive of his own life experience, and so skilled in a particular medium of expression which can communicate what for many remains incommunicable, is a fantastic gift and one for which we give thanks to God.

Selected (and annotated) Bibliography

For those whose appetite for Munch and his world has been whetted, there is no shortage of resources for study readily accessible in English language. In the following paragraphs, there are full bibliographical details of all the books mentioned in the chapter, and a wide selection of suggestions for further reading. First for mention must be the beautifully crafted publication which accompanied a Munch retrospective at the National Gallery in London: Mara-Helen Wood (ed.), *Edvard Munch: The Frieze of Life* (London: National Gallery Publications, 1992).

An equivalent, but more recent and on Munch's home territory, is Arne Eggum (ed.), *Munch: at the Munch Museum, Oslo* (London: Scala Books, 1998).

There are numerous monographs, which combine good selections of pictures with brief summaries of the artist's life. Of special note are John Boulton Smith, *Munch* (London: Phaidon Press, London, 1977); Thomas Messer, *Edvard Munch* (London: Thames and Hudson, 1987); and Ulrich Bischoff, *Edvard Munch: 1863–1944* (Cologne: Benedikt Taschen, 1988).

The Phaidon publication commends itself for the fine quality of its reproductions; the Taschen for extraordinarily good value for money and a large selection of images. A book that brings Munch's words and pictures into such an inspiring and creative juxtaposition is Bente Torjusen, *Words and Images of Edvard Munch* (London: Thames and Hudson, 1989, first published 1986).

Further study of Munch as printmaker is best aided by the work of Elizabeth Prelinger, whose name is associated with two outstanding books: Elizabeth Prelinger, *Edvard Munch: Master Printmaker* (New York and London: W. W. Norton and Company, 1983); and Elizabeth Prelinger & Michael Parke-Taylor, *The Symbolist Prints of Edvard Munch* (New Haven and London: Yale University Press, 1996).

For a deeper insight into Munch in his Scandinavian context, Øivind Bjerke sets his work alongside that of a fellow Norwegian Symbolist: Øivind Storm Bjerke, *Edvard Munch and Harald Sohlberg: Landscapes of the Mind* (New York: National Academy of Design, 1995).

For good quality biographical research, it is hard to better the work of Reinhold Heller, and two of his books have featured strongly in the making of this chapter: Reinhold Heller, *Edvard Munch: The Scream* (London: Allen Lane/ The Penguin Press, 1973); and Reinhold Heller, *Munch: His Life and Work* (Chicago: The University of Chicago Press, 1984).

Other reference works with authoritative standing are Ragna Strang, *Edvard Munch: the Man and the Artist* (London: Gordon Fraser, 1979); and Arne Eggum, *Edvard Munch* (London: Thames and Hudson, 1984).

For more background on Expressionism, both of the following books include informative essays and a good selection of pictures: Frank Whitford, *Expressionist Portraits* (London: Thames and Hudson, 1987); and Dietmar Elger, *Expressionism* (Cologne: Benedikt Taschen, 1991).

Any attempt to explore more fully the writings of Søren Kierkegaard, especially as they relate to Munch, will be helped by the work of George Pattison: *Kierkegaard: The Aesthetic and the Religious* (London: SCM Press, 1992); and *Art, Modernity and Faith: Restoring the Image* (London: SCM Press, 1998).

For a variety of other insights and interpretations of Kierkegaard's work, see Alistair Hannay & Gordon Marino, *The Cambridge Companion to Kierkegaard* (Cambridge: Cambridge University Press, 1998).

The book by Kierkegaard which it is believed Munch himself read in later life can be found in a variety of translations. Amongst them is Søren Kierkegaard, *The Concept of Anxiety*, edited and translated with Introduction and Notes by Reidar Thomte (Surrey: Princeton University Press, 1980).

The book that explores the therapeutic potential of Munch's pictures is Sandra Bertman, *Facing Death: Images, Insights, and Interventions* (Philadephia: Taylor and Francis, 1991).

Theological issues concerning the relation between God and suffering are
handled in Jürgen Moltmann, *The Crucified God* (London: SCM, 1974).

Notes

This chapter is primarily the work of Richard Kidd.

[1] From the so-called 'Moss Ledger', OKK (Oslo: Kommunes
Kunstsamlinger) T 2782-bw, late summer of 1892; quoted and translated in
Bente Torjusen, *Words and Images of Edvard Munch* (London: Thames and
Hudson, 1989), p. 119.

[2] From the 'Moss Ledger', OKK T 2782-j, late summer of 1892; quoted and
translated in Torjusen, *Words and Images of Edvard Munch*, p. 121.

[3] Edvard Munch, *Livsfrisens tilblivelse* (Oslo, 1929), p. 10; quoted and
translated in Torjusen, *Words and Images of Edvard Munch*, p. 65.

[4] Munch, OKK T 2772, autobiographical note, dated Saint-Cloud, 5
February 1980; quoted and translated in Torjusen, *Words and Images of Edvard
Munch*, pp. 55-7.

[5] Ms. Munch Museum Archives, Oslo, N 45, probably beginning of 1930s;
quoted and translated in Arne Eggum, *Edvard Munch* (London: Thames and
Hudson, 1984), p. 44.

[6] Ms. Munch Museum Archives, Oslo, N 122, probably end of 1920s;
quoted and translated in Eggum, *Edvard Munch*, p. 46.

[7] Eggum, *Edvard Munch*, p. 46.

[8] Munch, OKK T 2759, probably 1904; quoted and translated in Torjusen,
Words and Images of Edvard Munch, p. 50.

[9] Munch, OKK N 29, c. 1890–1891; quoted and translated in Torjusen,
Words and Images of Edvard Munch, p. 48.

[10] Elizabeth Prelinger, *Edvard Munch: Master Printmaker* (New York and
London: W. W. Norton and Company, 1983), p. 10.

[11] Quoted in Arne Eggum, 'The Theme of Death', in Reinhold Heller,
Edvard Munch: Symbols and Images. Exhibition Catalogue (Washington DC:
National Gallery of Art, 1978), p. 152; cited in Prelinger, *Edvard Munch*, p. 76.

[12] Prelinger, *Edvard Munch*, p. 76.

[13] Ibid., p. 88.

[14] Ibid.

[15] Ibid., p. 90.

[16] Munch, draft of a letter to Jens Thiis, c. 1932–1933, ms. in Munch Museum Archives, Oslo; quoted and translated in Reinhold Heller, *Munch: His Life and Wo*rk (Chicago: The University of Chicago Press, 1984), p. 21.

[17] See the section 'The Theology of the Cross and Atheism', in Jürgen Moltmann, *The Crucified God. The Cross of Christ as the Foundation and Criticism of Christian Theology*, trans. R.A. Wilson & J. Bowden (London: SCM, 1974), pp. 219-227.

[18] Laura Munch, letter to her children, 12 Jan 1868, ms. in Munch Museum Archives, Oslo; quoted and translated in Heller, *Munch: His Life and Work*, p.15.

[19] Ms. Munch Museum Archives, Oslo, N 5–N 16, probably December 1889; quoted and translated in Heller, *Munch: His Life and Work*, p. 55.

[20] Ms. Munch Museum Archives, Oslo, T 2761; quoted and translated in Heller, *Munch: His Life and Work*, p. 40.

[21] Ms. Munch Museum Archives, Oslo, T 2760, 8 Jan. 1892; quoted and translated in Heller, *Munch: His Life and Work*, p. 62.

[22] Edvard Munch, *Livsfrisens tilblivelse*, p. 17; quoted and translated in Heller, *Munch: His Life and Work*, p. 63.

[23] From Munch to Mrs Valborg Hammer, Paris, September 1896, OKK T 2782-ba; quoted and translated in Torjusen, *Words and Images of Edvard Munch*, p. 30.

[24] 1 Corinthians 13:12, KJV.

[25] From a pamphlet put together by Munch in Grimsrød, originally cited in Christian Gierløff, *Edvard Munch selv* (Oslo: Gyldendal norsk forlag, 1953), p. 43; reprinted and translated in Øivind Storm Bjerke, *Edvard Munch and Harald Sohlberg, Landscapes of the Mind* (National Academy of Design, New York, 1995), p. 21.

[26] Munch, letter to his family, printed in Inger Munch (ed.), *Edvard Munchs Brev: Familien* (Oslo: Johan Grundt Tanums Forlag, 1949), p. 270; reprinted and translated in Bjerke, Munch and Sohlberg, *Landscapes of the Mind* , pp. 22-3.

[27] Quoted and translated in Bjerke, Munch and Sohlberg, *Landscapes of the Mind*, p. 23.

[28] Reinhold Heller, *Edvard Munch: The Scream* (London: Allen Lane/Penguin Press, 1973), pp. 67-8.

[29] For example, Søren Kierkegaard, *Philosophical Fragments or a Fragment of Philosophy by Johannes Climacus*, trans. D. F. Swenson & H. V. Hong (Princeton: Princeton University Press, 1962), pp. 46-67; Kierkegaard's

Concluding Unscientific Postscript, trans. D. F. Swenson & W. Lowrie (Princeton: Princeton University Press, 1941), pp. 186-98.

[30] Kierkegaard, *Concluding Unscientific Postscript*, pp. 186-90.

[31] George Pattison, *Art, Modernity and Faith: Restoring the Image* (London: SCM Press, 1998), p. 24.

[32] Heller, *Edvard Munch: The Scream*, pp. 28-30.

[33] Quoted in Heller, *Edvard Munch: The Scream*, p. 27.

[34] Sandra Bertman, *Facing Death: Images, Insights, and Interventions* (Philadelphia: Taylor and Francis, 1991).

2
Marc Chagall: Playing With Fire

It is difficult to think of another artist who lived so long and experienced so much. Born into a poor Jewish family living in the town of Vitebsk within the borders of the Russian Empire, Marc Chagall (1887–1985) discovered early on what it was like to be part of a community constantly struggling to preserve its religious and cultural identity in the face of oppression and discrimination. Frequent pogroms — government sanctioned attacks by Christians against Jews — were a fact of life for those who lived in the area known as the 'Pale of Settlement'. Later Chagall would welcome the political revolution of 1917 led by the Bolsheviks that brought to an end the power of the Tsars and promised a measure of freedom and tolerance.

By the 1930s Chagall was living in Paris, and once again he experienced the full force of human brutality. He watched as the Nazis came to power and began to implement a policy designed to eliminate Jews from Europe. The task of rounding them up and despatching them to concentration camps was well under way when arrangements were made for Chagall to escape from France to America in 1941. He went with a mixture of relief that he was safe and guilt for those he left behind. He continued to follow the progress of the war, including news of the destruction of Vitebsk and of the terrible reality of the Jewish Holocaust.

Thus, in a life frequently overshadowed by the upheaval and conflict, fear and unrest, war and suffering that scarred the twentieth century, Chagall worked as an artist. He created paintings, etchings, murals, stained-glass windows, and set and costume designs, so giving expression to the world he knew and experienced. It would hardly surprise us, then, if his art was dominated by a sense of the world's darkness. But though, as we shall see, Chagall does indeed use paint to convey something of the dark and terrible events that took place in Europe under Nazi rule, just a brief glance through a selection of his work reveals a man in love with colour. His paintings, with their unique language and imagery, are a glorious celebration of life and love, and despite encountering so much pain and despair, he filled his world with mysterious, playful images designed to provoke us into laughter.

It is this ability to concern himself with both the tragic and the joyful that makes Chagall the kind of guide who might help us on the journey of faith, not least because human life almost invariably requires us to deal with these opposites. We know what it is to be surprised by joy and to be torn apart by despair, and our lives are often a struggle to make sense of these conflicting experiences. In Chagall we will discover a person who gave powerful expression to the universal experience of suffering, but who never let go of the faith and the hope that could dream of a deeper reality. He serves as a bridge, holding together opposites within his own life, and so encouraging us to search for a wholeness that is truly life affirming.

The two pictures to which we shall give particular attention are very different. They will serve to introduce us to the twin themes of tragic suffering and joyful play, enabling us to explore how these weave their way throughout Chagall's life and work. We shall then seek to show how they might be described as two sides of the same coin, providing us with the kind of 'language' that can nurture and enrich the journey of faith. One of the recurring motifs to emerge will be the way in which Chagall employed a gentle, almost mischievous, irony in his painting — and, indeed, recognized an irony in all of life and faith. Irony, of course, relies on a clash of opposites, as expression is given to different levels of meaning, one or more of which is invariably hidden from those who think they know it all. I do not believe Chagall had any desire to make us the victims of his irony, but he does invite us to open our eyes and to see.

White Crucifixion (1938)

The systematic extermination of the Jews had not yet begun, but clear signs had already emerged of Germany's intentions. Since coming to power in 1933, the Nazis had carried out street attacks on Jews, declared a national boycott of all Jewish shops, and brought in laws denying citizenship to German Jews. In his home in Paris, Chagall was all too close to these unfolding events, and visits to Vilna in Poland and to Palestine increased his awareness of the widespread anti-Semitism that was forcing so many Jews to flee for their lives. Added to which, his own work had been vilified in a Nazi exhibition of 1933, 'Images of Cultural Bolshevism', and in 1937 a large number of his paintings held in German public collections were confiscated. Chagall reacted by reasserting his Jewish origins, but he could not help but be fearful for the future.

Then in 1938 came waves of vicious attacks, culminating in the infamous Kristallnacht of 9 November — the 'night of broken glass' — when tens of thousands of Jewish homes, shops and synagogues were destroyed. It provided the immediate context for Chagall's magnificent painting, *White Crucifixion* (Plate 3).

This is typically 'Chagallian'! The immediate impression is of a profusion of disparate images that do not appear to belong together or to have much order: figures float in the air, houses are at odd angles, a boat appears from nowhere. The sense is of everything in motion, in a state of flux and turmoil. The style is 'primitive', displaying the kind of naïvety that might lead us to describe it as some kind of icon, and there is clearly no sense in which we could call this a realistic painting. The rules of perspective are deliberately ignored and there is no horizon. Instead, we are given the impression of entering another world, free from normal constraints, and yet this other world is never too far removed from the one known and experienced. Here, as elsewhere in his work, Chagall included numerous references to what he saw, but did so in a way that is intensely personal rather than formal. He wanted to evoke feelings, memories and sensations.

White is the colour of sorrow. It appeared strongly in other paintings of this period, most notably one titled *Solitude* (1933) that portrays a Jew sitting alongside a white heifer, cloaked in his white tallith — the traditional prayer shawl — lost in a deep and profound sadness. In *White Crucifixion* it is also the dominant colour, contrasting with small patches of brightness (particularly the flames of fire) that give life and balance to the composition. Around the central cross Chagall has placed a number of scenes reminiscent of the way many traditional images of the crucifixion include the various participants in the story, and these provide us with a particular historical context for the painting while enhancing the sense that this is iconography.

On the right, a synagogue has been desecrated, its contents scattered on the ground outside before the building is set on fire. It is clearly a

German soldier who is responsible as he wears the uniform of a
Brownshirt with a swastika on the armband, though this is not as prominent in the painting as was once intended and Chagall has avoided placing
a similar swastika on the flag. In the foreground distressed figures seek to
make their escape, fleeing in different directions. One of them is familiar
from some of the artist's other work: the man with the sack on his back
appears in *Over Vitebsk* painted in 1914 where he is most obviously the
archetypal Wandering Jew. In *White Crucifixion* he might also be the
prophet Elijah whose presence was awaited at each Passover meal as the
one who would bring news of the Messiah and the promise of freedom. In
his somewhat idiosyncratic autobiography, *My Life*, Chagall recalls childhood Passovers:

> My father, raising his glass, tells me to go and open the door.
> Open the door, the outside door, at such a late hour, to let in the prophet
> Elijah?
> A cluster of white stars, silvered against the background of the blue
> velvet sky, force their way into my eyes and into my heart.
> But where is Elijah and his white chariot?
> Is he still lingering in the courtyard to enter the house in the guise of a
> sickly old man, a stooped beggar, with a sack on his back and a
> cane in his hand?[1]

In *White Crucifixion*, Elijah steps over a burning Torah scroll; the very
basis of the community's identity and practice is being destroyed, and
there is no sign of a white chariot.

On the left, an army is entering the picture waving red flags. Some
critics have suggested that this should be seen as a liberating force — the
Red Army — arriving in time to help save the village from destruction, so
reflecting Chagall's committed involvement in the Communist
Revolution. The argument, however, is hard to sustain. It is true that
Chagall had hoped the Revolution would bring in a new era of toleration
that would allow artists like himself to flourish, and he did agree to take
up the position of Commissar for Art in Vitebsk in 1918. But by mid-1920
internal politics had forced him out, and from then on his standing with
the Soviet authorities rapidly declined. Chagall's own disillusionment set

in early. *My Life* tells of how he gathered together the house-painters in Vitebsk to make copies of his own sketches in order to decorate the town for the first anniversary of the Revolution. He writes:

> And on October 25, throughout the town, my multicoloured animals swung back and forth, swollen with revolution.
> The workers marched forward singing the International.
> When I saw their smiles I was sure they understood me.
> Their communist leaders appeared to be less satisfied.
> Why is the cow green and why is the horse flying in the sky? Why? What has that to do with Marx and Lenin?
> There was a rush to place orders with the young sculptors for busts of Lenin and Marx, in cement.[2]

The year before painting *White Crucifixion*, Chagall produced his only major composition dealing explicitly with the Russian Revolution. Divided into sections, *The Revolution* (1937) offers two contrasting ways of seeing and shaping the world. On one side the revolutionary masses are gathered, painted in reds and purples with their weapons of conflict and their tombstones; on the other side musicians, acrobats and lovers create a scene of joy and harmony where the dominant colour is a gentle blue; in the middle Lenin does a handstand! 'I think the Revolution could be a great thing,' wrote Chagall, 'if it retained its respect for what is other and different.'[3] But clearly it had failed to do so, and the idea that just a year later he would depict the Red Army as the bringer of freedom is impossible to accept.

It is more likely that this scene in *White Crucifixion* has echoes of the past and Chagall's dark childhood experiences of pogroms. The little group of houses was his familiar way of recalling with fondness the simple structures that filled the town of his birth. Now burning, they lie at strange and impossible angles, just as Chagall was now living in a world that had been turned upside down and had itself lost any sense of rational coherence and meaning. Below the houses a boat carries refugees who are shouting and gesticulating.

While some have used this painting to point to Chagall's political commitments, others have seen in it evidence that he had very little interest in politics of any description, even wanting to distance himself from current events. The two figures running away in the bottom left corner are seen as illustrative of this. One is carrying a scroll, while the other wears a piece of white cloth over his blue smock that in one preliminary sketch for the painting carried the German inscription 'Ich bin Jude' [I am a Jew]. Why did Chagall remove the wording? Was it because he wanted to avoid any clear political statement? Would it have tied him too closely to the plight of the Jews when in fact he had ceased to care much about the Jewish faith? We shall return to such issues in due course, though to try to distance Chagall from a concern for contemporary events or his sense of Jewish identity is no more convincing than the idea that he was actively promoting communism. This complex man makes us deeply aware of Jewish suffering while at the same time giving expression to a wider vision of reality.

At the top of the painting are several floating figures, perhaps prophets and teachers from the Old Testament, who lament the fate of the Jewish people. Two are wrapped in a tallith, or prayer shawl, while one wears tefillin, the small leather box on the forehead that contains passages from the Old Testament. Chagall repeatedly painted figures in the air who are both distant from and yet also part of the world. At the bottom a menorah burns as it would in Jewish worship, and appears to be the only solidly upright object in the painting.

In the centre of these swirling scenes of terror and destruction is, of course, the figure of the crucified Christ. He is very clearly a Jewish Christ, for the loincloth he is wearing is unmistakably a tallith, but there is also no doubt that this Jewish martyr is also the Christian redeemer of the world. Above his head are the Roman letters INRI and the Hebrew inscription provided by Pilate, 'Jesus of Nazareth, King of the Jews'; surrounding his head is a halo affirming the holiness of this victim of violence.

As we give our attention to this great painting, and particularly to the figure of Christ, it is clear that we have to begin to work with it at a number of different levels. We have noted that *White Crucifixion* is Chagall's response to specific events that took place in 1938, and yet we have also become aware that there are references to other times and places including, of course, the death of Jesus in first-century Palestine. The picture makes significant political comment on what was going on, but at the same time this is not allowed to become too obvious or too dominant. It is evidently a work of art that is about the darkness of pain and suffering. There is a deep sorrow and anguish here that is unprecedented in the rest of Chagall's works, and has led to the painting being compared and contrasted with *Guernica*, a frightening and fearful work of art executed a year earlier by Picasso in response to terrible events in the Spanish Civil War. Yet in the midst of suffering the figure of Christ conveys a deep peace and tranquillity. A shaft of light enters the painting and we are led to believe that there is a path of hope to be discovered amidst the wreckage of this world's events.

But undoubtedly the central issue to be faced is the fact that Chagall, a Jew, has painted a Christian symbol — the crucifixion — in order to express the suffering of his people. Here was a man who had himself experienced persecution at the hands of Christians, who now saw it happening once again, and who nevertheless dares to use the tradition of the oppressor to give a voice to the oppressed. We are left with a sense of deliberate irony, not least because the finished painting could so easily become an icon for use in Christian church worship. It is an irony that deserves to be explored in greater depth.

A universal symbol of suffering

It has been said that the crucifixion can no longer really serve as a symbol of universal suffering, both because there are so many other rich images now available from film and photography, and because the vast majority of those who suffer do not belong within the Christian tradition. But the evidence suggests otherwise. During the last century artists from all backgrounds have drawn on this image as a pathway towards understanding and compassion, including Chagall.

A brief encounter with a Rabbi, recalled in *My Life,* prompted Chagall to regret his failure to ask questions '. . . about Christ, whose pale face had been troubling me for a long time.'[4] From his earliest days as a painter he had been prepared to follow his own intuitions, and this led him to cross the kinds of boundaries that often made him an outsider. He was the child born in poverty who entered the sophisticated art world; the Russian who lived most of his life in the culture of the West; the Jew who rejected the ban on image-making even to the point of painting Christian symbols. His first rendering of the crucifixion was in 1912, a painting he called *Dedicated to Christ* that was Cubist in style and very different from what he would produce later on. It reveals, however, Chagall's early interest in the figure of Christ, and this was to surface with real force in the late 1930s and 1940s with *White Crucifixion* the first in a series of paintings in which the darkness of crucifixion was explored. Others from the period include *The Martyr* (1940), showing a man bound to a stake amidst images associated with sacrifice, *Yellow Christ* (1941), clearly influenced by Gauguin's painting of the same name, and *The Crucified* (1944), a winter scene showing poor Russian Jews nailed to crosses in the street running through their village. In a poem written to his wife, Bella, Chagall reflected that '. . . like Christ, I, too am crucified, fastened to my easel with nails.'[5]

Chagall was certainly not the first to use the crucifixion image in this way. The story of the *Isenheim Altarpiece,* completed by Matthias Grünewald in the early sixteenth century, is of how this immensely disturbing painting of Christ's crucifixion was used within a hospital context in order that patients might see in Christ one who could identify with their suffering and bring them healing. Francisco Goya was another artist who, in his *Third of May 1808*, famously used the crucifixion image in a portrayal of Napoleon's brutal execution of patriots in Madrid to confront issues of justice and injustice. In all kinds of contexts, the cross has become a way of representing and symbolizing suffering. But it is one thing for a Christian artist such as Goya to employ this symbol; it is quite another matter for a Jew.

The issues raised by Chagall's painting are graphically illustrated by the work of a Jewish writer, Chaim Potok. He, too, wrestled with the power of the cross as a symbol for suffering in his novel *My Name Is Asher Lev*. Asher Lev, a member of the strict Jewish community of Ladover Hasidim, is a brilliant artist whose gift contradicts the values and beliefs of his own people. In the book we are taken back to his childhood, through the experiences of love and conflict that accompany him as he learns to paint, to the time when he looks for a way to express on canvas all the anguish and torment felt by him and especially his mother during the course of those growing years. Despite the horror and exclusion he knows will result, he chooses to paint his mother on a cross. He cries out:

> For all the torment of your past and future years, my mama. For all the anguish this picture of pain will cause you. For the unspeakable mystery that brings good fathers and sons into the world and lets a mother watch them tear at each other's throats. For the Master of the Universe, whose suffering world I do not comprehend. For dreams of horror, for nights of waiting, for memories of death, for the love I have for you, for all the things I remember, and for all the things I should remember but have forgotten, for all these I created this painting — an observant Jew working on a crucifixion because there was no aesthetic mould in his own religious tradition into which he could pour a painting of ultimate anger and torment.[6]

As predicted, the two paintings Asher Lev produces evoke rage from his family and community. There is a deep sense of betrayal. They do not understand how he could have painted what for centuries had been a symbol of domination, persecution and death for Jews. And yet, for the painter himself, there seemed to be no choice.

This was the conclusion of an artist such as James Rosen, a devout Jew, who when asked why he had chosen the cross for a 1975 painting on suffering and love answered very simply that '. . . some symbols transcend particular traditions and strike a universal human chord.'[7] Such artists have shown remarkable courage in their willingness to step outside their own religious and cultural framework, and in doing so they have often faced criticism and rejection particularly from within their own community. Chagall is another who has walked this path. He believed that good art should be able to transcend a particular context and culture and to speak a universal message, and that in the face of people's shared pain and suffering the image of crucifixion is the one that most powerfully gives expression to this experience.

When we consider the meaning of *White Crucifixion*, however, there is something more to be said. In 1933 Chagall wrote:

> If a painter is a Jew and paints life, how is he to keep the Jewish elements out of his work! But if he is a good painter, his painting will

contain a great deal more. The Jewish content will be there, of course, but his art will aim at universal relevance.[8]

Those words could easily have been written about *White Crucifixion*, particularly if we take care to give weight to both sides of the argument. It is a painting that does set out to employ a universal symbol with universal relevance, but it also wants to speak directly into the Jewish experience of pain and suffering in Nazi Germany. It treads the line between the universal and the particular, and this is a key to its greatness.

Chagall succeeds in confronting us with a number of questions. Who is the person on the cross? Do we recognize him as a Jew? Is he a Jewish martyr in solidarity with the Jews pictured in the surrounding scenes of chaos and destruction? Or is he the instrument of Christian anti-Semitism? Is he the victim of violence, or the cause of violence, or both? Could he be the universal Christ, and if so, how is he redeemer for the victims of Nazi persecution? Whose tradition is at work in the picture? What is the symbol of the cross saying, and who is meant to be listening?

As Christians we take our lead from the Apostle Paul who decided to know nothing '. . . except Jesus Christ, and him crucified' (1 Corinthians 2:2). We regard the cross as central to the faith we proclaim and the life we live, and we want to go on and declare that it has a universal meaning and significance. The cross is the place where we are brought face to face with the human condition, and where we encounter the presence of God. It is not, of course, the only such place, but the Christian faith wants to affirm that the particular event of Jesus' crucifixion is in some way decisive for all humanity and for the nature of God. It is the death of Christ that allows God to share in the experience of human suffering and death in a deeper, more intense way than happens elsewhere in history. Moreover, we believe that this is decisive for us in enabling a discovery of the participative presence of God in all our individual and collective experiences of suffering.

Though we have made such universal claims for the cross of Christ, however, we have consistently lived and acted in ways that limit the cross to something whose power and meaning is made in our own image. It has become an instrument of exclusion and violence, and this is illustrated by the deep rift that grew up between Jews and Christians. Late in the second century, Melito of Sardis made the accusation that in crucifying Jesus the Jews were guilty of murdering God, and this charge of deicide took a fierce hold on the mind and heart of the Christian church. It was repeated by many of the 'Fathers' of the church, notably John Chrysostom who warned Christians tempted to celebrate Jewish festivals not to mix with those who killed Christ and so are 'dishonoured, abandoned by God'. By the twelfth century, verbal attacks had given way to physical attacks. The actions of the English crusaders, with the cross emblazoned on their tunics, included taking vengeance against the Jews and a number of massacres took place. One of the most infamous incidents happened in 1190 when a mob attacked the prosperous Jewish community of York, who took refuge in the royal castle before committing mass suicide. From then on Christian anti-Semitism became more general, and the cross a symbol that provoked fear and hatred. In the twentieth century this surfaced yet again in the Jewish Holocaust, or Shoah. In the heartland of Christian Europe six million Jews were murdered, and there is little doubt that such action was only possible because of centuries of Christian anti-Jewish teaching, including that experienced by Chagall in Russia. Tragically, even when the evidence of Nazi atrocities was undeniable, only a very few Christians actively resisted the policy of genocide.

White Crucifixion forces us to confront this history and challenges those of us who belong to the Christian tradition to look again at how we understand and use the cross as the ultimate symbol of our faith. The painting does not allow us to think of Jesus as anyone but a Jew with his distinctive prayer shawl wrapped around him. Further, in surrounding Jesus the Jew with scenes from history that record Christian anti-Semitism, we are faced with the inherent irony of the situation, an irony that demands a response.

To help us in this, we do not have to stray from familiar territory. Paul Duke has described the Fourth Gospel as having 'a quality and persistence of irony that seem unique in early Christian expression.'[9] He has gone on to explore the ways in which the writer consistently exploits this device, and this gives us the opportunity to place Chagall's painting alongside the insights he offers.

One example of the Gospel's irony noted by Duke has to do with the identification of Jesus' opponents. On one level it appears simple. John's fierce polemic against 'the Jews' surfaces with progressive intensity throughout the course of the Gospel, and while it is evident that those in mind are a selective group comprised of the religious authorities who were actively resistant to Jesus and his message, this has proved to be fuel for the fire of anti-Semitism over many centuries. But Duke shows that it is not as straightforward as this, not least because out of all the New Testament writings John's Gospel most clearly offers a universal vision of the meaning of the cross. It is for the sake of the whole world that Christ died and lives.

In John 1:11, right at the beginning of the Gospel, John writes that Jesus '. . . came to what was his own, and his own people did not accept him.' Who are his own people? Who are the guilty ones? It would be easy to conclude — somewhat smugly — that it was the Jews who failed to accept Jesus, but such an interpretation is far too neat! As the Prologue makes clear, Jesus' domain is the world; he embraces the whole of humanity as his 'own people', and those who fail to accept him are those whose imagination and understanding is too small and restricted by traditional boundaries. Now we have to wonder if it is not the Christian community that has too often been guilty of a narrow perspective, one that holds Jesus within a straightjacket of our own making and blames others for his rejection and death. John's universal vision demands that we stop pointing the finger, examine ourselves, and make our own effort to discover a new way of seeing.

When it comes to Jesus' trial and execution, the exchanges between Pilate, 'the Jews' and Jesus raise the fundamental question of authority, not least in the use of the ironic title 'King of the Jews'.[10] In one sense, Jesus is clearly not their king at all for he has no human mandate to rule. In another sense, we want to say 'the Jews' were wrong and that they should have recognized that Jesus is indeed their king. But in a further, deeper sense, John calls us to recognize that we too are wrong: Jesus is not ruler over one small province but ruler of the world. We should note that when Jesus is 'lifted up' on the cross, drawing all the world to himself, Pilate ensures the title is written in Hebrew, Latin and Greek so enabling the whole world to recognize his kingship. This is a universal vision that demands our faith and obedience.

The use of irony in the Fourth Gospel serves many purposes, but at least one of its achievements is to put readers on their guard against the human tendency to contain and define Christ — a theme to which we shall return at the close of this chapter. Jesus appears as one who breaks down barriers and crosses borders, who challenges conventional wisdom, who includes outsiders, and who in death draws all people to himself (John 12:32). And this is exactly the challenge of *White Crucifixion*. The image of the crucified Christ is at the centre of images of Jewish persecution, and we are put on our guard against any complacency that might lead us to believe that we have either learned or lived out the universal message of the gospel. We are reminded that, throughout history, those who should have known better did not, and a symbol of costly resistance to violence has too easily become exactly the opposite.

It has been argued strongly that Chagall's is not a Christian painting of the crucifixion. In Chagall's biography, Franz Meyer states:

> Christ's relation to the world differs entirely from that in all Christian representation of the Crucifixion. There it is not the world that suffers, except in grief for his death on the cross; all suffering is concentrated in Christ, transferred to him in order that he may overcome it by his sacrifice. Here instead, though all the suffering of the world is mirrored in the Crucifixion, suffering remains man's lasting fate and is not abolished by Christ's death. So Chagall's Christ figure lacks the Christian concept of salvation. For all his holiness he is by no means divine.[11]

It is an interesting comment. Certainly Chagall professed no Christian faith and so in this sense Meyer is right to say that *White Crucifixion* is not a Christian painting. Throughout his life Chagall remained a Jew, and when he did carry out commissions for Christian churches — such as stained-glass windows, one of which can be seen in Chichester Cathedral — he always felt a certain discomfort. Meyer is also right in suggesting that Chagall's representation is unlike others that belong firmly within the Christian tradition. His is not an idealized crucifixion scene, neither delicately layered in gold and rich colours in the Gothic style, nor set in the kind of peaceful landscape portrayed by the Romantic artist Caspar David Friedrich; it is, as we have seen, rooted firmly in twentieth-century history. We may want to question, however, whether Meyer has really understood the images and meanings that surround the cross when he suggests that the Christ of Christian faith abolishes suffering. In our search for a theology after Auschwitz, we have to discover a God present at Auschwitz, one who is there amidst pain and suffering and who, as Alan Paton reminds us in his novel, *Cry, The Beloved Country*, comes 'not to save us from suffering, but to teach us how to bear suffering.'[12]

In painting *White Crucifixion*, Chagall does face us with the horror of Auschwitz, and his vision of the cross and its meaning contains a greater depth than Meyer realizes. It is also a painting that redeems the cross as a universal symbol of suffering, for there is a real sense in which the past actions of Christians have meant we have forfeited the right to it. Only a Jew can once again give permission for the cross to be used in this way, enabling it to become an expression of the universal experience of suffering that also has the capacity to become a universal symbol of hope.

The Juggler (1943)

Here (Plate 4) is a painting that could not be more different. It is as distinctively 'Chagallian' as *White Crucifixion*, and yet it seems to belong to a different world designed to evoke the very opposite emotions within the viewer. Here is playful fantasy, magical imagery, and joyous colour.

It is true that by the time he painted *The Juggler* Chagall was enjoying the safety of life in America. In one sense he was a long way from the terror of war in Europe and so a different kind of painting might not be surprising. But we should note that the war was certainly not far from his mind, aware as he was of the course events were taking on the Russian front. It disturbed him greatly to learn that the Nazis had conquered Vitebsk in July 1941; the retreating Red Army had set fire to the city, and the 16,000 Jews who remained were being murdered. We should also recall that it was during this same period that Chagall painted a number of his crucifixion scenes, several of which have already been referred to. In many ways this was a time of darkness for the artist, and yet he produced *The Juggler*.

Chagall's time in America was a period of exile. He never felt at home living in the city of New York despite the presence of many other refugees, but in 1942 it did provide him with his first opportunity to work in ballet. The National Ballet Theatre commissioned Chagall to prepare sets and costumes for their production of *Aleko*, and because trade union difficulties prevented him completing the work in New York, the entire troupe moved to Mexico City for a month where the ballet was premiered to considerable acclaim. The resulting exposure to Mexican art, culture and landscape provided new sources of inspiration for Chagall, most particularly in the use of colour. Three years later, having completed a further commission to design the sets for Stravinsky's *Firebird*, he commented:

> I wanted to penetrate the spirit of Firebird and Aleko without illustrating them, without copying anything. I'm not trying to represent anything. I want colour to speak for itself and act alone.[13]

This renewed interest in colour inspired by time spent in Mexico found its way into a cycle of circus paintings completed by Chagall following his return to New York. *The Juggler* is the most important of these, and the intense colours that fill the canvas are immediately striking. The bright yellows, greens, blues and reds help give a dominating presence to the central figure, who appears to hold in balance all the various elements of the picture. Our attention is, of course, drawn towards the head of the bird placed on the body of a man. Here are fantastic images and symbols that are not obeying familiar rules, and we know that if we are to give sense and meaning to the painting, then we have to begin to enter another world — the world of the circus where the absurd is commonplace and everyone is at play.

The cock's head, with its eye staring out at us and its beak pointing cheekily upwards, is one of Chagall's characteristic animal motifs and appears in a number of his paintings of this period. It can be seen in *Listening to the Cock* (1944), *Cow with Parasol* (1946), and *Madonna with the Sleigh* (1947), all of which were painted during his time in America, and it provided the subject for a costume design for Scene IV of *Aleko*. There are many ways of responding to and interpreting the way Chagall includes the cock. On the one hand, it was simply a way of recalling the rural setting of his childhood where animals were a part of daily life. He frequently alluded to his memories of Vitebsk and gave expression to the ideal of peasant life where humans and animals lived together in harmony. On the other hand, it can be seen as a symbol of elemental forces, both sexual and spiritual. It is a reminder that for thousands of years the cock has played a part in religious ceremonies, and Chagall himself would have encountered its ritual sacrifice during the purification ceremony before the Day of Atonement. So our attention is directed towards the existence of another world — the world of non-rational forces, of the soul, of the unconscious, that has a dark and unknown dimension. It is interesting to note, too, that within the Jewish Hasidic tradition within which Chagall grew up, Rabbi Meier ben Baruch from the thirteenth century had interpreted the second commandment as forbidding the representation of human faces in the synagogue but allowing the depiction of animal heads in their place. This might also have been in Chagall's mind. None of the interpretations is mutually exclusive and each one may have contributed to this painting.

The figure of the juggler stands on one leg, the other thrown back up to meet his neck in a pose that is reminiscent of the acrobat in an earlier painting on the circus theme. On his right arm hangs a clock, another characteristic feature of Chagall's work. This is a fascinating symbol. It was one of those memorable objects from childhood, present in his parent's living room that seemed to the young Chagall to have a strange life of its own. The unremitting, uninterrupted ticking of time gave to it an unending quality that nothing could destroy. Yet at the same time, that ticking away of each minute marked out the limits of human existence, held as we are within the confines of time. Thus the clock became a frontier symbol, a bridge between this world and eternity. Often Chagall painted it flying through the air, most notably in *Time is a River Without Banks* (1930–1939), illustrating the passing of time. Here it is draped over the arm of the juggler in a way that reminds us of the limp, melting clocks in Salvador Dali's Surrealist painting *The Persistence of Memory* (1930), and so we sense that time is somehow being subverted; past and future are wrapped up in the present, the normal ordering of things is turned upside down, and life becomes subject to greater forces.

The juggler's green vest contains a further recurring image that never ceased to haunt Chagall: the fiddler. Almost always present at Jewish weddings, funerals and festivals, this legendary figure makes his first appearance of any note in *The Dead Man* (1908) where he sits on a roof playing his music, the kind of music that was always full of emotion and invariably contained a note of sadness and melancholy. It seems both the instrument and the way it was played captured the bittersweet nature of life. We know this enigmatic figure best, of course, from the stage play and screenplay *Fiddler on the Roof* telling the story of the Jewish community of Anatevka in the Ukraine.

The circus ring in which the juggler stands has at its base familiar village images from Vitebsk — little wooden houses, a picket fence, a tree. It is the world of Chagall's childhood that he always retained within him. On the upper levels occur various circus scenes, including a female rider who gallops across the ring and a female trapeze artist swinging through the air dressed in blue. On the right there is a woman and a horse entwined together such that they might be one creature. Like the figure of the juggler, this is human and animal coexisting on the same level in the kind of unity that might occur in children's paintings, so breaking down conventional barriers. This sense of longing for a oneness with the animal world comes across not only in Chagall's art. In writing about the circus he said:

> At the sight of horses, who are always in a state of ecstasy, I think: are they not, perhaps, happier than we? You can kneel down peacefully before a horse and pray. It always lowers its eyes in a rush of modesty. I hear the echo of horses' hooves in the pit of my stomach. I could race on a horse for the first time and the last time, to the brilliant arena of life. I would be aware of the transcendence, of no longer being alone among the silent creatures whose thoughts of us only God can know.[14]

The whole painting conveys a terrific sense of movement. There seems to be a whirlpool of warm and rich colours carrying everything and everyone with it except the juggler himself, who gives the impression of being a kind of orchestral conductor leading the joyous celebration of life. The intense colours that dress his figure have already been noted. The fiery yellow and red contrast with the cool blue, while green speaks of life. It is interesting that the ancient Egyptians used the colour green for the faces of certain gods, seeing it as representative of resurrection and life, and Chagall himself used it to colour the face of the violinist in his painting

The Fiddler (1912–1913). Meyer describes it all coming together in the figure of the juggler, such that 'he embodies elemental psychic force as organizer in the sphere of primeval humanity.[15]

In whatever ways our understanding and appreciation is enhanced by this deeper study of the painting, I believe it would be a mistake to forget that this is a circus scene. The circus is a place where the imagination is allowed to run riot, where normal thought processes can be suspended, where what matters is not rational explanation but the ability to live, move, feel, laugh and cry. It is in so many ways the world of the child. Interestingly, there have been a number of artists who have shown a fascination with the circus, including Seurat, Picasso, Lautrec and Rouault (the last of whom we will return to shortly). Chagall's own interest must have been aroused by encounters with travelling jugglers and acrobats, and this emerges in a number of early paintings. It was cemented, however, by Ambroise Vollard who had a season box at the famous Cirque d'Hiver in Paris and invited Chagall to make use of it. This he did, and it resulted in a series of etchings completed in 1927 and known as the *Cirque Vollard*.

The theme was to surface again and again, and it is just as evident when we look at Chagall's considerable involvement in the associated worlds of the theatre and ballet, for he did not hesitate to blur the boundaries between these various art forms. In the period after the 1917 Revolution he worked for the Kamerni Jewish State Theatre, bringing together his experience of the international avant-garde world of Paris with his love for the Jewish folk tradition. Chagall exercised an influence on just about every aspect of a production, allowing a new Expressionist style to emerge within Jewish theatre, and it is not hard to see how close it became to the wondrous, imaginary world of the circus. He covered the walls and ceiling of the theatre with murals, including *Introduction to the Jewish Theatre* (1920) with its images of acrobats and musicians. He did the make-up for the actors, which involved painting their faces as if they were clowns. He banned the use of realistic props, insisting that the actors drink imaginary tea and eat non-existent food. He made sure the costumes they wore became works of art. One delightful story recounts the way in which, just before the curtain was due to rise and the leading actor make his entrance, Chagall

. . . seized the actor by the shoulder and lunged at him frenziedly with his paintbrush as if he were a puppet, painting splodges on his costume and drawing birds and pigs on his cap so tiny that they would have been invisible from the auditorium even with binoculars . . . Chagall wept and muttered under his breath when we extracted the actor by force and pushed him on to the stage.[16]

It is hard to know whether this is theatre, pantomime or circus! It does reveal something of the unity of vision that inspired the artist's work wherever he was and whatever he was doing.

Why, then, this fascination with the circus? Why did Chagall paint *The Juggler*, and in what direction does he point us? Whereas the first painting we looked at drew us into the experience of pain and suffering, this second one invites us to participate in a world of fantasy and play. At the circus we encounter trapeze artists defying the laws of gravity, animals playing games with humans, painted clowns hiding behind their absurd masks, and jugglers making us gasp in wonder at impossible feats. So our minds, hearts and imaginations are set free and we are able to learn another way of seeing and engaging with reality — a way that is playful rather than logical, mystical rather than mechanical. This possibility is present so often in Chagall's paintings, whether or not the formal subject-matter is the circus. Lovers float through the air, cows dance with umbrellas, and there is the figure of the *Luftmensch* seen in a painting such as *Over Vitebsk* (1914) who lives and walks on air, surviving against the odds, expressing the precariousness of existence known by the circus performer who is trying to keep all the balls in the air at once. None of this is susceptible to mechanical reason.

I don't think Chagall was ever engaged in an attempt to *escape* from reality. His paintings included the ordinary, mundane details of human existence, and he never spoke of the circus as if it were a way of avoiding or running away from life. Rather, he seeks to offer us an alternative vision, a different kind of perspective, another language for engaging with reality. He wanted to give expression to Shakespeare's message that 'All the world's a stage', and at the circus he found a world where the drama of life was played out with peculiar intensity. He said:

For me a circus is a magic show that appears and disappears like a world. A circus is disturbing. It is profound . . . It is a magic word, circus, a timeless dancing game where tears and smiles, the play of arms and legs take the form of a great art . . . Through the centuries, it has been the most poignant cry in man's search for amusement and joy. It often takes the form of high poetry.[17]

It appears, then, that far from being a frivolous means of escape, the circus is a place of searching and discovery. It takes us to the heights and depths of human endeavour. Indeed, for Chagall it is nothing less than a place of spiritual journeying. He went on to say:

I have always thought of clowns, acrobats and actors as tragically human beings who, for me, are like characters in certain religious paintings.
Even today, when I paint a crucifixion or some other religious scene, I experience almost the same emotions I used to feel painting circus people . . . it is very hard to explain why . . .[18]

This is a deeply revealing and provocative comment. It asks us to recognize that in some strange, ironic way *White Crucifixion* and *The Juggler* belong together. Despite the fact that the world of fantasy and play that we encounter in the circus seems so distant from the suffering figure on a cross, the truth is found in their unity. The clown and the crucified are one; laughter and tragedy go hand in hand, and play becomes the serious business of spiritual growth.

The importance of play
The Nonconformist religious tradition has a well-founded reputation for earnestness and ugliness. The hallmark of chapel culture has been sober respectability aimed at self-improvement, and the buildings used for worship have been plain and functional. There has never been much room for anything as trivial as art. In the fierce words of the Welsh Nonconformist poet, R. S. Thomas:

Protestantism — the adroit castrator
Of Art; the bitter negation
Of Song and dance and the heart's innocent
joy.[19]

Those of us who belong within this tradition have been used to seeking
the presence of God in careful exposition of the Word, in rigorous doctrinal debate and dispute, and in frequent meetings of church members. The
last place we have been taught to look is the circus — which may be just
as true in other traditions, for as early as the fourth century male theologians like John Chrysostom and Ambrose were condemning playful
activities and preparing the ground for the emergence of a strong and per-
vasive work ethic.

Yet if we allow ourselves to enter the world of *The Juggler*, we might
be surprised at how easily it can take on the marks of the kingdom of
God. As we have discovered, the circus is a place of rich colour where life
in all its fullness is celebrated and affirmed. All are welcome to join in the
fun irrespective of age, ability or appearance: there is room for those
whose bodies are deformed, for clowns who want to shed tears, for those
who struggle with their masks. It is inclusive, of the animal world as well
as all humanity. The circus challenges familiar power structures as it
becomes a place where, in Chagall's words, those who earn no more than
'a piece of bread' are those who lead the rejoicing, and only those who
nurture the child within can enjoy the games. Time ceases to matter, as
the riotous absurdity of life is embraced rather than controlled. It is all a
long way from church meetings and synods!

Perhaps most distinctive of all is the way in which, just as the circus
invites us to enter another world, so the kingdom of God asks us to imagine another reality. Both are, in one way or another, at odds with the
prevailing culture and express the unfulfilled human longing for a world
of harmony and joy. Chagall, of course, would not have had any commitment to Christian eschatology, but from within his own Jewish Hasidic
tradition he could draw on similar hopes and beliefs. It was a tradition
suspicious of reason as a way of understanding God, preferring to nurture
the emotions and allow the power of dance and music to lift the heart
towards Paradise. Hasidic teachers would deliberately engage in playful

activities such as turning somersaults in the market place, exactly as if they were in a circus. It is not too surprising, therefore, that Chagall should feel that an affinity exists between the world of the circus and the world of the Bible, the two themes that provided the main axes for his work.

These parallels between circus and kingdom help us to understand the importance for play, not least because it has been suggested that at the root of all genuine play is our hope for another life and another world. In his book, *Man at Play*, the Jesuit scholar Hugo Rahner argues that:

> To play is to yield oneself to a kind of magic, to enact to oneself the absolutely other, to pre-empt the future, to give the lie to the inconvenient world of fact. In play earthly realities become, of a sudden, things of the transient moment, presently left behind, then disposed of and buried in the past; the mind is prepared to accept the unimagined and incredible, to enter a world where different laws apply, to be relieved of all the weights that bear it down, to be free, kingly unfettered and divine. Man at play is reaching out — as has been said — for that superlative ease, in which even the body, freed from its earthly burden, moves to the effortless measures of a heavenly dance.[20]

We are aware that as we get older we participate in the kind of games where rules are carefully agreed and set down, and winning becomes little less than a compulsion. But our earliest and purest experiences of play are not like that at all. They have to do with creating imaginary worlds; they are free expressions of a desire to reach beyond ourselves, breaking apart the confines of known reality with new wonder and joy. We might dare to say that any quest to reach out to what is other, including our journeying towards God, has to involve us in this activity we call play. As Jesus said, 'Whoever does not receive the kingdom of God as a little child will never enter it.'[21]

This is in no way to trivialize the spiritual journey. Just as it would be wrong to see play as a mere escape from reality, it would also be wrong to see it as lacking in seriousness. A child's play-world cannot be dismissed lightly as of no consequence, and as adults it is worth noting how often we continue to use terms such as 'play' and 'game' in very serious contexts. Our use of expressions such as 'fair play', 'war games' and 'playing around' almost always refer to matters of considerable importance. But at this point we so often go one step too far by thinking that serious play must be something we work hard at, with the inevitable result that we lose a sense of genuine playfulness and our playing becomes tied to what is possible for us to achieve. It ceases to be the vision of something unpredictable and unexpected; it ceases to give us a window into another world. That is why the kingdom of God can never be something we achieve by our own efforts, but must emerge out of a playing with genuinely new possibilities for a transformed future that break apart the old order.

One prominent theologian, quoted in the previous chapter, who has discussed the importance of play is Jürgen Moltmann. Drawing on the Old Testament wisdom literature, he argues that the genesis of the world is best understood as having the character of play with God creating freely in joy and delight.[22] So in Proverbs 8:30-31, we hear Wisdom declare that 'I was daily his delight, rejoicing before him always, rejoicing in his inhabited world and delighting in the human race.' Creation is a divine game because it is born in freedom. It is not necessary for God to create, nor is it some kind of chance accident; rather, the ground of creation is God's good pleasure and reflects God's own nature. The act of creation is serious because it is meaningful, but it does not have the character of necessary work that has to be accomplished.

God's creation of humankind means that we become part of the game. We are invited to be players with God. We have freedom to participate and so discover for ourselves the joy that is at the heart of life. Just as we need to reject concepts of God that use God as a problem-solver in difficult situations or a stop-gap when our knowledge runs out, so Moltmann urges us not to measure our own lives by how much we are used or prove useful. In the words of the Westminster Catechism of 1647, our chief purpose is 'to glorify God and to enjoy Him forever', and it is this that justifies and makes beautiful our existence before anything that we might do or achieve.

One of the consequences of being created in freedom and living in freedom is that not everything is determined. True creative play has an openness that always allows what is new and incalculable to emerge.

Thus the symbol of the world as play stands in direct opposition to the Enlightenment symbol of the world as machine, for a machine suggests a closed system with an unbroken chain of causality determining everything that happens with no room for chance. When we play we have to be ready to dance to different and unexpected tunes, and this brings us back to the vision of an alternative world, the hope of the kingdom of God as that which offers radically new and surprising possibilities rather than being merely the fulfilment and ending of what already is. It is worth noting that just as the creation narrative in Genesis offers us a picture of Eden as an idyllic place where there was opportunity for joyous play with a freedom unhindered by sweat and toil, so when the prophet Zechariah looks forward to the coming age of salvation he describes it as a time when 'the streets of the city shall be full of boys and girls playing in its streets' (8:5). Play and Paradise are words that belong together.

One of the crucial players in the game is Christ. Christ is God's response in love to human misery, not because God needs to respond but because God wants to, and in doing so God liberates us to a new future. Again, the theme is repeated: this is not simply the repairing of the ancient play of creation, but the beginning of a new game of a new creation born out of the gloriously uncontainable, unfathomable love of God. But it is just at this point that Moltmann appears to lose faith in the symbol of play, for while he is happy to speak of Easter as the beginning of dancing and festivity, of the laughing of the redeemed, of joyous liberation from the bonds of slavery, he is unwilling to see the pain and anguish of the cross as part of the game. He suggests we can do nothing else but leave it out. 'It is difficult,' he says, 'to consider the sufferings of the forsaken Christ and his pain of death a serious loving game of God.'[23]

That is an unsurprising comment. I wonder, however, if it is an adequate comment, and whether we must be prepared to allow our imaginations to continue to live with the symbol of play even in the face of the cross. This is partly because we must always be wary of separating the events of cross and resurrection as if they can be interpreted in isolation from each other; but it might also be because this is the point at which we are required to encounter the irony at the heart of our faith. The cross is where nothing is as straightforward as it should be, where losing suddenly becomes winning, where everything is revealed and everything is hidden. In all kinds of ways, we find we are playing games with our language and ideas, trying to comprehend the ironic clash of opposites that challenges those who have too easy an understanding of truth. We describe the cross as a place of glory and of beauty, while at the same time knowing it to be a place of darkness and despair; we want to speak of the suffering figure on the cross as one with our humanity and also as the crucified God; and we recognize that what is no more than foolish, absurd and laughable failure becomes a means of grace and hope. It is reminiscent of the way Sydney Carter in his memorable hymn continues the theme of joyous, playful dance on into and through the events of Good Friday, describing how

> I danced on a Friday when the sky turned black;
> It's hard to dance with the devil on your back.
> They buried my body and they thought I'd gone;
> But I am the dance and I still go on.[24]

So we too are invited to join in the continuing dance of life.

Could this be why Chagall had the same emotions painting circus people as painting scenes of crucifixion? It is more than likely, for he would be part of a long tradition of those who have seen a link between the figure of Christ and that of the fool or clown. One is the artist Georges Rouault, a Catholic who sought to express in his paintings an anger with the violence and ugliness of life. He did this in part by painting some startling images of Christ with the characteristics of the clown and of a clown with Christ-like features, so making the link between the two. Thus, in some strange way the suffering of the cross becomes part of the game of life with its power to open the window into another world of joyous dance and riotous laughter.

It is time to return to Chagall and his painting of *The Juggler*. Throughout his life Chagall was a person at play, sometimes living as a clown within his own magic world, paying scant attention to what was going on around him. He didn't always bother to date his paintings in conventional ways, and nor did he allow his autobiography to be too tied to what actually happened! These things were of little account. What did matter to Chagall was the life of the spirit. 'Art', he declared, 'is an act of faith.'[25] It should be born not of doctrine, but from the depths of the artist's soul, and his powers of composition and flow of colour are used in the quest to make room for a spiritual reality that can enrich the lives of all.

We have explored how the circus directly contributes to this quest, as a place that invites us into a joyous world of play that echoes with the sights and sounds of the kingdom of God. Such playful activity is, as we have seen, characterized by freedom. Dance and laughter, games and celebrations, are only possible for those who are free, and for the Christian this freedom is not what we can make of and for ourselves but is always the transforming gift of God's grace. In the light of this, it is worth looking at *The Juggler* again to consider whether it might be open to further interpretation and offer additional insight. Let us ask the question: could the juggler in the painting in any way offer us a picture of God?

The juggler is certainly the central figure, the pivot around whom everything else revolves. He appears to hold and shape time, and give harmony and balance to the painting. But though the juggler is central, he is by no means controlling. We have already described him as a kind of orchestral conductor — perhaps even the ringmaster — who is intimately involved in the whole performance, forming and shaping it, but at the same time allowing the various participants themselves freely and fully to express who they are and what they can be. Indeed, he would not only allow them; he would help them. Without dictating or manipulating, he would work with them, and this mutual sharing enables a creative overcoming of obstacles and the continual discovery of new and unexpected possibilities that can enrich the final performance.

I believe this provides a picture of God that can enrich our spiritual journey. It is one that allows us to participate with God in a free and dynamic way. It is one marked by openness and creativity, as God invites us to play and dance to the rhythm of a new creation. Most significantly, it is a picture that enables us to encounter the persuasive love of God, a love that is powerful yet non-coercive — what Norman Pittenger so vividly describes as 'the lure of the divine love'[26] — involved with us yet protective of our freedom, able to renew all creation yet needing us to share in the task. Did Chagall intend us to see God in the figure of the juggler? It is a question that cannot be answered with certainty and does not need to be, but I am struck by the fact that, in the painting, the juggler appears to have nothing to juggle with! Maybe his task is to hold together in love the various images that whirl around him, both from past and present, enabling the joyous game of life to go forward into the future. One thing is certain: Chagall always retained a moving faith in the power of love. He said:

> More clearly, more precisely with the years, I have come to feel the relative righteousness of our ways, and the ridiculousness of anything that is not produced with one's own blood, and one's own soul, and which is not saturated by love.
> Everything is liable to change in life and in Art and everything will be transformed when we pronounce, unconstrained, this word 'Love' . . . In it lies the true Art: from it comes my technique, my religion; the old and the new religion that has come to us from far distant times.[27]

The figure of the juggler does not threaten us. Rather, he makes us laugh. God's love does the same, for divine love is the ultimate circus act, full of absurd joy and amazing wonder. It is the kind of love Anne Sexton describes in her poem, 'The Awful Rowing Toward God', as God's 'wild card'. She imagines herself playing a game of poker against God, and as she lays out a royal straight flush, God produces five aces to win the game and cause them both to break into smiles! It is a poem that brings together in images full of irony and truth the themes of divine play and human laughter, of the gloriously unpredictable hope of God's future and the love that makes everything possible. It ends with a kind of prayer:

> Dearest dealer,
> I with my royal straight flush,
> love you for your wild card,
> that untamable, eternal, gut-driven ha-ha
> and lucky love.[28]

How can we sing the Lord's song in a strange land?

The question asked by the writer of Psalm 137 strikes at the heart of the human condition. It asks how we are able to hold together a joyous engagement with life amidst the reality of suffering, and whether there is still room for any kind of faith in God. Chagall's two paintings, *White Crucifixion* and *The Juggler*, face us with these two polarities of human experience, but instead of holding them separate we have seen the way in which the artist embraces both and does learn to laugh, play and sing even when faced with the strange and evil rule of Nazi Germany. *White Crucifixion* is a fearful painting, born out of harsh experience, but it is not without hope as is evident both from the streaming white light that illuminates the cross and the serene way in which Christ himself is depicted. Chagall saw the figure of Christ as of profound significance: he was Jewish martyr and prophet, the ultimate expression of human loneliness and isolation, and the one who — even when nailed to a cross — reached the heights of true freedom and peace. Chagall believed that this universal symbol of suffering also offers a path to hope. In the same way, the circus that is the scene of so much joyous play is not without its pain. Those who participate with deformed bodies can also be the objects of ridicule and the note of melancholy is always present in the music of the fiddler and the tears of the clown, such that the artist went so far as to describe the circus as 'the most tragic show on earth.'[29] It is evident that irony is never far below the surface in both paintings.

How was it that Chagall was able to 'sing the Lord's song in a strange land', weaving together so much that is mutually contradictory while continuing to use art to voice his personal commitment to tolerance and love? What might we learn for our own Christian journey?

One word that is often used to describe Chagall, and that he frequently used of himself, is the word 'poet'. One of his close friends, particularly during the American years, was Raissa Maritain, whose husband was the Catholic philosopher Jacques Maritain. She said:

> Each of Chagall's canvases — in its serenity, pictorial solidity, and infallible science of colour — lives on the stir of poetry, I mean that poetry which is the soul of every work of art, and which calls for an assent, a response of our whole being, as every great work of art does. Poetry, in this sense, is the manifestation of a mysterious knowledge, an experience full of savour, which is born in the depths of the soul . . .[30]

Such a view is echoed again and again, and is confirmed by just a cursory glance at a selection of Chagall's work. The visual language is widely regarded as that of the poet, allowing ideas to take flight within the human imagination and making use of tools such as symbol and metaphor, analogy and irony. His paintings are clearly opposed to sterile rationalism; his emphasis is not on the way formal elements interact, but on the inner experiences and feelings expressed. It is interesting to note, however, Chagall's response when the Surrealist movement, officially launched in 1924, eagerly approached him in order to enlist him as a member. The movement took a determined anti-rationalist stance and was committed to exploring and illustrating the unconscious mind. However, whilst Chagall clearly agreed with many of the ideas expressed by the Surrealist Movement, in fact he refused. The reason for this is that he could not fully agree with the idea that a painting can automatically create itself through the surrender of the conscious will; he also believed in making clear choices as to how to organize and colour images on a canvas, much as a poem requires the careful organization of words.

As well as using the language of colour, Chagall also wrote poetry. In his early life he dreamed of being a poet, recording in *My Life*:

Night and day I wrote verses.
People spoke well of them.
I thought: I'll be a poet, I'll go to . . .
I no longer knew where to let myself go.[31]

As soon as I learned how to express myself in Russian, I began to write poetry. As natural as breathing . . .
I longed to show my verses to a real poet, one of those who get their poetry published.[32]

Chagall did spend a great deal of time with poets throughout his life, often preferring their company to that of other painters, and he continued to write poetry until the end of his life. One of the clearest indications of how he saw himself is a beautiful painting from just after his marriage to Bella in 1915 called *The Poet Reclining*, in which the artist identifies himself as the poet. It has a deeply tranquil and meditative feel to it, a reminder that Chagall always wanted the experience of seeing his paintings to have the same effect as reading poetry.

This poetic 'language' that is so evidently central to Chagall's art is also, I believe, a key to understanding how it is possible for him — and us — to 'sing the Lord's song in a strange land'. Poetry spans the gulf between reality and possibility. It gives close attention to the material of ordinary life in order to open our eyes to what is, while at the same time it liberates the imagination to dare to see things differently. It articulates the complex nature of truth. It is a response to the way the world is and the way the world might be. Moreover it has the power, as Seamus Heaney has suggested, to redress balances by meeting reality with a counter-reality, 'a glimpsed alternative, a revelation of potential that is denied or constantly threatened by circumstances,'[33] and in this way poetry becomes a subversive force for integration and harmony. This is seen most clearly in those who, without in any way compromising their artistic discipline and integrity, have used their poetry to promote political and social change — women and men such as Irina Ratushinskaya and Wilfred Owen. Heaney suggests that for such people poetry becomes 'an exercise in the virtue of hope',[34] where this hope reaches beyond the world that is immediately experienced and finds its roots in the transcendental.

Lionelle Venturi, a close friend during his time in America, wrote of Chagall:

> Gifted with an imagination that is both boundless and at the same time ineffectual against external events, what can this child do, lost as he is in a world more and more alien to him? He replies to war, massacres, martyrs by his painting — the only language of which he is master — by a defiance ever more obstinate. He conjures away the spirit of evil by tenderness and hopes that are sweeter as they are more unrealizable. Thus he escapes into poetry as in a refuge to find himself in losing himself.[35]

It is surely a mistake to say that Chagall 'escapes' into poetry. That misses the truly subversive nature of poetry with its daring ability to give voice to the present order and to dream of new realities. His art is indeed a statement of 'defiance', an act of resistance, a refusal to accept the way things are, and that is why it becomes the kind of poetry that can produce both the paintings we have looked at. While *White Crucifixion* never allows us to forget evil, *The Juggler* never allows evil to suppress hope; with the help of such poetic tools as irony we are given a language of liberation not only to express our contradictory experiences but to argue for redress in a cruel world.

It is clear that poetry and play share much in common, including this ability to be a subversive force. If we picture a carnival we will think immediately of music, laughter, dance and colour all brought together in playful celebration, but we are also aware of how threatening that act of play might appear, particularly to those in authority. It treads the fine line between being a procession and a march, a joyous gathering and a dangerous riot. There is something uncontrollable about it, such that within the act of play there is always an unspoken statement of resistance and rebellion. As we have seen, both play and poetry delight in imagining future alternatives, and this gift is always fearful for those who want to protect and guard the status quo.

We need this kind of 'language' for the journey of faith. Poetry can take us to those places where formal expressions of doctrine find it hard to go, offering a defence against that which we find unbearable, a way of replying to the pain of this world, and a means of nurturing the hope that is at the heart of Christian belief. Let us conclude by identifying more clearly two ways in which this needs to be worked out within the journey of faith.

First, our worship needs to be poetic. If we reduce the language of liturgy to the level of rational discourse or ethical argument, it will be impoverished; what is more, it will fail in its task of enabling the people of God to encounter the presence of God. We have to make room for all kinds of speech, from praise and joy to anger and lament, from affirmation and acclamation to pleading and despairing, for these reflect the range of experiences that shape and form the worshipper. It is poetic discourse that not only gives expression to such contradictory emotions and experiences, but allows them to be held together in tension, dramatizing the story of God's involvement in our lives. Further, it is poetry that then enables us to transcend who we are, as in worship we seek a sense of that which is infinitely greater than ourselves, the source of all our hopes and dreams.

This places a number of requirements on those who lead and participate in worship. Language has to be used thoughtfully, such that words are not cheapened by over-use or careless use. Imagination requires the use of such tools as symbol and metaphor, analogy and irony, in order to provide depth and meaning. There must be room for doubt as well as belief, struggle as well as certainty. Perhaps most importantly, worship needs unashamedly to engage in the games of ritual and ceremony. Of course, they are not useful in an obvious way, any more than other forms of play, but as has been argued this does not make them any less serious. The words and actions that surround the sacraments, for example, are charged with potency, challenging the social and political realities of this world and pointing us in the direction of a new world, but their revolutionary nature will be lost on those who fail to play the game and cannot see with the eyes of the poet.

Earlier we noted the way in which *White Crucifixion* could so easily have been meant as an icon for use in worship. Chagall was certainly influenced by the iconic tradition — a tradition that unites art, faith, ritual, and the desire to see through a window into another world.

Second, we need poetic language to speak of our faith in Christ. In our ways of speaking and understanding, the view persists that the truest form of language is 'factual', offering an objective and scientific account of the way things are, but it is clear that this will prove inadequate when we seek to give expression to who Christ is for us today. Our study of Chagall's paintings has warned us against any attempt to contain Christ within a particular definition, reminding us that such a path leads to exclusion and ultimately violent persecution. Instead we have glimpsed something of the power of poetic devices such as irony to confront us with the truth about this man who fits no single formula. We need to be able to picture him as human and divine, as Jewish martyr and Saviour of the world, as prophet and teacher, as clown and juggler at play, and it is poetry that can provide us with the imaginative resources to do so.

Truth of all kinds — and certainly the truth of Christ — has to be appropriated with our bodies and our souls as much as our minds. It is relational rather than propositional, inviting us to respond in love to the story of death and resurrection. It can appear as absurd and fantastical, enabling joy and grace to take root in the heart even in the midst of pain and suffering. It always has the power to defy logic in just the same way as art, for there are no boundaries that can control it. Thus, all our attempts to know, follow and serve Christ must be provisional, and faith becomes a continuing journey of imaginative discovery.

In speaking about his own spirituality, it is striking how often Chagall used the word 'mystical'. He gave a lecture at around the same time as he painted *The Juggler* in which he said:

> Some people are wrongly afraid of the word 'mystical', they give it an overly orthodox religious meaning. We must strip this word of its old-fashioned, stale appearance: it must be taken in its pure form, intact, strong! . . . without mysticism, would there be even one great painting in the world, a single great poem or even a single great social move-ment?[36]

The spirit of mysticism present within Hasidic Judaism was a guiding influence on Chagall, with its emphasis on the intuitive, emotional response to God. It taught him that everything natural should be regarded as holy and that the presence of God is to be found in all people. It also taught him that the weak are especially rich in heart and that power and self-confidence are barriers to a living relationship with God. So while Chagall held back from identifying with any particular religious tradition and adhered to a general ideal of tolerance and universal love, he saw Christ in weakness on the cross as being a central figure in the encounter with the mystery at the heart of life. The final irony of his life is that he should have been buried as a Jew in a Catholic cemetery.

Chagall was an immensely complex individual not least because, as we have seen, he crossed all kinds of borders — national, social, political and religious. His art, too, defies any easy categorization for it is hard to think of anyone who has painted in the same style with the same use of colour. The result has been paintings that help us sing songs and see suffering without diminishing the reality of either. Indeed, his contribution to the journey of faith is to help us live creatively with both, celebrating colour and playing with fire.

Selected (and annotated) Bibliography

It is not difficult to locate resources that will deepen appreciation for and understanding of Chagall's artistic achievements. These will also reveal the way in which he worked and experimented with all kinds of artistic mediums, even though this chapter has concentrated on his paintings with oils. Perhaps one of the most comprehensive and interesting books available is one that not only reproduces a large number of his works of art but has also collected together lectures, essays, reviews, poetry, and interviews, both by Chagall and about Chagall. It is edited by a friend of his: Jacob Baal-Teshuva (ed.), *Chagall: A Retrospective* (New York: Hugh Lauter Levin Associates, 1995).

Chagall wrote his autobiography when he was thirty-five years old. It has appeared in various editions over the years. The text referred to in this chapter is an unabridged version, and it also includes a number of plates Chagall prepared to illustrate his life story: Marc Chagall, *My Life* (New York: Da Capo Press, 1994).

There are a number of excellent monographs available that concentrate on reproducing a selection from Chagall's vast artistic output. They also provide a brief introduction to his life and a commentary on the work reproduced. Included amongst these are: Gill Polonsky, *Chagall* (London: Phaidon Press, 1998); Werner Haftmann, *Marc Chagall* (London: Thames and Hudson, 1985); and Marie Therese Souverbie, *Chagall* (London: Spurbooks, 1975).

For a more detailed study of the artist's life, it is possible to consult a number of biographies. These vary considerably in form and content. There are two older ones: Franz Meyer, *Marc Chagall* (London: Thames and Hudson, 1964); and Sidney Alexander, *Marc Chagall* (London: Cassell, 1979). The one by Meyer is beautifully produced and very detailed, containing colour prints and analysis of a large number of works as well as small black and white reproductions of many others. Alexander's might be termed a more standard biography: it concentrates on Chagall's life and does not include any reproductions. Both these biographies were produced some years before Chagall died and so are not able to provide a complete overview of his life and work.

More recent and more readily available are Monica Bohm-Duchen, *Chagall* (London: Phaidon Press, 1998); Andrew Kagan, *Marc Chagall* (New York: Abbeville Press, 1989); and Ingo F. Walther & Rainer Metzger, *Marc Chagall 1887–1985: Painting as Poetry* (Cologne: Benedikt Taschen, 2000). The biography by Bohm-Duchan is part of Phaidon's *Art and Ideas* series and is a joy to handle and read. It is thorough without being detailed and is very accessible. The book by Kagan is a useful introduction, though it suffers from the fact that a number of paintings only appear in black and white, while Taschen has produced a briefer but helpful survey of the artist's life and work with high-quality images. There are one or two books available that deal with specific projects undertaken by Chagall, and one outstanding production looks at his work for Russian theatre 1914–1922. It has several fascinating essays and a fine catalogue of pictures: Susan Compton (ed.), *Chagall: Love and the Stage 1914–1922* (London: Merrell Holberton, 1998).

For further background to Jewish themes and concerns during the last century, it is worth consulting a volume that accompanied an exhibition at the Barbican Art Gallery in London: Avram Kampf, *Chagall to Kitaj: Jewish Experience in 20th Century Art* (London: Lund Humphries/Barbican Art Gallery, 1990).

The novelist Chaim Potok is quoted in this chapter. A number of his novels are set within the Hasidic Jewish community of New York, and while New York is a long way from Vitebsk, it is hard to imagine a better way into this particular faith tradition: Chaim Potok, *My Name is Asher Lev* (London: Penguin, 1973).

The key text for exploring the presence of irony in John's Gospel is by an American author: Paul Duke, *Irony in the Fourth Gospel* (Atlanta: John Knox Press, 1985).

The theme of play can be explored from different perspectives. Particular reference is made in this chapter to two theologians: Jürgen Moltmann, *God in Creation* (London: SCM Press, 1985); Moltmann, *Theology and Joy* (London: SCM Press, 1973); and Hugo Rahner, *Man at Play* (London: Burns and Oates, 1965).

A discussion and celebration of the significance of poetry appears in a series of lectures delivered by Seamas Heaney while Professor of Poetry at Oxford University: Seamus Heaney, *The Redress of Poetry* (London: Faber and Faber, 1995).

Notes

This chapter is primarily the work of Graham Sparkes.

[1] Marc Chagall, *My Life* (New York: Da Capo Press, 1994), p. 39.

[2] Ibid., p. 139.

[3] Ibid., p. 156.

[4] Ibid., p. 128.

[5] Marc Chagall, *Poèmes*, 1909–1972, trans. Philippe Jaccottet (Geneva: Gerald Cramer, 1975), p. 36; quoted in Andrew Kagan, *Marc Chagall* (New York: Abbeville Press, 1989), p. 69.

[6] Chaim Potok, *My Name is Asher Lev* (London: Penguin, 1973), pp. 287f.

[7] James Rosen, quoted in Terrence Dempsey, 'Images of Jesus in Modern Art: Contemporary Representations of Jesus', *Proceedings of the Centre for Jewish-Christian Learning* 10 (1995), p. 58.

[8] Quoted in Ingo F. Walther and Rainer Metzger, *Marc Chagall 1887–1985: Painting as Poetry* (Cologne: Benedikt Taschen, 2000), p. 62.

[9] Paul Duke, *Irony in the Fourth Gospel* (Atlanta: John Knox Press, 1985), p. 155.

[10] John 18:33-40; 19:12-22.

[11] Franz Meyer, *Marc Chagall* (London: Thames and Hudson, 1964), pp. 414f.

[12] Alan Paton, *Cry, The Beloved Country* (Harmondsworth: Penguin, 1958), p. 193.

[13] Quoted in Marie Therese Souverbie, *Chagall* (London: Spurbooks, 1975), n.p.

[14] Marc Chagall, 'The Circus', in Jacob Baal-Teshuva (ed.), *Chagall: A Retrospective* (New York: Hugh Lauter Levin Associates, 1995), p. 197.

[15] Meyer, *Marc Chagall*, p. 443.

[16] Abram Efros, 'Les artistes du Théâtre de Granovski', in Marc Chagall: *Les anneés russes: 1907–1922*. Exhibition catalogue (Musée d'art moderne de la Ville de Paris, 1995), pp. 248-51; cited in Didier Schulman, 'Painting as Theatre, or Theatre as Painting?' in Susan Compton (ed.), *Chagall: Love and the Stage 1914–1922* (London: Merrell Holberton, 1998), p. 10.

[17] Chagall, 'The Circus', pp. 196f.

[18] Ibid., p. 198.

[19] R. S. Thomas, 'The Minister' in *Collected Poems 1945–1990* (London: Phoenix, 1995), p. 54.

[20] Hugo Rahner, *Man at Play*, trans. B. Battershaw & E. Quinn (London: Burns and Oates, 1965), pp. 65f.

[21] Mark 10:15.

[22] Jürgen Moltmann, *Theology and Joy*, trans. R. Ulrich (London: SCM Press, 1973), pp. 40-2.

[23] Moltmann, *Theology and Joy*, p. 50.

[24] Sydney Carter, 'Lord of the Dance', from *Songs of Sydney Carter in the Present Tense*, Book 2 (Great Yarmouth: Galliard, 1963).

[25] Marc Chagall, 'Art and Life', in Baal-Teshuva (ed.), *Chagall: A Retrospective*, p. 178.

[26] This is the title of his well-known book: Norman Pittenger, *The Lure of the Divine Love* (New York: Pilgrim Press; Edinburgh: T. & T. Clark, 1979).

[27] Marc Chagall, 'Art and Life', in Baal-Teshuva (ed.), *Chagall: A Retrospective*, p. 179.

[28] Anne Sexton, 'The Awful Rowing Toward God' in Diane Wood Middlebrook and Diana Hume George (eds.), *Selected Poems of Anne Sexton* (New York: Mariner Books, 1988), p. 243.

[29] Chagall, 'The Circus', p. 197.

[30] Raissa Maritain, 'On Chagall's Surrealism', in Baal-Teshuva (ed.), *Chagall: A Retrospective*, p. 145.

[32] Chagall, *My Life*, p. 35.

[33] Ibid., p. 93.

[34] Seamus Heaney, *The Redress of Poetry* (London: Faber and Faber, 1995), p. 4.

[35] Ibid.

[36] From Lionello Venturi, *Chagall* (Geneva: Skira, 1956), quoted in Sidney Alexander, *Marc Chagall* (London: Cassell, 1979), p. 357.

[37] Marc Chagall, 'Some Impressions Regarding French Painting', in Baal-Teshuva (ed.), *Chagall: A Retrospective*, p. 174.

3
Stanley Spencer:
Looking for Resurrection

'I believe . . . in the resurrection of the body and the life everlasting.'
These words do not always flow easily from modern lips and many contemporary believers find themselves pulled in contrary directions, both affirmation and intense questioning. How refreshing, therefore, to meet another traveller on the journey of faith who understands both our hopes and our fears in these matters. Stanley Spencer (1891–1959) became famous as a painter of 'resurrections', but his biography is a continuous narrative of lived uncertainty and self-doubt. In the following pages we shall draw on some of his many documented experiences and the remarkable inheritance of his pictures to strengthen our own confidence for the journey.

In Spencer's art we find one of the strongest affirmations of human embodiment in the work of any recent English painter; he really does take human bodies seriously. In so doing, of course, he continues in the great Christian tradition of beginning with incarnation, the ultimate symbol of just how important embodiment is to God. As we shall see, this takes him, almost inevitably, onto the precarious and often controversial border between religion and sexuality; and, whilst we shall find the artist at times both confused and damaged by his own experiences, there is much here we can learn from him too. Ultimately, however, our lasting impression will take the shape of an affirmation: a potential for the resurrection of all things. This is a wonderful gift to leave us; but to feel its full force, we shall need to divert on a lengthy excursion.

The Dustman, or *The Lovers (1934)*
The Dustman is, if nothing else, a delightfully exuberant and witty painting (Plate 5). It exudes fun — and all the joys of heaven. We must enjoy its colourful delights before we feel for its darker tones. It is a 'resurrection' picture. It belongs in a series which Spencer painted during a

particularly disturbed and disturbing phase in his life, under the heading
Last Day or *Last Judgement,* and was intended for exhibition in the
'church-house' — of which more will be said later. We can pick up point-
ers toward the final image in a letter from Spencer to Gwen Raverat in
December 1932.

> Dustbins are looking up . . . It appears that I became so enamoured of
> the dustman that I wanted him to be transported to heaven while in the
> execution of his duty. So I got a big sort of wife to pick him up in her
> arms while children in a state of ecstasy hold up towards him an empty
> jam-tin, a tea-pot, and a bit of cabbage stalk with a few limp leaves
> attached to it. This scene occurs — Cookham people will say: 'We have
> seen strange things today' — a little away from the centre of the road in
> the village . . . The left group is a sort of washerwomen onlookers, the
> right group is the other dustman and a poor old ragged man expecting
> and hoping for a ride also. This is all very nice in its way, but some sort
> of terrible quality has crept in.[1]

Indeed it has. Amidst all the jollity, there is also an intense air of strangeness — even in excess of Spencer's other strange and better-known
figurative paintings. When Spencer submitted this picture for the 1934
Summer Exhibition at the Royal Academy it was rejected, and its rejection became the occasion of his formal resignation — although there is
more to that story than this painting alone.

The catalogue for the 2001 Spencer Exhibition at the Tate speaks of
this picture as a 'transitional work'. It connects back into the (relatively)
more conventional resurrection paintings of Spencer's Cookham and
Burghclere days, and it paves the way for themes that were to sustain his
work through the remainder of his career. His own explanation of its resurrection motif ran as follows:

> Nothing I love is rubbish and so I resurrect the tea-pot and the empty
> jamtin and the cabbage stalk, and as there is a mystery in the Trinity, so
> there is in these three objects and in many others of no apparent conse-
> quence . . . The picture is to express a joy of life through intimacy. All
> the signs and tokens of homelife and place, such as the cabbage leaves
> and the tea-pot, which I have so much loved that I have resurrected

them from the dustbin . . . As a child I always looked on rubbish heaps and dustbins with a feeling of wonder . . . In this *Dustman* picture I try to express something of this wish and need I feel for things to be restored.[2]

What, then, are the roots of this fascination with resurrection?

Connecting back — the story so far

Spencer had grown up in the sheltered environment of Cookham, a small village near Maidenhead. William Spencer, his father, was the organist at Hedsor church and a teacher of music. Nearly all of Stanley's early education was provided by his two older sisters in a schoolroom behind the house, and his extensive knowledge of literature and the arts was largely self-acquired in later life. It was rare for him to leave the village before 1907 when his father, still somewhat reluctantly, enrolled him at Maidenhead Technical Institute where he had his first formal instruction in drawing. So successful were these beginnings that a year later he was at the Slade School in London, where Henry Tonks began to give real substance to his drawing — a skill that remained key to all his future work.

Cookham, however, remained all important. It was the place to which he would return again and again, the place that fired his imagination and creativity. It was Cookham that provided a kind of 'religious' base from which he could explore wide-ranging, often religiously unconventional, ideas. *The Dustman* is just one in a long series of paintings which take Cookham and its residents for their primary context. Through the years, a great variety of famous biblical moments — annunciation, nativity, triumphal entry, crucifixion and resurrection — all took shape in his pictures around the familiar forms of his beloved village. The result is one of the most consistent and powerfully evocative efforts at the contextualization of gospel narratives produced anywhere in the twentieth century, and a lasting challenge to all for whom this remains a significant hermeneutical tool.

Spencer's comment soon after painting his first oil, *Two Girls and a Beehive* (c. 1910), is telling with regard both to Cookham and to the religious sense he associated with it: 'My feeling for things being holy was very strong at this time . . . It marks my becoming conscious of the rich religious significance of the place I lived in.'[3] It is this meeting of spirituality and place which also fascinates me most strongly and which resonates with elements of my own experience. My guess is that, even for Spencer, it could have been another place — though Cookham was uniquely pregnant with potential for his particular sensibilities. It is, however, a sensitive response to early childhood experiences and an irresistible urge for creative expression that combine in Spencer's art to form such an extraordinary collection. After living with his pictures for a while, we feel that we know Cookham and its people; as also we feel we know Spencer and his deep, almost compulsive, sense of belonging — secure belonging which makes possible and sustains his own risky spiritual journeying.

Like many of his contemporaries, Spencer's life was significantly shaped by the 1914–1918 war. Being slight in stature, his attempts to join the infantry were unsuccessful and much of his time was spent as a medical orderly. Sadly most of his sketches from this period were destroyed before his return to England, but an oil, *Travoys with Wounded Soldiers Arriving at a Dressing Station at Smol, Macedonia* (1919), commissioned by the Ministry of Information at the War Office, was preserved and is one of his most striking images.

Back in England marriage to Hilda Carline, also a student of the Slade, and the major project at Burghclere were the dominant features of the following years. Much has been written about Spencer's agonizing relationships with women. His sheltered upbringing gave him little confidence, and his engagement to Hilda was broken off several times before their eventual marriage in 1925. Sources suggest that the marriage was always turbulent, largely due to Stanley's irritability and easily provoked anger; but he and Hilda were for many years dedicated companions known for their intense debates and conversations, especially concerning Spencer's work as an artist. Through these years and even after her death, Spencer wrote copious letters to Hilda to accompany their equally exhaustive conversations. He was known to speak with pride about a hundred-page letter he wrote during what was no more than a brief period of separation. One result of this literary proliferation is an extensive Spencer-archive, held today by the Tate and as yet only partially classified and documented. Spencer became deeply committed to the creation of his own memorial, both literary and visual, but the imagined project was always one step beyond his ability to deliver; so that today there exists a vast collection of letters, notes, sketches and pictures that it will take many research-years fully to explore. It is an interesting question, one to which we must return, as to why someone so committed to the theme of resurrection should find it necessary to try and build such a comprehensive memorial to his own life and work.

The Burghclere project was a major achievement and occupied several years of dedicated work. Louis and Mary Brehend commissioned a comprehensive series of war paintings and decided to build an oratory in which it could be housed. The altar-piece includes a massive exploration of the theme of resurrection, in this case the resurrection of soldiers killed in the trenches of the First World War. Whilst awaiting the chance to begin, however, Spencer undertook another large-scale project, the one for which he is probably best-known today, *The Resurrection, Cookham* (1924–1927). This work is striking not least for its sheer size, 9 feet high and 18 feet in length. Spencer's recollection of painting this enormous work is very much bound up with visits from Hilda, who would explore its latest development in great detail and then engage in intense dialogue. Hilda herself appears no less than five times at different points in the picture.

The Resurrection, Cookham is so important in the sequence of Spencer's resurrection images that I need to give some account of it here. I have not, however, included the picture in this book — although I hope readers will search one out for reference. The image is so large and complicated that reproduction on a small page is never really satisfactory, and it is so well-known that it is not difficult to gain access to a larger copy.

Spencer's earliest biographer, Maurice Collis, was amongst the first following his death to explore the artist's copious writings. There he found four attempts to explain the picture, but confesses that, after several readings, he himself remained little the wiser.[4] It is indeed a complex work. Here I pick up my own four themes, which interweave and build upon each other in ascending significance.

First, at the simplest level, the picture draws on traditional Christian symbols that invite reflection on the theme of resurrection. In a place associated with death, the Cookham churchyard, graves are opening as might be expected in traditional representations of Judgement Day. Some of the figures are clothed, others naked, suggesting a meeting between those still living and those long dead. There had been even earlier paintings in Spencer's *oeuvre* which featured the idea of opening graves: a diptych from as early as 1914–1915 titled *The Resurrection of the Good and the Bad* and an early much smaller draft also titled *The Resurrection, Cookham*, painted back in 1920–1921. The inspiration for this picture, then, begins with the painter's deep immersion in the world of church and its traditions, and crucially its credal testimony to the resurrection of the dead. But that is only a beginning, the starting point from which traditional connections begin to reach out.

Second, there is an emphasis on the intimate connectedness between the heavenly and the earthly. As any of the locals would be quick to recognize, this really is Cookham, the Thames flowing in the background, and a host of familiar faces both living and dead. Not only are there multiple appearances of Hilda, but also the artist himself (twice), his mother, Hilda's brother Richard, and other characters familiar from the world of Cookham and its environs. Even so there is considerable license in Spencer's interpretation. The church does not strictly follow the architecture of Holy Trinity, Cookham; the Thames is not located in quite its literal geographical relationship to the church, and the figures are variously exaggerated in their forms. So it seems that there is here a creative attempt to bring together a very particular idea of resurrection, familiar from biblical narrative and historical iconography, and a more general notion of resurrection as something already happening in the known world of Cookham and its surroundings. It is as though the artist has found a new way of seeing the familiar, which uncovers a dimension of resurrection normally hidden from the casual observer. That all this should come to focus in a churchyard is usually associated with Spencer's reading of John Donne's description of a churchyard as 'the holy suburb of heaven'. Rather than wait for heaven to be revealed once and for all at the last day, the possibility is waiting in one of heaven's suburbs to glimpse it in the here and now. Perhaps Spencer would say more than glimpse; here it is waiting to be seen by any who have eyes that can see.

Third, there is a strong sexual motif in this picture which needs to be understood in the light of a particular moment in the artist's own story. *The Resurrection, Cookham* was painted in the wake of Spencer's life-changing introduction to adult sexual experience. This image is a celebration of a kind of 'new birth' experienced through sexual initiation, brought about by the marriage that took place within the span of painting this picture. The multiple appearances and prominence of Spencer and his first sexual partner, Hilda, is no mere coincidence. The very energy breaking open the tombs has something joyfully orgasmic about it. Spencer himself described this picture as the first of his 'sex pictures'; however, as we shall see, the way sex informs his later pictures becomes ever more prominent and ever more tortured with the passage of years. The restful contentment and well-being that floods the whole picture is that of post-coital tranquillity. This is a vision of the heavenly life as it might be experienced here and now in the after-glow of good sex.

Finally, however, there is more to be said about the universality of this understanding of resurrection. What, for example, is the significance of the Africans rising from their own appropriately dusty contextualized graves, or the detail of Spencer's mother brushing down the jacket of her husband, said to be reminiscent of familiar daily rituals around his departure for work? Certainly Spencer did not want to limit this way of seeing to Cookham alone, nor to his particular relationship with Hilda. For Spencer, the joy of resurrection seen in the midst of life is global in its dimensions; it happens in Africa as much as it does in an English country churchyard. And it happens in the little events which take place in people's lives everywhere and become stored away as the characteristic memories which most obviously keep the dead alive amongst the living. That special ritual of dusting the jacket and an unforgettable moment in which Spencer recalls Hilda crossing a stile on the path to the Thames are moments that bring resurrection pleasure, comparable with the deep well-being experienced through total relaxation by immersion in a good book — hence his own self-portrait like a bookmark in the open pages of a volume at the right-hand corner.

What these moments of memory have in common is the way in which they evoke a sense of loving and being loved, of security and untroubled well-being. This then is an image of resurrection that invites the viewer to recall such moments, and in them to taste, in the midst of life, a similar pleasure in all that is implied through the image of resurrection.

Back to the dustbins

The Dustman was, of course, painted many years later, after prolonged and tortuous experiences associated with his marriage. But motifs already identified in *The Resurrection, Cookham* give added dimensions to our understanding. Part of the 'strangeness' referred to earlier has to do with the ambivalence expressed in its alternative titling *The Lovers*. This is another picture that might be seen primarily as a portrayal of sexual ecstasy. There is something wildly ecstatic about the way the dustman is lifted high in the arms of his beloved. There is a mixture of voyeuristic pleasure and prudery in the eyes of those who behold this scene. And the juxtaposition of what some interpret as dirt with what others associate with joy is not at all unusual around the subject of sex. Dirt and sex are frequent partners in discussions about the formation of attitudes to human sexuality. It is remarkable that for all his frustration, broken relationships and damaged experience, Spencer is repeatedly able to find pleasurable affirmation in picturing a sexual encounter. More than that he is able to find in all manner of bodily expression something of the transcendent wonder of heaven and resurrection.

The Dustman clearly bears all the other layers of significance identified in *The Resurrection, Cookham*. It is supremely an affirmation of the resurrection of all things — right down to the rubbish in our bins. One way in which Spencer lived out this affirmation was through his almost obsessive collection of souvenirs from his own life-experience; it is as though he feared the loss of anything which might one day add to the fullness of his own resurrection. Then there is also a strong contextual motif in this picture; once again the location is quite clearly Cookham, and many of the figures would be recognizable in the local community. What might have remained unrecognized, unless first we had looked at some of his earlier paintings, is the measure to which this should be seen as a resurrection picture at all — certainly if we are looking to traditional Christian iconography as a point of reference. Perhaps there is at least some resonance between the images of open dustbins and Spencer's earlier version of *The Resurrection, Cookham*, in which the opening graves might well be compared to lids pushed open on bins.

Some theological connections

The connection that most strongly comes to my own mind is with H. A. Williams's spiritual classic, *True Resurrection*. In its day Williams's bold affirmation of resurrection 'in the now' was a daring challenge to the sterility of much received orthodoxy. As he explained in his opening chapter, the problem with resurrection in much western Christianity has been its relegation to another time or another place: a garden tomb some two millennia past, or a final judgement in an unknown future. No wonder it had become the focus of so much nineteenth- and twentieth-century scepticism. New sciences for the study of the past made it vulnerable to legitimate historical criticism, and new understandings of possible futures for the world threw traditional iconographic images of a cosmic end-time into the realm of remote speculation. What is needed, Williams argued, is a robust experience of resurrection in the present. The following is a classic passage amongst writings about resurrection:

> An artist, at first only painfully aware of an utter emptiness and impotence, finds his imagination gradually stirred into life and discovers a vision which takes control of him and which he feels not only able but compelled to express. That is resurrection. Or a scholar or scientist as he pursues his research finds a favourite theory breaking up in his hands. He is left with no home in which to house the quantities of evidence he has collected. Then a new more adequate theory gradually takes shape in his mind that makes him more at home with his material even than he was before. That is resurrection. Or a married couple find their old relationship, once rich and fulfilling, slowly drying up into no more than an external observance to the point where it seems impossible that these dry bones should ever live again. Then a new relationship emerges, less superficially high powered and less greedy than the old one, but deeper, more stable, more satisfying, with a new quality of life which is inexhaustible because it does not depend on the constant recharging of emotional batteries. That is resurrection. Or an individual finds life less and less rewarding, not on its public and professional side, where he may be very successful, but in its failing to bring in an adequate degree

of personal fulfilment. He seems to get less and less of what he wants and values most, although he does not know what it is. He feels intolerably isolated on a rubbish dump he cannot get off. He has identified what he is with a limited and false portrait of himself, which he was successfully sold by an unconscious conviction that limitation means safety. But the supposed claims of safety are emptying his life of content. Yet in the midst of his despair he discovers a broader basis on which to establish himself, and, in spite of the threatening danger, fills up more of his own space, lets himself in for more of what he is, and thus finds a richer more satisfying life. That is resurrection . . . .[5]

So it goes on, naming where resurrection can be seen and experienced in the here and now. It is hard to believe that Williams could have written with such sharpness unless, like Spencer, he was also dipping into actual life-experiences. Williams recalls in this passage the painful experiences of real life which lead to frustration, broken relationships, suffering and potential despair; but they are also experiences in which and out of which resurrection's domain is tasted. Williams sums it up as follows:

> Resurrection is always a mystery. It is always a miracle. It is always the creative act of the Eternal Word. Because that Word is spoken now in the present in terms of what we call the common circumstances of life, there can be nobody who at some time or other has not thus been raised from the dead. But more often than not our eyes are holden and we do not know it. We do not recognize resurrection when it comes to us. The presence of the Eternal Word is unnoticed, and evidenced only in the new life made available; just as at Cana of Galilee the guests enjoyed the good wine but did not know whence it was.[6]

This is all much more 'spiritually' told than would have flowed comfortably from Spencer's pen; but my own sense is that it taps into one and the same reality.

It is striking that Williams begins with the illustration of an artist in search of inspiration. How closely bound is the content of Spencer's artistic vision with his own struggle, along with that of so many other artists, to achieve that vantage point which releases in an artefact a new way of seeing the world. It is also striking that Williams names the constant struggle through which human beings battle with the sense of emptiness and lack of fulfilment to discover fresh sources of renewal and pleasure. This is Spencer's story through and through, as is Williams's focus on marriage as a locus par excellence for the continual energy of resurrection. Spencer could have read this with firsthand understanding.

At the core, both for Williams and for Spencer, is an affirmation concerning the universality of resurrection experience. In more recent times and from a now popular source of spiritual renewal, I am reminded of that familiar way of speaking about the island of Iona, usually attributed to the Community's founder, George McLeod, which speaks of Iona as '. . . "a thin place", only a tissue paper separating the material from the spiritual.'[7] On Iona pilgrims can learn to develop their ability to see their more normal environments in which they live and work in new ways. Cookham might well be described as Spencer's Iona; the striking difference, however, is that Cookham is an ordinary village and not a sparkling and isolated isle like Iona.

The Scorpion (1939)

The second painting chosen for display in this chapter has become a popular favourite and reveals the artist in a very different mode of operation. *The Scorpion* (Plate 6) is a scene from Spencer's *Christ in the Wilderness* series, painted in a time of self-imposed isolation as he emerged from a long period of personal disorientation and distress. Around that time he wrote:

> My life seems to go in cycles, the beginning & end of each finding myself alone. I am like some already discarded implement or utensil whose original home is a rubbish heap, but because I looked as if I might be some use was picked up by some passer by & was carried & inspected by him until he decided I was useless & threw me on one side . . . . I seem to have the same disability to help myself as a broken pot has . . . .
> There is reason why I have been given a broken appearance. There are things in this world which are whole & and complete but which have the appearance of a broken utensil. The real purpose I am meant to serve is dependent on my apparent uselessness . . . .

The good I have to give is through this sort of disappointment in dis-
covering I am a broken pot. My life's journey, & what is to me
interesting in it, is expressed by . . . apparent uselessness as far as I am
supposed at first to be, picked up, chucked away, picked up and chucked
away again. That is the path my soul treads.[8]

These are heavy words written out of a strong sense of self-pity and personal brokenness. The image of discarded rubbish connects us once again
to *The Dustman*. But what has happened to the vision of resurrection? At
first sight brokenness seems to have won the day — but not entirely so.
Towards the end of the quotation there begins to emerge a theme of hope,
a discovery of life-giving meaning actually embedded in the broken experience of personal suffering.

By the end of 1938, his first marriage to Hilda was long ended and his
second marriage to Patricia Preece was in tatters. Exhausted by the cease-
less production of commercially saleable landscapes in an attempt to
escape from debt and, finally, excluded by Patricia from his home at
Lindworth, Spencer fled to London. For the first six weeks he stayed with
his friends, John and Elizabeth Rothenstein. From there he moved into a
top-floor bed-sitting room at 188 Adelaide Road, also in Swiss Cottage,
and it was there he spent several months in near isolation, living through
his own 'wilderness experience'.

The *Christ in the Wilderness* series forms a highly original collection
of images. Initially Spencer had planned to create a sequence of forty
paintings, one for each day of Lent. His intention was that they should
decorate the ceiling of his intended church-house, modelled on the
squared pattern of the choir ceiling in Cookham Church. In the end
Spencer completed only nine, another example of his tendency to set himself impossible goals. It is the small square format of these paintings (just
56 cm. by 56 cm. each) that, amongst other things, makes them so distinctive. The size might well have been determined as much by
circumstances as by design, in that the rented room did not have the space
of his earlier studio. Spencer initially sketched all forty in small squares
and then worked them up into larger studies. In the nine finished works,
the Christ figure typically fills the entire canvas, often with striking compositional ingenuity. This is in marked contrast with his highly crowded

figure paintings of earlier years. Spencer's Jesus in these pictures is a thoroughly human young prophet, with strongly Jewish features. Each picture is based on a biblical text, some from the parables, many from the Sermon on the Mount.

The text for *The Scorpion* can be found in Luke 10:19, which reads, 'I give unto you power to tread on serpents and scorpions, and nothing shall by any means hurt you.' Spencer's angle on the text is unusual. Rather than portray the conquest of treading unharmed on a scorpion, this is a benign and sensitive image in which Christ's victory over the scorpion is achieved through relationship rather than violence. The scorpion has its sting at the ready, curled over as if for an attack, but more probably out of frustration at the disarming effect of Christ's loving caress. Spencer is concerned to express the intimate relationship between Christ and the animal world, rather than callous domination over it. Indeed the whole image is designed to demonstrate how integrated the young Christ is with the environment in which he is set. His garment is surfaced like one of the pebbles that litters the desert floor, and his flesh blends without contrast into the setting where he is found. Spencer wrote concerning *The Scorpion*: '. . . although there are none about I feel this is Christ giving himself to the fleas and bugs and lice department . . . .'[9] It is like a return to the familiar theme from *The Dustman*; namely, that there is no creature sufficiently unworthy as not to merit the attention of God's Christ. If we were to look for Spencer's own presence in this picture, he is both the prophet enduring his wilderness experience and the scorpion, at odds with much of God's world, but nonetheless still at home in it.

Recalling these days of isolation as a time of profound self-examination, Spencer wrote: 'I used sometimes to go to bed after lunch because I wanted to live my inner self.'[10] During these months he also read Thoreau's *Walden*, a text which provided him with images of retreat into nature, some of which clearly fed, if only obliquely, into his own wilderness pictures. These were difficult days, but Spencer writes of pleasure as well as pain through the experience of isolation: 'After sweeping the floor and dusting a bit, I would sit down on one of the two chairs and look at the floor. Oh, the joy of just that.'[11] Clearly the experience of retreat was, as it has been for others, a significant source of therapy. Like the young Christ in his pictures, Spencer too experienced the wilderness sojourn as a time of transition, from one kind of childhood into a new phase of maturity. In a later chapter, we shall see Georgia O'Keeffe also exploring the desert as a place of deep spiritual significance.

Some writers have suggested that the *Christ in the Wilderness* pictures indicate temporary abandonment of Spencer's emphasis on sexuality, which had so evidently dominated his work through the previous seven years, replacing it with a return to more evidently religious interests. It is clear that these works do mark a new departure, not only in painting but also from his personal agony of sexual confusion. My own view, however, is that it is possible to over-stretch this analysis. I do not see Spencer abandoning his struggle to integrate sexual and religious sentiments in these images. These pictures are by no means free from eroticism in the broader sense; Spencer's Christ is very much an embodied human, fully integrated into an earthed and richly sensuous environment. What does seem clear, however, is that these pictures suggest a greater degree of sexual self-acceptance than the artist had experienced for some years, and we shall see him emerge from this time with a renewed ability to bring religious and sexual motifs towards a new and significant unity.

Back-tracking again

So what had brought Spencer to such an extraordinary point in his life-experience? What had happened to the elation of first-love and long-awaited sexual union with his beloved Hilda? It is a complex story, supported by a wealth of literary and pictorial allusions still ripe for further research and interpretation.

In later life Spencer recalled with pleasure a time when, newly-wed, '. . . we groped our way peacefully about each other',[12] but their romantic idyll was disappointingly — though predictably — short-lived. By the November of 1925, the same year as their wedding earlier in February, Shirin was born and with her arrival their lives began to change. Indeed, it is not long before Spencer is writing about Hilda most typically in terms of irritation and anger. The way in which he describes her behaviour as a young mother fits well a more modern diagnosis of post-natal depression. She was lacking in energy, frequently tired, and incapable of responding to Stanley's immature and insatiable desire for attention. His own letters allude to prolonged periods of enforced sexual abstinence, a discipline that he almost entirely associates with her commitment to Christian Science. All the ingredients of a recipe for disaster were gathered and waiting. 'You cannot serve Stanley Spencer & Christian Science',[13] he wrote in one of his more angry and pained letters; but the attack on her religious beliefs feels very much like a cover for his own inadequacy in personal relationships.

As if all this were not enough, enter at this point Patricia Preece, a woman Spencer first met casually in a Cookham teashop in 1929. Patricia, who shared a home with her partner Dorothy Hepworth in a cottage by Cookham Moor, was seemingly everything that Hilda failed to be. A veneer of elegance, sophistication and her flattering attention to Spencer's continual tirade of ideas soon left the artist hopelessly infatuated. *The Meeting*, a cryptic picture, painted somewhat later in 1933, set in the back yard of Spencer's home, powerfully depicts the intensity of his obsession. In the picture, we see Spencer greeting Patricia, her back turned from the viewer. But there is also an enigmatic third figure, usually interpreted as his own alter-ego, who witnesses what had by the time of painting become in memory a charged and intimate moment.

One consequence of Spencer's strongly egocentric disposition was that, from the beginning, Hilda becomes drawn into the confused and confusing exploration of his own sexual feelings. By the early 1930s, the toll on her too great, Hilda withdrew to London and Stanley found himself plotting a course to marry Patricia at the earliest legal convenience, pathetically unaware that he had constructed for himself a trap already set to guarantee his own future unhappiness.

In retrospect it seems clear that Patricia had always viewed Spencer more as a saviour from her own financial difficulties than as a potential companion and lover. Soon he was providing her with a stream of lavish gifts, and it is no surprise to find him signing over to her the rights to Lindworth, the family home in Cookham. This, it seems, was a last ditch attempt to secure certainty about their forthcoming wedding. It is probable that the marriage, solemnized at Maidenhead Registry Office in May 1937, was never consummated. With extreme naïvety Spencer, we now know, assumed that he could have both women 'serve' him at one and the same time, two wives instead of just one. From his own perspective, divorce from Hilda remained little more than a legal formality, incapable of disturbing the fundamental feelings, which he trusted they would always have for each other. Perhaps it would have been wise to consult Hilda herself on this matter at an earlier stage! Almost immediately the reality was that both women had abandoned him to the loneliness he so much dreaded, Patricia returning to her home with Dorothy, Hilda struggling to build a new life for herself and Shirin with other members of the family around London.

It is these events that form the backdrop for what Spencer came to call his 'sex pictures'. Amongst them are portraits of Patricia, many nude, a variety of erotic drawings and a series of paintings he called *The Beatitudes of Love* depicting caricature couples exploring the potential for their own sexual fulfilment.

The Beatitudes of Love is peculiarly haunting. The simple titles of its individual components, *Nearness, Knowing, Seeing, Contemplation, Consciousness, Worship* and *Age* give no hint of the erotic intensity of their content. At first sight they seem to depict the sexual experimentations of people with various physical and/or social disabilities. The juxtaposition of disability and sex was taboo enough in the society of Spencer's day, even before deeper layers of meaning are allowed to surface. In fact, further attention suggests that each picture in some measure explores Spencer's own disabled attempts to form meaningful relationships: with Hilda, Patricia . . . and whomever. That these images are so intensely sexual is simply testimony to the ultimate focus of his own continuing struggle.

Actually, more than half a century later, I, like others, find these pictures strangely moving. Necessarily long-hidden from public view, in this later age it is possible to read them as a challenging affirmation of the sexual identity of people with various kinds of disability — still a topic which rouses strong and polarized opinions in twenty-first century Britain. Even, however, as expressions of the painter's own unresolved sexual longings, there is every reason today to respond to these pictures with empathetic understanding rather than prurient hostility.

There is also much to be learned from the nudes that Spencer painted at this time: those that depict Patricia alone, as well as those that bring Patricia and Stanley together in a single picture. All are painted in a distinctive, tonally harsh style. There is no doubting the fleshiness of the flesh in these pictures — so that when Patricia and Stanley are painted alongside a leg of mutton in the same picture (1937), there is no difference in colour or texture between any two of the three prominent subjects. Not until Lucien Freud does another painter tackle human flesh with such energetic and graphic realism.

Once again these are images that can be read in a variety of ways. At one level, it is not unreasonable to see them as a straight expression of the painter's intense sexual frustration. It is as though Spencer had found a way to incarnate his unfulfilled sexual desires onto canvas through the very act of painting. Patricia's flesh is meticulously replicated as if his eyes had systematically consumed her centimetre by centimetre. At another level, however, these paintings might be seen as pioneering explorations of human embodiment which, viewed retrospectively through the lens of Francis Bacon, Lucien Freud and others, lose most of their contemporary shock-value and can be re-read as significant sacramental celebrations of a truth about our embodied lives.

Two motifs become inseparably intertwined through this period. Spencer's personal life falls ever further into a state of collapse, and his over-truthful representations of himself and his relationships push him ever further beyond the bounds of acceptable art in his day. Spencer had already fallen foul of the artistic powers-that-were at the Royal Academy as early as 1935. It seems odd now that the paintings that caused such offence should be *The Dustman* (or *The Lovers*), which we have already considered in some detail, and the now much-loved work titled *St Francis and the Birds* (1935). A heated exchange between Spencer and the authorities at the Academy, soon blown out of all proportion and filling the newspapers, rapidly enhanced Spencer's reputation as an artist people either loved or despised. On Spencer's side such energetic expressions of anger were all part and parcel of his personal turmoil at this time. From the Academy's side, there is evidence of significant myopia, and a foolish unwillingness to seek compromise. When put to the test it was hard to show that the defects in *St Francis and the Birds* stretched much further than the comical displacement of a thumb on St Francis' left hand. Basically the paintings were too thoroughly 'Spencerian' for the committee of the day. Maurice Collis' commentary on these events, however, is not without significance:

> Reflecting on the whole episode three years later, Spencer observes that if he had not resigned in 1935, he would have been forced out of the Academy in 1938, for it would have refused to hang a single one of his dozen or so sex pictures of 1937-38.[14]

In reality, the two double portraits were rarely exhibited until after Spencer's death. It is fascinating, however, to see how public attitudes can shift so significantly with the passage of only a brief span of years. Personally, I do not think this is anything at all to do with the slipping of public 'standards'; rather, it is a healthy shifting of attitudes towards greater realism concerning the truth about many people's lives.

None of us would have wished on Spencer the personal torment of those years nor, probably, would we have rushed to extol the quality of his ethical decisions; but we should perhaps be grateful that, at great cost to himself, we now have access to images which, read from a fresh perspective, can be instrumental in helping others to live through their own wilderness experiences. Not only that, they actually provide resources that can help to bring people through to new and better times. All of which brings us full-circle back to the *Christ in the Wilderness* series of 1939.

More theological connections

I am not alone in connecting Spencer's *Christ in the Wilderness* series with that other spiritual classic from the pen of H. A. Williams, *The True Wilderness*. Indeed my own copy of the 1965 edition, published by Constable, has one of the series reproduced on its paper jacket. For that printing, the publishers chose *Rising from Sleep in the Morning*, a beautifully crafted composition in which the garment of the kneeling Christ, arms stretched toward heaven in prayer, takes the shape of a lotus flower, familiar from Hindu and Buddhist spiritualities in the East.

As in his account of 'resurrection', Williams wants to emphasize that 'wilderness' is not an experience remote from us in our everyday lives. It

is not enough to distance it from ourselves as something that happened to
Jesus in the dim and distant past. Williams wrote:

> . . . the wilderness belongs to us. It is always lurking somewhere as part
> of our experience, and there are times when it seems pretty near the
> whole of it. I'm not thinking now of people being ostracized, or without
> friends, or misunderstood, or banished in this way or that from some
> community or other. Objectively, as a matter of actual fact, these things
> happen to very few of us. Most people's wilderness is inside them, not
> outside. Thinking of it as outside is generally a trick we play upon our-
> selves — a trick to hide from us what we really are, not comfortingly
> wicked, but incapable, for the time being, of establishing communion.
> Our wilderness, then, is an inner isolation. It's an absence of contact. It's
> a sense of being alone — boringly alone, or saddeningly alone, or terri-
> fyingly alone. Often we try to relieve it — understandably enough, God
> knows — by chatter, or gin, or religion, or sex, or possibly a combina-
> tion of all four.[15]

This is not a bad description of what had happened to Spencer and, what
is more, an insight into why his own period of isolation was so effectively
therapeutic. Williams' own Lent Book became so significant in the 1950s
because of who he was. How refreshing it is to hear a respected cler-
gyperson testify so freely to the experience of wilderness. If it can happen
to him, we say, then there is no reason why it cannot happen to us; indeed
we might do well to embrace it rather than evade it. What Williams did
for respectably religious people in the 1950s, Spencer can do for others
amongst today's pilgrims who find it easier to listen to the testimony of a
painter than that of someone bound up with the institutions of formal
religion.

In his chapter 'The True Wilderness', Williams goes on to elaborate
the dimensions of wilderness that we commonly experience. Finding one-
self left outside in a culture of success, failing to live up to romantic
fantasies of sexual bliss in the cold light of a real and enduring marriage,
being robbed of the securities of childhood religion with its clear-cut
answers and no-nonsense certainties; these are all experiences to which in
some measure Spencer gives testimony in both words and pictures — but

they are all at the heart of our normal human experience too. What we all need, Williams argues, is a true Lent:

> . . . which has nothing to do with giving up sugar in your tea, or trying to feel it's wicked to be you. And this Lent, unlike the ecclesiastical charade, this sense of being isolated and therefore unequipped, is a necessary part, or a necessary stage, of our experience of human beings. It therefore found a place in the life of the Son of Man. Because He is us, He too did time in the wilderness. And what happened to Him there shows us what is happening to ourselves. Here, as always, we see in His life the meaning of our own.[16]

Surely this is precisely what Spencer was describing when he wrote about himself using the image of a broken pot. That this particular pot is broken does not make it useless. Rather it is, as Spencer suggests, the basis of its peculiar strength and potentially, for us as for the artist, the source of our most profoundly creative contribution to the world.

Into the church-house

In drawing towards the end of this chapter we will return to two themes that have been important throughout our exploration of Spencer's *oeuvre*: the relationship between religious and sexual experience and the universality of resurrection. Concerning the former, Spencer often expressed his concern that people misunderstood his life journey as one from religion to sexuality. He wrote:

> It is a mistake to suppose that because my recent pictures have a clear emphatic relationship to sexual love that they are for that reason neither spiritual nor religious. Sex is as much an illusion as religion or any other mystery.[17]

I take this as a pointer towards integration and relatedness rather than mutual exclusion. In a letter to Hilda as late as 1950, Spencer was still trying to explain himself, distancing himself from some of the baggage which comes with a sexual label on his work, and setting it within the larger framework of relationships as a whole. He wrote:

I always dislike, for some reason, to use the word 'sexual' in explaining my desires & I rather think I know why. The physical part of my desire is aroused by consciousness of a degree of harmony & nearness reached between myself & and another simply.

Because of Nature's arrangement & production, the part of love that induces physical desire has been thought to be exclusively & only between men and women. I have often felt the inadequacy of this & how arbitrarily would such a condition be that says only between sexes can the supreme emotion be felt & explained.[18]

It is these boundaries against which Spencer was pushing throughout his life, and nowhere do we see him doing so more consistently than in his vision for the church-house. Probably from as early as the years of the First World War, and certainly from the years of his work on the chapel at Burghclere, Spencer began to conceive the idea of a specially designed architectural space within which his life work could be displayed. Needless to say, as ever, the project was on a scale beyond his own capacity, financial and otherwise; but that did not stop him from working at continual revisions of its plan. From the start, the vision was massively symbolic, and became in concept the ultimate synthesis of his integration of religion and sexuality.

As its name, the 'church-house', suggests, the structure is conceived as a fusion of the sacred and the secular. At the centre is a chapel, the altar piece being his *The Resurrection, Cookham*, lastingly recognized as the true summit of Spencer's work. The walls of the nave, which also symbolize the High Street in Cookham village, are lined with Spencer's biblical paintings, the ceiling patterned with the forty images of *Christ in the Wilderness*.

So far, then, there is little to stun the imagination of the potential visitor. At various points, however, the central chapel is connected into the domestic environment of a house. Its larger rooms and corridors also map the layout of the village of Cookham, and include all the necessary facilities for domestic life — bedrooms, kitchen, bathrooms, toilets — all of which are integral to the artistic vision. In particular, bedrooms and lavatories become focal points for the meeting of sacred and secular. Bedrooms, individually dedicated to the memory of Spencer's various wives and lovers, become shrines to the celebration of sexual love. Spencer also planned small rooms for meditation on *The Beatitudes* sequence that, as we have already heard, was designed to explore something of the breadth of sexual experience. Once complete the church-house would offer hanging space to all the major sequences of Spencer's paintings, creating an integrated environment in which the celebrations of religion, domesticity and sexual pleasure are connected into a seamless whole.

Now, there is little doubt that the project lurches at times into the absurd — maybe even the obscene — especially in those seasons of Spencer's life when his own sexual life became so tormented and damaged. But at root there is much that rightly challenges some of the inherited social attitudes of his day. There is no doubt, for example, that the gulf between sacred and secular had become hopelessly widened, and many contemporary artists, from a variety of disciplines, have also explored this theme. The novelist Iris Murdoch readily comes to mind. In his letters and scribblings, Spencer often returned to explore the relationship between religious and sexual experience — and always he found them to have a great deal in common. With hindsight, he finds his own early religious paintings manifesting intimations of the same sensuality that becomes explicitly sexual in his later work. That the domestic and the religious are one and the same had been the constant refrain of his work, famous biblical stories being repeatedly contextualized in the familiar scene of his own home and of his village. Of that special experience he once wrote:

When I lived in Cookham I was disturbed by a feeling of everything being meaningless. But quite suddenly I became aware that everything was full of special meaning, and this made everything holy. The instinct of Moses to take his shoes off when he saw the burning bush was very similar to my feelings. I saw many burning bushes at Cookham. I observed this sacred quality in most unexpected quarters.
What I saw was to me miraculous: compared to what I had seen previously, it was full of unexpected and surprising meaning and fullness. Ever since these Cookham experiences every tomorrow has seemed as the world to come.[19]

This comment is a good excuse for one final rehearsal of the over-arching theme, resurrection.

And finally . . . the resurrection

At its deepest level Spencer's *oeuvre* is an extended testimony to the all-pervasive theme of resurrection — the resurrection of all things, uniquely perceived as the true locus of energy for the sacred. One series that Spencer did manage to complete in later life, *The Resurrection, Port Glasgow* (1947–1950), again succeeds in exploring this theme. Commissioned as War Artist in the Second World War, Spencer was sent to Glasgow to record the efforts of the Clyde shipbuilders in making their distinctive contribution to the war. In Spencer's hands the result is a series of panels that find their natural home in the framework of a traditional Christian chapel. There is a sanctifying of this heavy and punishing work which, without becoming patronizing, honours it and locates it in the domain of God's redeeming care.

The points in Spencer's life at which his vision for resurrection becomes distorted and spoiled coincide with those times when dependence of memory (the well-spring of his art) becomes, as it were, trapped in the snare of painful images of the past. There is an unredeemed sense of tragedy associated with some of the late pictures of Hilda to whom, as we have noted, he continued to write extensive letters long after her death. This is nowhere more poignantly represented than in the picture *Love Letters* (1950) which had been reserved its own special place in the 'Hilda chapel' of the church-house. Another, *Hilda and I at Pond Street* (1954), finds the artist presenting flowers from a shroud-lined coffin-shaped box to his now long-estranged and long-deceased bride. These remarkable images represent in visual form the unremitting cry of a soul trapped by unprocessed grief — a cry that many have felt, but few have managed to express with such power.

Spencer often spoke of his work in intensely religious language, although he was always concerned lest people should misunderstand this language as literal rather than symbolic. There is an enigmatic extract from his jottings in which he tries to explore this insoluble tension:

Conversation today in which words of a religious or spiritual nature occur is just a shambles . . . If I use some words such as 'Heaven' then the reader (other than a Catholic) gets into the corner of his mind, where the vaguest most insubstantial half-crazed unformed ambiguous notions exist & then says 'yes' confidently to me to encourage me to say something further on the subject. But I can see from his subservient attitude, a rather proud one, that he is now completely incapacitated for understanding anything further I may have to say about it. I do not want people to . . . get into their Sunday clothes the moment I use such a word any more than they would if I said Basingstoke. But if, in order to get them out of this corner of their minds, I said that Heaven was like Basingstoke . . . then there would be the assumption that Heaven was ordinary & nothing to wonder at, or feel any sense of wonder at. & again I and the reader would be wrong.[20]

I am reading this to be Spencer's way of saying that people consistently refuse to understand that all reality, and that includes Basingstoke, is so wonder-ful, that those who have eyes to see will see the reality of heaven in it. The problem is twofold: people assume that heaven is disconnected from ordinary reality and, in any case, few are graced with the eyes to see it.

So, he says, scenes and figures are portrayed as if already in heaven, already energized by the life of resurrection. Be it dustmen with their bins, soldiers in the trenches or shipbuilders in the yards, all carry the signs of resurrection life. Put another way we might say that Spencer has a peculiar power to recognize a deeper truth in all that he sees — what the poet Gerard Manley Hopkins once called 'the dearest freshness deep down things.'[21] It is as though his eyes are privileged to catch a glimpse of the divine depth in all reality. In all this we might rush to think him blessed, sensing how much we ourselves are privileged to share it with him. But it all came at a terrible price, the price of intense personal anguish, something we have seen in the lives of many other artists too.

But what a gift for the traveller on a journey of faith! Would that we all might enjoy the gift of sight, in-sight even, which can see in and through the surface of domestic, embodied reality and celebrate the energy and life of God, shot through the whole of creation. This is the stuff that enables people to endure a great deal; for all the contradictions of his life, of which no doubt there are many, Spencer sustained his visual testimony to the fundamentally graced nature of human life, through to the end.

There are, then, several things that I believe Spencer leaves with us which can become valuable markers on our own faith journeys. I would like to learn from him how best to train my own eyes to see the world in the 'depth' he so often seems to see it. I would like to learn with him how best to recognize 'value' even in the broken pots which form the basic fabric for our lives. I would like to be able to sustain his undefeated 'optimism' through all the variety of human experience. And I would like to learn how never to lose sight of the fundamental 'goodness' of human embodiment, however easy it is to lose it to distortion and corruption. Spencer's, then, is a truly remarkable testimony to the resurrection of all things.

Selected (and annotated) Bibliography

Much has been written about Spencer, especially since his death in 1959. For those wishing to follow up the themes that we have begun to explore in this chapter, nothing can better the cluster of resources published in association with the Tate Britain exhibition of late spring and early summer 2001. Fundamental is the catalogue: Timothy Hyman and Patrick Wright (eds.), *Stanley Spencer* (London: Tate Publishing, 2001). In addition, however, there is a much briefer and incisive summary of his life and work: Kitty Hausser, *Stanley Spencer* (London: Tate Publishing, 2001). There is also a new edition of extracts from his prolific writings: Adrian Glew, *Stanley Spencer: Letters and Writings* (London: Tate Publishing, 2001).

Together, these three form an excellent lens through which to view the ways in which this artist has recently come to be understood. There were two major earlier works that provide crucial source material, a catalogue and a monograph. The catalogue, accompanying an earlier exhibition at the Royal Academy, was the first to list all the then-known works attributed to him: *Stanley Spencer RA* (London: Royal Academy of Arts, 1980). It is impossible to miss the irony that the Academy should honour one it had callously discarded, and that so soon after his death. The monograph is significant because it gathers in one place the largest single collection of colour pictures: Keith Bell, *Stanley Spencer* (London: Phaidon, 1992).

Of earlier historical interest are two biographical sketches. The first, by Spencer's friend Elizabeth Rothenstein, was an early attempt to put his work on the wider artistic map. It is very sympathetic to his life, if a little naïve at times: Elizabeth Rothenstein, *Stanley Spencer* (London: Phaidon, 1945). The other, written soon after his death, provided the first serious access to his letters and other unpublished papers. It is also written sympathetically with a sensitive eye to the needs of his living relatives: Maurice Collis, *Stanley Spencer* (London: Harvill Press, 1962).

In this chapter, there has also been reference to the writings of Harry Williams. In particular, H. A. Williams, *The True Wilderness* (London: Constable, 1965); and Williams, *True Resurrection* (London: Mitchell Beazley, 1972).

Notes

This chapter is primarily the work of Richard Kidd.

[1] Quoted in Timothy Hyman & Patrick Wright (eds.), *Stanley Spencer* (London: Tate Publishing, 2001), p. 183.

[2] Spencer Archive (Tate Gallery), 733.3.74; quoted in Hyman & Wright (eds.), *Stanley Spencer*, p. 183.

[3] Quoted in *Stanley Spencer RA* (London: Royal Academy of Arts, 1980), p. 11.

[4] Maurice Collis, *Stanley Spencer* (London: Harvill Press, 1962), p. 85.

[5] H. A. Williams, *True Resurrection* (London: Mitchell Beazley, 1972), pp. 10-11.

[6] Ibid., pp. 11-12.

[7] Quoted in Ron Ferguson, *Chasing the Wild Goose* (London: Fount Paperbacks, 1988), p. 16.

[8] Spencer Archive (Tate Gallery), 733.2.67 (c. 1939); quoted in Adrian Glew, *Stanley Spencer: Letters and Writings* (London: Tate Publishing, 2001), p. 192.

[9] Quoted in Keith Bell, *Stanley Spencer* (London: Phaidon, 1992), p. 464.

[10] Quoted in Hyman & Wright (eds.), *Stanley Spencer*, p. 180.

[11] Quoted in Bell, *Stanley Spencer*, p. 164.

[12] Quoted in Collis, *Stanley Spencer*, p. 83.

[13] Stanley Spencer to Hilda Spencer, Lindworth, October 1933; quoted in John Rothenstein (ed.), *Stanley Spencer the Man: Correspondence and Reminiscences* (London: Elek, 1979), p. 53.

14 Collis, *Stanley Spencer*, p. 117.

15 H. A. Williams, *The True Wilderness* (London: Constable, 1965), pp. 29-30.

16 Ibid., p. 31.

17 Essay One, Notebook (c. 1936), TAM 16B; quoted in Glew, *Stanley Spencer: Letters and Writings*, p. 175.

18 Spencer, letter to Hilda Spencer, Clivedon View (c. 1950), Spencer Archive (Tate Gallery), 733.1.1672; quoted in Glew, *Stanley Spencer: Letters and Writings*, p. 235.

19 'Sermons by Artists', Notebook (1934), Spencer Archive (Tate Gallery), 8055.44; quoted in Glew, *Stanley Spencer: Letters and Writings*, p. 164.

20 Writings 1932–1937, Spencer Archive (Tate Gallery), 733.2.7; quoted in Glew, *Stanley Spencer: Letters and Writings*, p. 150.

21 Poem, 'God's Grandeur', in W. H. Gardner & N. H. Mackenzie (eds.), *Poems of Gerard Manley Hopkins*, fourth edition (London: Oxford University Press, 1967), p. 66.

4
Georgia O'Keeffe:
Imaging the Depths

There are artists who immediately suggest themselves as guides, teachers and companions for the spiritual journey. Their life and work reflect such concerns and commitments, inviting us to see with eyes of faith and so to walk the same road. Other artists appear at first sight unlikely to provide significant resources for this journey of faith and, like Edvard Munch, Georgia O'Keeffe (1887–1986) could easily be regarded — and discarded — as one of these. Widely accepted as one of the most prominent American artists of the last century, O'Keeffe is best known for her depictions of flowers and bones, somewhat unpromising material for those engaged on the spiritual journey, and for a number of reasons she might be seen as a strange and problematic choice for our deeper reflection.

An initial problem is attempting to explore O'Keeffe's work with the help of just two paintings. Her most common way of working was to paint a series, or even a series of series, that approached the same subject in a number of different ways, sometimes over a considerable period of time. As we shall see, such an approach can be extraordinarily creative, allowing the artist to develop all kinds of pictorial possibilities, but it does make it particularly difficult to examine one painting in isolation from others. It may be that readers will want to make use of one of the monographs mentioned in the bibliography in order fully to appreciate O'Keeffe's aims and intentions.

A further difficulty is O'Keeffe herself. During her lifetime she became something of a celebrity, initially as a result of her intimate relationship with the pioneer photographer Alfred Stieglitz, who eagerly presented her as a sensual woman artist, and more latterly by promoting herself as the solitary, independent visionary. Celebrity status rarely encourages balanced, insightful understanding of a person's achievements, and such projected images have often served to obscure and confuse rather than reveal. O'Keeffe remains an elusive figure whose

work defies straightforward categorization. Moreover, she did not believe
in offering words of clarification and explanation, declaring that

> I think I'd rather let the painting work for itself than help it with the
> word.[1]

> It is easier for me to paint it than to write about it and I would so much
> rather people would look at it than read about it. I see no reason for
> painting anything that can be put into any other form as well.[2]

Such a warning might cast doubt on the wisdom of pursuing a study of
O'Keeffe, except that for someone so uncomfortable with words she did
in fact write a great deal, mostly in the form of letters, often providing
crucial if enigmatic insights into the nature of her work.

Her lack of any formal religious commitment confirms O'Keeffe as a
strange companion to choose for our journey. Her father was a Catholic
and her mother Episcopalian but neither attended church regularly, and it
is only following her first visit to New Mexico in 1929 that O'Keeffe's
paintings reveal any sign of interest in the Christian church. It is, however, an interest limited to landscape and culture, provoked by the sight of
Penitente crosses belonging to a lay brotherhood of Hispanic Catholics
that marked places of worship for isolated communities without a priest.
The appearance of these austere crosses, the scene of somewhat bizarre
rites of flagellation at Easter time, provided subject matter for a number
of paintings, as did the adobe church on the village square of Ranchos de
Taos.

But if O'Keeffe had little concern for religious faith, she certainly
possessed a genuine spirituality that pervaded the whole of her life. It
shines through her paintings as she journeyed both inwards, developing a
deep sense of self, and outwards, encountering the world's infinite horizons. It is a journey marked by contemplation and the continual search for
beauty, simplicity and harmony. It is O'Keeffe's spirituality that makes
her an artist deserving our attention, not least for the ways in which she
can nurture and challenge our own Christian journey.

The influence of new ideas

In 1905, O'Keeffe was enrolled at the Art Institute of Chicago. It was the beginning of her formal art training that continued, after an enforced break due to illness, at the Art Students League where she was taught by the noted American painter William Merritt Chase. O'Keeffe proved to be a more than able student, winning a prize from Chase for one of her still-life studies. But at both these institutions the training she received followed long established patterns that required students to study and copy what was put in front of them, to imitate the styles of the Old Masters, and so to produce realistic representational images. Such a conservative approach to art could not hold O'Keeffe for long. In fact, she lost interest for a time, and it was not until 1912 while taking a summer course at the University of Virginia that she encountered someone who could give her art meaning and direction — Arthur Wesley Dow.

Though he did paint, Dow's main influence was as a writer and teacher, bringing a fresh and radical approach to the discipline. He rejected the kind of art that aimed at realism and encouraged students to give attention to the elements of composition — colour, shape, line, space — in ways that sought to bring harmony and balance. The calling of the artist, he believed, is to not to teach us to see facts but to feel harmonies. Above all, this requires the active involvement of the artist who is not there merely to copy what already exists, but to make free and personal choices about how to present an image, rooted in a developing awareness of how to create a harmonious design. Art should express not imitate.

O'Keeffe's initial contact with Dow was indirect. She was taught his ideas by Alon Bement, a disciple, but in 1914 she returned to New York to study under Dow himself. Recalling the effect his thinking had on her, O'Keeffe said:

> This man had one dominating idea: to fill a space in a beautiful way — and that interested me. After all, everyone has to do just this — make choices — in his daily life when only buying a cup and saucer. By this time I had a technique for handling oil and watercolour easily; Dow gave me something to do with it.[3]

Dow did not, of course, develop his ideas in a vacuum. The transforming moment in his life came when he discovered Asian art and subsequently met Ernest Fenollosa, an expert in the field from the Museum of Fine Arts in Boston. This was how Dow came to adopt the Japanese design concept known as *notan*, a method of patterning based on the opposition of light and dark, that he was to pass on to O'Keeffe. Indeed, we shall discover a number of ways in which Asian art and philosophy had a continuing part to play in O'Keeffe's life, proving to have a major influence on her painting. It is worth noting that her library included Fenollosa's two volumes, *Epochs of Chinese and Japanese Art: An Outline History of East Asiatic Design*, and that one of her favourite books was Kakuzo Okakura's *The Book of Tea*.

While studying under Dow, O'Keeffe encountered another book that would prove to be a guiding influence throughout her life. *Concerning the Spiritual in Art* by Wassily Kandinsky was first published in Germany in 1911, and following its appearance in translation in 1914 Bement suggested she ought to read it. She did so, many times.

In the face of what he described as 'the nightmare of materialism, which has turned the life of the universe into an evil, useless game',[4] Kandinsky's aim was to present art as the way forward in humanity's search for moral and spiritual renewal. But such renewal could only be achieved by art that takes seriously the inner life of the soul that celebrates the emotions and creates forms of internal harmony rather than being tied to reproducing objects from the tangible world. What this means is that the true artist, the 'priest of beauty',[5] will move towards producing abstract forms, for it is through abstraction that we are set free from the limits of the material world in order to give expression to deeper, inner truth. Artists should always work in a way that is guided by inner necessity. He wrote:

> The artist must be blind to distinctions between 'recognized' or 'unrecognized' conventions of form, deaf to the transitory teaching and demands of his particular age. He must watch only the trend of the inner need, and hearken to its words alone. Then he will with safety employ means both sanctioned and forbidden by his contemporaries. All means

are sacred which are called for by the inner need. All means are sinful which obscure that inner need.[6]

Kandinsky knew this approach required a radical break from the past, and he used music to press home his arguments. He described music as having the advantage of being the most non-material of the arts, able with ease to engage the inner life and so give voice to the spiritual. Painting needs to learn fundamental lessons from music by setting itself free from a dependency on natural forms that serve as boundaries, and embracing abstraction in order that a direct encounter with the spiritual can become possible.

A considerable part of what is a short book is taken up with a discussion of colour, for Kandinsky believed that different colours influence the soul in deep and intense ways. He goes through them in turn, making divisions on the basis of warm and cold, light and dark, proposing the kind of feelings they create on their own and when mixed. He also suggests how different forms can enhance or distort the effect a colour has. So, for example, he describes yellow as having 'a disturbing influence . . . an insistent, aggressive character'[7] best suited to sharp forms such as triangles, while blue is 'the typical heavenly colour' that creates a feeling of rest most suited to round forms. This is not meant to be restrictive, for Kandinsky encouraged the exploration of all kinds of combinations, including those that appear to be discordant, in order that through manipulation fresh harmonies might be discovered. Indeed, the striving for harmony lies behind the entire project; it is to be a harmonization that improves and refines the human soul, expressing the inner being of the artist and striking a corresponding chord of recognition in the soul of the viewer.

Unsurprisingly, Kandinsky did not expect art to abandon natural forms in favour of the abstract overnight. The natural world would still provide means of expression, but the artist must go as far as emotion would allow in altering forms and colours, and he looked towards a day when the ultimate ideal would be achieved:

When we remember . . . that spiritual experience is quickening, that positive science, the firmest basis of human thought, is tottering, that

dissolution of matter is imminent, we have reason to hope that the hour
of pure composition is not far away.[8]

Concerning the Spiritual in Art had considerable impact on the development of modern art. It is fascinating to read it alongside Kandinsky's
own highly abstract compositions so as to begin to understand what he
was seeking to achieve, and then to detect the effect his ideas had on the
work of other artists. O'Keeffe was certainly one of these. Together, Dow
and Kandinsky were seminal figures in her development as a mature
artist, representing as they did a number of new ideas: a rejection of materialism and an openness to the inner world of the soul; the expressing of
emotion as having greater significance than the reproduction of an external object; an emphasis on composition that knows and feels beauty,
rather than a style that concentrates on the imitation of natural forms; a
move away from realism towards abstraction; and the search for harmony
and for balance. All this struck a chord with O'Keeffe. It gave her foun-
dations upon which to build her art and a way of bringing her art into the
whole of life. She took from Dow and Asian culture the conviction that
painting well and living well should form an integrated whole, and so she
says that when teaching her high school students:

> I liked to convey to them the idea that art is important in everyday life. I
> wanted them to learn the principle: that when you buy a pair of shoes or
> place a window in the front of a house or address a letter or comb your
> hair, consider it carefully, so that it looks well.[9]

It is worth taking a moment to place these new and influential ideas
that were emerging within the art world into a wider context, for without
doubt they were at least in part a response to developments in other fields
of enquiry. In science, Rutherford's work on the atom had shown that
there is a real sense in which the world as we see it does not exist. His dis-
coveries called into question a reliance on the visible world of matter as
the basis for human thought and action, suggesting that what is real is not
simply the visible, and it was this that prompted Kandinsky to reject the
material in a quest for the spiritual. Psychology, too, was making the journey inward that was revolutionizing understanding of the human psyche.

Freud's ideas were increasingly well known, opening up the uncharted waters of the unconscious and engaging in an analysis of human sexuality (in ways that, as we shall see, were to haunt O'Keeffe). Again, the message was clear: the concrete image of the world around us has been destroyed, what is real is more than the visible, and truth must be sought within as well as without.

Related ideas were also emerging in literature. The poet Ezra Pound, like Dow, gained inspiration from Fenollosa with the result that he developed different forms of writing (circular rather than narrative) in works like the *Cantos*, and spoke up forcefully for the freedom of the human spirit. At the same time D. H. Lawrence was writing in ways that advocated the inherent power of human intuition, most notably expressed as emotions and feelings, and was read and admired by many artists including O'Keeffe. If we add into this melting pot the political movement campaigning for women's right to vote, and the specifically American tradition of landscape painting that sought the spiritual in nature and viewed with suspicion an over-reliance on the power of rational analysis, then we have a time that is ripe for the emergence of new movements in the art world.

We must take note of one more vital influence that shaped O'Keeffe's life as an artist — the development of photography. As we have already noted, the most significant relationship in O'Keeffe's life was with the photographer, Alfred Stieglitz, whom she eventually married. He saw his mission as gaining acceptance of photography as an art form, arguing that, like painting, it should be about much more than producing realistic images. The feelings and inspiration of the photographer have to be involved for it to be art, he suggested, and technical knowledge follows strictly as a secondary requirement.

Having received her first exhibition at Stieglitz's gallery and then benefited from his ongoing sponsorship, O'Keeffe inevitably came into contact with the circle of photographers associated with him, and perhaps the most influential among them was Paul Strand. She wrote to him:

> I've been wanting to tell you again and again how much I liked your work — I believe I've have been looking at things and seeing them as I

thought you might photograph them . . . making Strand photographs for myself in my head.[10]

How exactly did his photography — and that of Stieglitz and others — shape O'Keeffe's work? We can see the way in which his close-up pictures of ordinary objects that were so magnified as to become abstract studies of shape and pattern and line are reflected in her paintings of flowers and shells. We can also see how her knowledge of the way the camera lens works, compressing distance and removing the middle ground, is used to give her paintings fresh power and perspective. O'Keeffe, however, never painted pictures like photographs. She was well aware of — and committed to — the special qualities of painting that create texture with a brush stroke and are able to carefully select what to include and what to leave out. She had her own independent vision to pursue.

It is time to turn our attention to O'Keeffe's work. As we do so we shall be able to see how the various influences are played out in her desire to express 'the wideness and wonder of the world',[11] and so trace the issues they raise for our own spiritual journey.

Jack-in-the-Pulpit No IV (1930)
In the autumn of 1915 while teaching art in South Carolina, O'Keeffe wrote to her friend Anita Pollitzer: 'I am starting all over new — Have put everything I have ever done away and don't expect to get any of it out ever again — or for a long time anyway.'[12] Several years later she was to give a brief account of this crossroads moment in her life:

> I said to myself, 'I have things in my head that are not like what anyone has taught me — shapes and ideas so near to me — so natural to my way of being and thinking that it hasn't occurred to me to put them down.' I decided to start anew — to strip away what I had been taught — to accept as true to my own thinking.[13]

The result was a series of beautiful charcoal drawings that she called her 'Specials'. They are full of life and motion with flowing lines and circles, many of them suggestive of growing plants and swirling water, and all of them moving very clearly in the direction of abstraction. Charles

Eldredge, a commentator on her work, suggests that it is these crucial drawings that provided O'Keeffe with the formal vocabulary she needed for future compositions, and that they proved to be a source of continuing inspiration over several decades.[14]

Growing plants had certainly been drawn to O'Keeffe's attention early on in life. Her art teacher at high school had brought in a flower — a Jack-in-the-Pulpit — for the students to study, and the possibilities it offered to the artist caught her imagination. She recalled how her teacher drew attention to:

> ... the strange shapes and variations in colour — from the deep, almost black earthy violet through all the greens, from the pale whitish green in the flower through the heavy green of the leaves. She held up the purplish hood and showed us the Jack inside. I had seen many Jacks before, but this was the first time I remember examining a flower . . . she started me looking at things — looking very carefully at details. It was certainly the first time my attention was called to the outline and colour of any growing thing with the idea of drawing or painting it.[15]

In the 1920s O'Keeffe began to transfer this fascination to canvas, painting a large number of magnified views of flowers that filled the available space — pictures of calla lilies, irises, poppies, roses, petunias, tulips, and many others. They clearly dominated her own imagination and caught the imagination of those who saw them. When first exhibited they drew a generally enthusiastic response from public and critics, and ever since these highly distinctive images have been closely associated with the name of O'Keeffe. In 1930 this period of flower painting culminated in a series of six *Jack-in-the-Pulpit* pictures that recall the early high school encounter. There is no doubt that O'Keeffe herself believed that this was a particularly significant series of paintings because she retained ownership of four of them and bought another back in 1973; they also have importance for us in our search for spiritual insight and resources.

As far as I am aware, the most readily available monographs and illustrated biographies of O'Keeffe do not reproduce the complete *Jack-in-the-Pulpit* series, though all of them can be found in one or other of the books mentioned in the bibliography. Britta Benke does, however, provide us with the second, third, fourth and sixth in *Georgia O'Keeffe 1887–1986: Flowers in the Desert*, and this is sufficient to reveal the way in which this series moves in a steady progression from representation to abstraction. O'Keeffe wrote:

> I work on an idea for a long time. It's like getting acquainted with a person and I don't get acquainted easily . . . Sometimes I start in a very realistic fashion, and as I go on from one painting to another of the same thing, it becomes simplified till it can be nothing but abstract.[16]

The first is the smallest in the series, and it is also the most realistic representation of the flower. As is typical, it is enlarged and magnified to fill the canvas, and so we find ourselves drawn into the centre of the flower. The bulbous pistil dominates. The purples, reds and greens are somewhat dark and oppressive.

The second is much larger, but the flower is painted to a smaller scale and so its setting becomes more visible. This has the effect of focusing attention on the Jack-in-the Pulpit, particularly as it is framed with the use of lighter colours. The swirling shades of green that surround the flower contribute to making this a less realistic painting. The lines radiating outwards from the pulpit are striking.

The third moves us in the direction of abstraction, as the flower becomes the central feature of a radically simplified picture. Folds of green gently unfurl on both sides to sweep up and surround a Jack-in-the Pulpit that appears to occupy a much more elevated position. Similar spaces on both halves of the canvas are filled with blue and white, so giving the whole painting a more formalized appearance.

The fourth (Plate 7) we shall return to in a moment. Just a brief glance reveals that this is a long way from being an attempt to provide a straightforward image of the flower.

The fifth is the largest of the six paintings and is almost entirely abstract in design. It is full of curves flowing through the painting from top to bottom, conveying movement and growth. The painting is dominated by strong, deep purples and greens, but there are no recognisable leaf forms and the form of the pistil is taken up into the sweeping flow of colour.

The sixth reduces the original flower to its simplest and most abstract. It could not be recognized as associated with the Jack-in-the-Pulpit except as part of this series. A dark pistil-like shape is all that remains, filling the central section of the canvas. It is surrounded by a bright white halo that slowly fades away. The use of colour is also greatly simplified.

As suggested at the beginning of this chapter, it is difficult to look at one of O'Keeffe's paintings in isolation. *Jack-in-the-Pulpit IV* has been reproduced for our attention, partly because it is the one I have found peculiarly arresting, and partly because it does serve to highlight a number of issues that are central to our exploration of this artist's work. It will help to consider in turn three basic questions.

To begin with, let us simply ask: what do we see when we look at this painting? The most arresting feature is clearly the presence of light. It is at the heart of this strong image, surrounding the pistil — much as it does in the last of the series — and streaking upwards through the painting. Without that light, the composition would not hold together.

Several critics have commented on the way in which O'Keeffe makes use of light, Bowman going so far as to say that 'light — in both its formal and metaphorical aspects — forms a consistent thread and one that helps to define her achievement as an artist.'[17] It is certainly not hard to find evidence to support such a view. During her time as head of the art department in a college at Canyon in Texas from 1916–1918, where wide open plains allow the sky to come down to meet the horizon, O'Keeffe was inspired to produce two notable watercolour series that are all about light. The explosive *Evening Star* pictures are full of vibrant reds and yellows that find their energy source in the light of the star that O'Keeffe used to see high up in the sky long before sunset, while her more gentle *Light Coming on the Plains* images try to capture the first signs of morning light arching across the sky like a pulsating halo. Much later, O'Keeffe would again make light the prevailing subject in paintings that resulted from the flights she took in her trips around the world. Her *Sky Above the Flat White Cloud II* (1960–1964) is one of a number in which the bottom two thirds of the canvas is left white while the top part consists of horizontal bands of pale colour, so creating for us the sense of an infinite world that is filled with light shining up from below.

For O'Keeffe, light became symbolic of the renewing life and growth present in all of nature, and *Jack-in-the-Pulpit IV* expresses this deep belief. As she moves towards abstraction, searching for ways of allowing the essence of the flower to emerge, she places light at the centre — the living force at its heart. It is clearly light that comes from within rather than from any external source. We look at what might be a crack allowing a shaft of light from deep inside, from the very source and origin of the plant's life, to break through. It is the light of life, there at the beginning, without which nothing has come into being.

In her biography of O'Keeffe, Roxana Robinson says:

> Early spring in the Adriondacks is a brown, bleak time, and green plants are rare. One of the earliest to appear is the strange, retiring jack-in-the-pulpit, which rises fresh and vivid from the sere brown leaves on the forest floor. By the springhouses in the woods, Georgia found a patch of jacks. They were the dark-veined variety, with dramatic purple-green stripes on the inner leaves that surround the smooth central shaft . . . The jack series is a powerful celebration of the strong thrust of spring and of the dark secret tower enfolded in green.[18]

To add meaning to the presence of the light, the remaining colours in *Jack-in-the-Pulpit IV* are much darker when compared with the earlier paintings in the series — and, indeed, when set alongside many of O'Keeffe's other flower paintings. In a letter, she commented on the importance of colour saying:

> . . . the flower is painted large to convey to you my experience of the flower — and what is my experience of the flower if it is not colour . . . Colour is one of the great things in the world that makes life worth living to me and as I have come to think of painting it is my effort to create an equivalent with paint colour for the world — life as I see it.[19]

To stand and look at O'Keeffe's flowers is to look at colour. She used colour to express the spirit of her subject (as she had been taught by Kandinsky), believing it to be fundamental to seeing, and she was not afraid to use a range of rich, striking tones. While this painting lacks the more vibrant colours that characterize so much of her work, the heavy greens and browns set against the blue have their own beauty and do achieve their purpose. They are basic to the experience she wishes to convey. We are given the feeling of looking into the still depths within the flower, as the outer layers that contain and protect life are pulled back, and everything is distilled.

The kind of shapes and lines we see used in *Jack-in-the-Pulpit IV* are of significance. References have already been made to O'Keeffe's abstract work and of the move towards abstraction within this painting, but we need to define more carefully what this meant.

The forms she used were almost always ones derived from nature. Marjorie Welish describes her notion of abstraction as that of 'condensation, not imagination'; it was a 'deliberative process of abstracting from nature'[20] and therefore very different from Kandinsky's freer and more arbitrary vision, however much she was influenced by him.

Jack-in-the-Pulpit IV is testimony to this. The line and pattern of the dark layered colours retain the image of the unfurling of leaves surrounding a plant, while the swelling form isolated by the light is evidently the plant's pistil. At the same time, however, these forms that derive from one particular flower become capable of other associations and so begin to take us towards abstract and, O'Keeffe would argue, universal forms. We can see in the painting canyons and crevices, voids and solids, gentle folds and black holes, round buds and lapping waves. Messinger has suggested that these recall the shapes and lines found in one of O'Keeffe's 'Specials', *Drawing XIII*,[21] but while this may be so we should not lose sight of the fact that they are exactly the kind of forms that continually appear within her work. Moreover, it has been suggested that they reflect a distinctively feminine reading of the world, and this is an issue we must shortly address in greater detail.

A second basic question needs to be answered: what were O'Keeffe's aims and intentions in choosing to paint flowers? There was an American tradition of flower painting long before O'Keeffe, but there is no doubt that she took it to a new level, and that her first enlarged canvases in 1924 were the result of two specific events. On the one hand, she was spending part of her time in New York where life was fast and hectic, and the urban environment of concrete and steel seemed to squeeze out the presence of the natural world. The rapid growth in technology, symbolized by the ever increasing height of new buildings, left no room for something as simple and small as a flower and she reacted against this. On the other hand, O'Keeffe came across a painting of flowers by Fantin-Latour that stimulated her to consider what she herself might do. She said:

> In the twenties, huge buildings sometimes seemed to be going up overnight in New York. At that time I saw a painting by Fantin-Latour, a still-life with flowers I found very beautiful, but I realized that were I to paint the same flowers so small, no one would look at them because I was unknown. So I thought I'll make them big like the huge buildings going up. People will be startled; they'll have to look at them — and they did.[22]

It was, suggests Robinson, the dynamic tension between the pace and noise of city life, and the quiet, fragile beauty of a flower that provided the necessary impetus.[23]

O'Keeffe gave a very moving account of what lies behind her paintings of flowers. She said:

> A flower is relatively small. Everyone has many associations with a flower — the idea of flowers. You put out your hand to touch the flower — lean forward to smell it — maybe touch it with your lips almost without thinking — or give it to someone to please them. Still — in a way — nobody sees a flower — really it is so small — we haven't time — and to see takes time, like to have a friend takes time. If I could paint the flower exactly as I see it no one would see what I see because I would paint it small like the flower is small.
>
> So I said to myself — I'll paint what I see — what the flower is to me but I'll paint it big and they will be surprised into taking time to look at it — I will make even busy New Yorkers take time to see what I see of flowers.[24]

It is an account that links us, I believe, with vital spiritual themes and insights. Behind O'Keeffe's words is not just a search for oneness with the natural world (though she identified with those who felt a deep affinity with nature), but a spirituality that is rooted in a loving attention to detail and that leads towards an encounter with a deeper reality.

The fact that she portrays flowers in such a magnified form immediately bestows importance on them, reminding us that they should not be lightly ignored and dismissed. In a similar way, O'Keeffe succeeds in giving these fragile flowers a permanence that belies their inherent transience, refusing to allow them to die and be forgotten. They have an undiminished strength, gained in part from brushwork that removes much of the detail from the surface of petals and leaves, leaving the impression that they might almost be plastic. When we look at her large images we see no signs of wilting; rather, the flowers are suspended in time in a way that enables them to be ever present to us, encouraging us to grasp the moment of seeing in a full and complete way. Thus O'Keeffe makes us take the flower seriously, however ordinary and small it may be, and demands that we give it proper attention.

'To see takes time' she tells us. It is a conviction shared with many others, and Barbara Novak helps make the link both with O'Keeffe's Asian influences and with another artist featured in this book. She tells us:

> Vincent van Gogh has eloquently reminded us that the Japanese artist spends his time studying 'a single blade of grass.' 'Come now,' he wrote, 'isn't it almost a true religion which these simple Japanese teach us, who live in nature as though they themselves were flowers?' O'Keeffe studies the flower as the Japanese studied the blade of grass. Van Gogh envied the Japanese 'the extreme clearness which everything has in their work. It is never tedious, and never seems to be done too hurriedly.'
> I suspect he would have admired O'Keeffe's 'extreme clearness' as well. It is, as he said of the Japanese, 'as simple as breathing.'[25]

They are comments very reminiscent of the American poet Walt Whitman (a particular inspiration to Stieglitz and his circle), who finds the eternal in the ordinary when he writes: 'I believe a leaf of grass is no less than the journey-work of the stars.'[26]

More significantly for us, as we explained in our 'Preview', this commitment to careful and loving attention demands effort and is one that Christian mystics and theologians have often spoken of as at the heart of our search for God — particularly those whose spirituality emphasizes

God's immanence in creation and in the ordinary human experiences of everyday life. The Lady Julian of Norwich, the fourteenth-century anchoress, wrote of her conviction 'that God is everything that is good, that God made everything, and that "in God is all".'[27] A simple encounter with a hazel-nut caused her to reflect deeply on the presence of God sustaining this one tiny, delicate aspect of creation, and to recognize that in the end everything that is flows out of the love of God. She developed a theology of creation that sees God as the ground of all that is in being, so giving a very positive place to the material as the outpouring of God's own nature. Quiet contemplation of even the smallest part of creation becomes a moment of revelation leading to wonder, awe and praise.

The twentieth-century monk Thomas Merton was another who learned that the art of seeing is a way of encounter with God. Like the Lady Julian, much of his life was spent in solitude, deprived of what we would regard as normal engagement with people and places. But this served only to heighten Merton's awareness of the sacredness of what is common and ordinary. In his *Seeds of Contemplation* he speaks of learning to realize that 'the love of God seeks us in every situation',[28] that everything is holy, and that creation mirrors the glory of God. A look at some of Merton's photographs reveals the depth of attention he would give to ordinary, natural objects, inviting us to engage in the inner spiritual journey through seeing. We shall have cause to mention Merton again before the end of this chapter.

Both the Ignatian and the Franciscan traditions lead us in the same direction. They, too, affirm the sacredness of creation as a place of encounter with the transcendent for those who take the time and effort to look. And while both would stress that there should be no confusion between the Creator and the created, there is a genuine reverence for what can be seen, felt and touched. Matter is the language God uses to communicate; through it is revealed truth and meaning. So we are called to a way of life that, in a phrase attributed to the Jesuit Jean-Pierre de Caussade, affirms 'the sacrament of the present moment'.[29] Each moment is an invitation to see with new eyes, truly to value what is experienced, and so to glimpse the wonder and mystery that lies half-hidden in the world around us. The fact that so often we fail to live with such loving attention points to our need of the artist in our midst, as one who looks at reality as if for the first time, seeing with sacramental eyes that penetrate beneath the surface, and allowing us to see the holy in what is ordinary. This is what we already encountered in the work of Spencer; here it is again with fresh force in the work of O'Keeffe.

It is her loving attention to the flower, then, that allowed O'Keeffe to go on a journey of exploration. She spoke of the way 'You paint from your subject, not what you see . . . I rarely paint anything I don't know very well.'[30] She directed her gaze towards the Jack-in-the-Pulpit, and from that concentrated looking she developed many different ways of understanding and interpreting the flower, including that portrayed in *Jack-in-the-Pulpit IV*. It took her into another world, the inner world both of the plant and of herself, searching for the reality behind the reality. It is this journey that leads us directly to our final question: what is being sought and achieved in the move from representation to abstraction?

Ways of seeing and knowing

The painting of such objects as apples, shells and flowers is often described as still life. The way O'Keeffe did it, however, defied the traditional understanding of this term, for not only did she look at these objects with an extraordinary intensity, she also deliberately removed them from their context in order to explore forms and colours. She opened them up and took them apart with her artist's eye, enabling new ways of seeing to emerge, and the Jack-in-the-Pulpit series illustrates the kind of steps that are involved.

O'Keeffe believed that these are steps in the search for what is real. She wrote: 'Nothing is less real than realism. Details are confusing. It is only by selection, by elimination, by emphasis that we get at the real meaning of things.'[31] To understand what she meant by these words takes us back to the ideas we encountered at the beginning of this chapter. For O'Keeffe there was no point in following in the footsteps of those who had tried faithfully to reproduce on canvas an exact replica of a flower, partly because the camera could now do that far more effectively, but also because the artist has the ability — and duty — to explore more significant levels of meaning. Thus, if we were to look at one of O'Keeffe's flower paintings and describe it as an accurate imitation of the real thing, and therefore a good painting, we would be missing the point entirely.

Her aim is not realism, for realism only serves to distract and restrict, preventing us from embracing the different ways of knowing that are opened up to the human mind and spirit by the work of an artist. The artist has the freedom to select colours, eliminate patterns, emphasize forms, and it is this ability that can help us see in new and revealing ways.

In his book, *Ways of Seeing*, John Berger reminds us that how we see things is never fixed.[32] It will be determined by context and culture; it will be affected by what the viewer knows and believes. So, as an example, he suggests that the sight of fire in the Middle Ages had particular meaning for people who believed in hell as a place of consuming fire. Their religious worldview shaped their experience of seeing. Likewise, when a picture is painted, there is a complex network of relationships and connections at work, involving the artist and viewer as well as the work of art, and always this involves interpretation. To believe there is one 'pure' way of seeing a painting is to go in search of realism. To recognize, however, that the process of interpretation is at the creative heart of any work of art is to look for 'the real meaning of things', and so be caught up in a much more exciting journey of discovery.

This is what lies behind O'Keeffe's flower paintings. They express her own interpretation, her inner emotional response to the natural world around her. She believed that was all she could do, declaring in a letter to William Milliken:

> I know I can not paint a flower. I can not paint the sun on the desert on
> a bright summer morning but maybe in terms of paint colour I can convey to you my experience of the flower or the experience that makes the
> flower of significance to me at that particular time.[33]

To succeed in this task of communicating her particular experience and knowledge of a flower, O'Keeffe moved away from representation in order to concentrate on that which for her was essential. That certainly meant paintings dominated by colour for — as we noted earlier — colour was central to her experience. Notice how in a list of her work O'Keeffe so often identified her paintings not just by the flower's name but by the colour: *red* canna, *black* and *purple* petunia*s*, *white* iri*s*. The enlarged flowers become studies in colour with almost everything else eliminated.

She plays with colours in ways that do not — and need not — resemble those of the actual plant, for the meaning of the painting is contained in the colour.

It also meant a concentration on form for this, too, is basic to O'Keeffe's interpretation of the world. The journey she makes in the *Jack-in-the-Pulpit* series is one that searches for the lines, shapes and patterns that not only express her understanding of the essence of the flower, but that she also sees repeated in all of nature because they have universal meaning. So, as we have seen, she slowly reduces and simplifies form, making the move from the flower's existence to its essence, and *Jack-in-the-Pulpit IV* is in many ways pivotal to the whole process. It is in this canvas that certain forms become dominant, the darker colours deliberately eliminating much of the diversity that expressed the life of the flower within the previous painting in the series, so allowing us to begin to see more than just the flower. This was what O'Keeffe wanted to achieve as she moved towards abstraction — to reach for universal forms and motifs that captured the way she saw and knew a world so full of wonder.

As will be evident, such a path requires the artist to make choices. The eye has to look for and select those forms that this artist perceives as portraying the essence of life, that point towards meanings with universal significance, and then decide how they can be committed to canvas. The act of painting becomes an act of self-revelation. It draws on the unique vision of the artist, showing us how she chooses to see things. O'Keeffe expressed something of this when, in trying to describe what good painting is, she argued that it has nothing to do with accurately reproducing a hill or tree. Rather:

> It is lines or colours put together so that they say something. For me that is the very basis of painting. The abstraction is often the most definite form for the intangible thing in myself that I can only clarify in paint.[34]

These words draw attention to O'Keeffe's conviction that her art reveals herself, becoming a means of self-discovery as she uses paint to interpret her own experience and emotions.

It is possible to take this one step further. In her consideration of O'Keeffe's flower paintings, Marjorie Balge-Crozier suggests that not only do they serve to uncover the inner life of the artist, but they also make us see more of ourselves. She points to the way that the enlarged flowers remove the distance between the viewer and the image, so making it hard to remain disengaged. She says of O'Keeffe:

> Her radical, close-up views make vision synonymous with the self, thereby opening the way for more emotional interpretations and reactions on the part of the spectator, who can no longer comfortably maintain the distance necessary for voyeurism. The viewer ends up feeling exposed in much the same way the artist has revealed herself, her vision, and her emotions. She has made us look — not at nature, but at what she has seen and made of it — a self-portrait that implicates the viewer.[35]

When O'Keeffe's early abstract paintings began to appear, they quickly provoked a reaction. In a society becoming used to making all kinds of Freudian associations, where art now saw itself as seeking to express hidden realities, her images were inevitably open to different interpretations — including sexual interpretations. O'Keeffe went out of her way to discourage such readings of her work, and following an exhibition in 1923 she made a deliberate decision to paint in a way that was 'as objective as I can make it'[36] in order to refute such interpretations. Her subsequent paintings of clam shells and flowers, however, could hardly be expected to achieve such a result. Later in life, she explained how she understood her own work by saying:

> Eroticism! That's something people themselves put into the paintings. They've found things that never entered my mind. That doesn't mean they weren't there, but the things they said astonished me. It wouldn't occur to me.[37]

It was certainly a reaction to critics who only looked at her paintings in this way, as if sex can be separated off from the rest of life. It was also a rejection of those who made too close a connection between the paintings and her own sexuality, instead of recognizing that their interpretation inevitably said as much about themselves. But it would be a mistake to ignore what is clearly there. Flowers are made for sex, often with both female and male parts clearly visible, and the fact that they bear a resemblance to human reproductive organs is a product of nature that could not be disguised. In addition, the flower has a symbolic place in human society, and in the early part of the century, at a time when misogyny took many forms, it had come to represent the dangerous, sensual, alluring power of a woman; O'Keeffe would have been well aware of this.

So while we must never reduce her flower paintings to sexual symbols, we cannot pretend that they lack sexual meaning. This is part of what gives them their depth and their strength. O'Keeffe affirms our inherent sexuality, to be celebrated in as simple an object as a flower, and never to be isolated from the natural streams of life. What is of real significance is that, in a culture dominated by men where women artists received little recognition, O'Keeffe brought a distinctive feminine way of seeing and knowing the world. She searched for universal forms that reflected her experience as a woman, remaining true to her vision despite being dismissed and trivialized by critics who would never have taken the same attitudes to a male artist. In a letter from the mid-1920s, O'Keeffe said:

> I have never felt a more feminine person — and what that is I do not know — so I let it go at that till something else crystallizes . . . What I want written . . . I have no definite idea of what it should be — but a woman who has lived many things and who sees lines and colours as an expression of living — might say something that a man can't — I feel there is something unexplored about women that only a woman can explore — Men have done all they can do about it.[38]

If we look again at *Jack-in-the-Pulpit IV*, the strong sexual connotations are evident, not just in the phallic shape of the jack or pistil, but even more so in the labia-like folds of the leaves and the crack of light that leads to the womb of life. Through her study of the flower, O'Keeffe abstracted what she believed to be universal forms of the kind we recognized earlier, and so developed a distinctive feminine visual language. As Anna Chave observes:

> O'Keeffe's imagery — with its myriad canyons, crevices, slits, holes,
> and voids, its effluvia, as well as its soft swelling forms — . . . describes
> abstractly what differentiates female bodies: the roundness, the flows,
> and above all, the spaces.[39]

It is worth looking at a selection of O'Keeffe's paintings so as to see the
way in which these forms recur. Look, for example, at *Inside Red Canna*
(1919), *Corn, Dark I* (1924), *Open Clam Shell* (1926), *Pelvis IV* (1944),
and *Black Place III* (1944). They are paintings that help us recognize the
power of female forms.

Should we, therefore, describe O'Keeffe as a feminist? If by that we
mean she allied herself with a feminist movement whose voice was
increasingly heard during the latter half of the twentieth century, then we
would be wrong. O'Keeffe could be very dismissive of those who wanted
to claim her for their cause, maintaining a strong insistence that she
should never be described as a 'woman artist'. But there is no doubt that
throughout her life, she was very conscious of how her gender shaped her
work, and she certainly modelled a life of pioneering independence that
inspired many who were engaged in the social struggle of women in society.

What is of greater significance for our own study is the way in which
O'Keeffe's art serves as a helpful place of dialogue with themes and concerns that emerge in contemporary feminist theology. A number of
possibilities emerge.

Essentialist theories that attempt to differentiate and define gender
according to certain preset characteristics have dominated the way we
understand human nature. Typically we have labelled men and women
with opposing traits, so the ability to reason and the capacity to be
assertive are regarded as 'masculine', while qualities such as intuition and
receptivity are seen as 'feminine'. But though this view may persist in
popular thinking, it is now recognized by psychologists as highly problematic. In particular, feminists have questioned the theory that there are
certain qualities that constitute the essence of what it is to be feminine,
not least because they have recognized the way it has been used to suppress and control the place of women in society. It is men who have

Plate 1: Edvard Munch, *Melancholy*, 1892 (oil on canvas : 64.5cm by 96cm),
Nasjonalgalleriet, Oslo © Munch Museum/Munch - Ellingsen Group, BONO, Oslo;
DACS, London 2003.

Plate 2: Edvard Munch, *The Sick Child,* 1885–1886 (oil on canvas : 119.5cm by 118.5cm), Nasjonalgalleriet, Oslo © Munch Museum/Munch - Ellingsen Group, BONO, Oslo; DACS, London 2003.

Plate 3: Marc Chagall (1887–1985), *White Crucifixion,* 1938 (oil on canvas : 155cm by 140cm), Art Institute of Chicago, Chicago. Gift of Alfred S. Alschuler, 1946.925. © ADAGP, Paris and DACS, London 2003.

Plate 4: Marc Chagall (1887–1985), *The Juggler,* 1943 (oil on canvas : 110cm by 79cm), Art Institute of Chicago, Chicago. Gift of Mrs. Gilbert W. Chapman, 1952.1005 © ADAGP, Paris and DACS, London 2003.

Plate 5: Stanley Spencer, *The Dustman (The Lovers),* 1934 (oil on canvas : 114.9cm by 122.5cm), Laing Art Gallery, Newcastle upon Tyne (Tyne and Wear Museums).

Plate 6: Stanley Spencer, *The Scorpion*, 1939 (oil on canvas : 56cm by 56cm), Art Gallery of Western Australia, Perth. © Estate of Stanley Spencer 2003. All Rights Reserved, DACS.

Plate 7: Georgia O'Keeffe (1887–1986), *Jack-in-the-Pulpit IV,* 1930 (oil on canvas : 102cm by 76cm), National Gallery of Art, Washington DC, Alfred Stieglitz Collection, Bequest of Georgia O'Keefe. © ARS, NT and DACS, London 2003. Image © 2003 Board of Trustees, National Gallery of Art, Washington DC.

Plate 8: Georgia O'Keeffe (1887–1986), *From the Faraway Nearby,* 1937 (oil on canvas : 91cm by 102 cm), The Metropolitan Museum of Art, The Alfred Stieglitz Collection, 1959 (59.204.2). Photograph by Malcolm Varon. Photograph © 1984 The Metropolitan Mueseum of Art. ARS, NY and DACS, London 2003.

Plate 9: Jacob Lawrence (1917–2000), *The Migration of the Negro,* 1940-41, Number 15 (casein tempera on hardboard : 12in by 18in), The Phillips Collection, Washington DC © Gwendolyn Knight Lawrence, courtesy of the Jacob and Gwendolyn Knight Lawrence Foundation

Plate 10: Jacob Lawrence (1917–2000), *A Mother tells the Story of Moses, Harriet and the Promised Land,* 1967, Panel 4 (gouache and tempera on paper : 11.5in by 11.25in), Abigail Kursheedt Hofman and Jane Hoffman Paress © Gwendolyn Knight Lawrence, courtesy of the Jacob and Gwendolyn Knight Lawrence Foundation

Plate 11: Vincent van Gogh (1853–1890), *The Potato Eaters,* April 1885 (oil on canvas : 81.5cm by 114.5cm), Amsterdam, Van Gogh Museum (Vincent van Gogh Foundation).

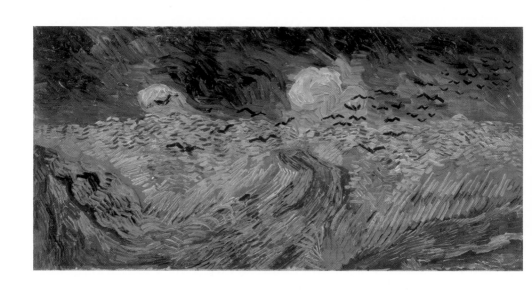

Plate 12: Vincent van Gogh (1853–1890), *Wheatfield with Crows,* July 1890 (oil on canvas : 50.35cm by 103cm), Amsterdam, Van Gogh Museum (Vincent van Gogh Foundation).

defined the 'feminine', and too often this has reduced women to little more than a function of masculine identity, consigning them to supportive nurturing and caring roles, and so enabling a patriarchal culture to prosper on the basis that this is just the way things are meant to be.

The myth of 'the eternal feminine' has resulted in an ongoing feminist debate between those who argue that gender identity is entirely a construct of our society and should be treated as such, and others who find strategic value in engaging with the world as it is and so are happy to make certain essentialist claims. All are agreed, however, that we need to refigure our understanding of human nature if women are to find liberation, and to do this it is vital that the starting point is the actual lived experience of women themselves. As Mary Grey says in her attempt to describe a new model of salvation:

> What we need to discover is whether the actual experience of real women, the way they see the world, feel, think, act and arrive at their own self-definition, as described by women themselves, can provide a firmer base on which to build a redemption theology.[40]

This was exactly the starting point for O'Keeffe as she learned to see and paint what is real. She began with her actual experience of a Jack-in-the-Pulpit and allowed this to shape and direct her representations on canvas as she made the journey towards an abstract, universal interpretation of the flower. The starting point was crucial, for it ensured that O'Keeffe never painted in a way that merely imitated cultural norms and expectations for women, and it meant that as she then gave expression to her own essentialist, feminine reading of the world, this was the result of her own genuine search for full personhood rather than any determinist gender theory. Her art thus contributes to the liberation of women — and so also of men.

O'Keeffe's deep sense of relatedness takes us further along this path. If the real experience of women is allowed to speak, it is Mary Grey's contention that they 'have been carrying the torch for all humanity's need and longing for deeper and more satisfying relationships, more effective patterns of affiliation.'[41] Redemption, she says, is about right-relation, and this requires a level of intimacy not only with God and with one another, but also with the natural world and with ourselves. Western society has failed to nurture such relatedness. It is dominated by competitive, aggressive patterns of behaviour that suffocate and destroy our relationships, and result in the exploitation of the poor and the abuse of the environment. In the face of this power-based ethic, it is women who have preserved the relational strengths that are in fact the key to our salvation — our wholeness — calling us to renewed recognition of the interdependency and mutuality that is at the heart of life. The world is about relationships; God is not distant and separate but immanent; everything is connected.

Again, I believe this is exactly where O'Keeffe leads us. She was engaged in a search for universal forms that expressed something of the unity of the world, and so her paintings help us to make vital connections: a landscape becomes a self-portrait, nature maps the unconscious mind, a flower reveals the female body. It is a vision that holds within it a mystical reverence for creation, expressing O'Keeffe's sense of the divine within everything. She nurtures ways of relating, and because she works at allowing these relationships to flourish O'Keeffe becomes an active participant in the work of healing and redeeming, bringing together what has been held apart. Creation and redemption are seen as part of one process, echoing the model that underlies Grey's theology.

Of course, the feminist sense of living in a world where relating is fundamental to all life makes it impossible to ignore our sexuality. Despite the fact that our faith is incarnational, much within Christian tradition has been based on a destructive dualism rooted in patriarchal thinking that elevates the mind above the body. The created order including our physical nature has been seen as something to be transcended and overcome, and women have been particular victims of this ever since the telling of the early Genesis stories. Their physical experiences have been undervalued, and their bodies have often been the objects of men's desire to dominate and control. But just as it is women who have experienced the body as the place of oppression, so it is they who are now enabling us to recover a sense of mutuality that includes a genuine celebration of our sexuality as integral to right relating. Feminist theology is leading the way towards a renewed sense of connectedness with the created order rooted in our embodied sexuality.

Not surprisingly, O'Keeffe also makes this journey — as we have seen in *Jack-in-the-Pulpit IV*. It could not be otherwise. As Robinson says:

> The sexuality in O'Keeffe's paintings is inextricably linked to her integrated view of life. Sexuality was a central force, celebrated but not separated from the rest. O'Keeffe expressed a natural sexuality, one inherent in flowers, landscapes, food, and relationships.[42]

The real meaning of things is not to be found 'out there', whether it is in an encyclopaedia of facts or a series of doctrinal statements. When we make the spiritual journey, truth is discovered as we learn to connect with all that is within us, around us, beneath us, above us, and beyond us.

From the Faraway Nearby (1937)

In 1929 O'Keeffe made an extended visit to New Mexico. It was to prove a decisive step. As a result of that visit she discovered how much she needed the wild, magnificent wide open spaces of the Southwest, and from then on she regularly spent time there until making a permanent move in 1949 to a house she had purchased and rebuilt in Abiquiu.

This period has been described as O'Keeffe's most fertile, and without doubt it took her in new directions that provide a vivid contrast to what went before. She completed the *Jack-in-the-Pulpit* series and continued to paint other close-ups of flowers, particularly those such as jimson weed that are common in the Southwest, but what really began to catch her imagination was the landscape. Instead of magnifying what was small, she now faced the challenge of conveying on canvas the broad expansive wilderness that filled her horizons and her heart. She wrote in 1939:

> A red hill doesn't touch everyone's heart as it touches mine and I suppose there is no reason why it should. The red hill is a piece of the badlands where even the grass is gone. Badlands roll away outside my door — hill after hill — red hills of apparently the same sort of earth that you mix with oil to make paint . . . You have no associations with those hills — our waste land — I think our most beautiful country.[43]

It took her back to early days as an art teacher in West Texas where the vast plains and the immense sky had a similar effect, giving her spirit a new sense of freedom and exhilaration. It reflected, too, her disaffection with New York where she had painted a number of cityscapes, and even with Lake George where she had spent so much time with Stieglitz and found inspiration for many of her earlier landscapes. Now she wanted to find once again the distinctive qualities of the desert. In her paintings, she began to try to capture the sense of limitless space, the sheer scale of the hills and the wild open spaces, the sharp bright light that produced a unique clarity and beauty, and the silence and solitude she encountered there. In some ways, O'Keeffe's earlier work prepared her. The natural contours and lines of the mountain formations mirrored the abstract forms she had drawn many years earlier. But in other ways it was a slow learning process, and the subjects she chose to paint during her early visits to New Mexico tend to have a more selective and contained focus. There are beautiful paintings of the Ranchos church with its adobe surface, and a number depicting the dark ritual Penitente crosses found in the region.

Increasingly, however, the land itself became the real subject. It was the kind of place where 'It seemed as though no matter how far you walked you could never get into those dark hills, although I walked great distances.'[44] Devoid of almost all signs of human presence and activity, this wilderness place took on monumental significance for O'Keeffe as a place of strength and sustenance for the soul, and something of this spirit is to be seen in one of her great paintings from this period.

During the course of her time in New Mexico in 1937, O'Keeffe described her day in a letter to Stieglitz. She wrote:

> I was up early — painted all day — out in the car from 7 till 11 — then the rest of the day indoors — and there it hangs on the wall looking at me — and I don't know what it looks like but I think I will paint it again tomorrow — just some red hills — At 5.30 I went out and walked — just over the queer coloured land — such ups and downs — so much variety in such a small space.[45]

Out of this deep affinity with the land O'Keeffe produced *From the Faraway Nearby* (Plate 8). The immediate impression created by the painting is of different elements brought together in unnatural and unreal ways within the same composition. We might easily describe it as strange and surreal — and very hard to make sense of! An enormous animal skull rests gently on a narrow strip of landscape. On the one hand the skull and antlers are painted in great detail, filling a large part of the canvas and appearing to dominate; on the other hand the landscape is distant, leading our eyes away towards a receding horizon while at the same time controlling the entire structure of the painting. There is a stark clash of perspectives, making us wonder what we are meant to be looking at and how the different pieces come together, and this almost bizarre juxtaposition clearly requires exploration. Yet after only a few moments of looking, it is also possible to begin to make some interesting connections. Notice, for example, how the colour and shape of the antlers correspond with the colour and shape of the tops of the mountains. The painting has a unity, far more so than slightly earlier paintings such as *Ram's Head, White Hollyhock — Hills* (1935) and *Summer Days* (1936), which also contained combinations of bone and land forms but in ways less connected. In both those paintings the skull hovers above the landscape rather than resting on it. In *From the Faraway Nearby* both skull and land belong to one another, so challenging the way we see both.

Let us begin a more careful consideration of this painting with the skull. Very soon after her visits to the desert began, O'Keeffe started to collect animal bones during the course of her long walks, shipping many of them back to New York in order to use them in her work. She was fascinated by these objects, including the way they allowed her to explore the relationship between a solid and a void, and she produced a number of still-life paintings. In a moving statement, O'Keeffe explained a little of why these bones became important to her:

> I have wanted to paint the desert and I haven't known how . . . So I brought home the bleached bones as my symbols of the desert. To me they are as beautiful as anything I know. To me they are strangely more living than animals walking around . . . The bones seem to be cut sharply to the centre of something that is keenly alive on the desert even

tho' it is vast and empty and untouchable — and knows no kindness
with all its beauty.[46]

Despite what we might think (and some have claimed), the skull in *From
the Faraway Nearby* is not, therefore, a symbol of death. It would be
more accurate to describe it as symbolic of that which transcends time,
holding within itself the past and enduring on into the future. Hard, white
bone has an undeniable strength and endurance, and for O'Keeffe it had a
living beauty as well. The skull's overarching embrace of landscape with
crystal blue sky is gentle and graceful, as well as powerful. In fact, as has
been pointed out by Marjorie Balge-Crozier, the horns could not possibly
be real for 'no deer or elk ever carried such a rack.'[47] The lower pair of
antlers is the product of the artist's imagination, giving added weight to
the beast that thus becomes a kind of kingly representative of all the other
beasts who belong in the wilderness.

Not only do bones represent an eternal beauty, but they also serve as
a symbol of the land. Maybe O'Keeffe was reflecting the historical link
between animals — particularly buffalo — and the wide-open spaces of
the west. Certainly she used the skull in *From the Faraway Nearby* to
capture the moods and feelings prompted within her by the desert experience. She described her aim as to portray the 'wideness and wonder of the
world as I live in it',[48] and so this aspect of the painting draws us into
some of the mysterious inner contradictions of encountering this landscape. We have both the harsh jagged edges of the skull with its
somewhat fearsome appearance, and the smooth beauty of the antlers that
long to be touched and caressed. We have something that is majestic in
size, but humbled by the conditions that overcame it. We have an object
that is both splendid and exotic, yet at the same time a commonplace
product of the wild terrain. In the beautifully precise and intricate painting
of teeth, eye socket, forehead and spreading antlers, we are faced with the
glory and desolation of the desert.

When we turn to consider the rest of the painting, we move from a
detailed object to a distant vista. The landscape that fills the bottom part
of the canvas is broad, open and empty, with little that might distinguish
it, while the bands of colour that form the background emphasize the
vastness of both the sky and the landscape. There is warmth in the gentle,

smooth contours of the slopes that make up the hills, flowing outwards and away beyond our sight. They are coloured red and brown, unlike the mountain peaks that appear as white as the bone.

One of the writers that O'Keeffe most admired was D. H. Lawrence, and it is revealing to note the similar ways in which they responded to the landscape of the southwest. Lawrence had spent more than a year living there, and in 1925 wrote a short story titled *St. Mawr*. Put briefly, it tells of a woman's escape from the artificiality of European society, and one of the main players in this is a horse named St. Mawr. The horse appears to be untameable, and this prompts the woman — driven on by her mother — to leave Europe with St. Mawr in search of the mountains of America, and the end of the story finds them living on a ranch in New Mexico. Lawrence's narrative evokes the natural beauty of the wide-open and wild place, and his vision matches that of O'Keeffe. He writes:

> It was autumn, and the loveliest time in the south-west . . . when the winds of the desert are almost still, and the mountains fume no clouds . . . For the moment, the brief moment, the great desert-and-mountain landscape had lost its certain cruelty, and looked tender, dreamy.[49]

Again he writes of it a little later:

> . . . it seemed to her that the hidden fire was alive and burning in this sky, over the desert, in the mountains. She felt a certain latent holiness in the very atmosphere, a young, spring-fire of latent holiness, such as she had never felt in Europe, or in the East. 'For me,' she said, as she looked away at the mountains in shadow and the pale-warm desert beneath, with wings of shadow upon it: 'For me, this place is sacred. It is blessed.'[50]

When O'Keeffe visited in 1929 one of her first paintings was *The Lawrence Tree*, a wonderfully mysterious picture of a tree in the grounds of Lawrence's house in Taos under which he would sit and write. It is a sign of her affinity with the writer, who sensed that this landscape held a special power and meaning.

At first O'Keeffe called her painting *Deer's Horns Near Cameron*, a reference to a visit she made to Arizona with, amongst others, the photographer Ansel Adams. However, when she later renamed it *From the Faraway Nearby*, she gave it a title that not only loosens its connection with one specific location, but poetically captures a vital aspect of what is going on in the painting. Between the nearby skull and the faraway landscape, there is nothing; there is no middle ground. In removing this middle ground, O'Keeffe is drawing our attention to the way in which, when looking through the lens of a camera, a viewer is able to keep in focus both the near and the far, particularly in a desert landscape such as the southwest with its very distinctive clear air and bright light. She used this experience of immense depth of field to create a powerful painting — one that presents a unified way of seeing, bringing together a vision of distant beauty that appears to go on forever with a careful attention to close up reality.

A connection with *St. Mawr* is once more revealed when towards the end of the story Lawrence writes of the beauty of the vast 'great circling landscape', and then says:

> And if it had been a question simply of living through the eyes, into the distance, then this would have been Paradise, and the little New England woman on the ranch would have found what she was always looking for, the earthly paradise of the spirit. But even a woman cannot live only into the distance, the beyond. Willy-nilly she finds herself juxtaposed to the near things, the thing in itself. And willy-nilly she is caught up into the fight with the immediate object. The New England woman had fought to make the nearness as perfect as the distance: for the distance was absolute beauty.[51]

This is the juxtaposition O'Keeffe paints. She, too, looks into the distance and describes it as 'a beautiful, untouched lonely-feeling place — part of what I call the Far Away.'[52] For her, too, it is a place of the spirit. Yet as for the New England woman, this vast and wild openness is not all there is, and so she paints the skull as the near thing she encounters.

It is at this point, however, that I believe Lawrence and O'Keeffe begin to move in opposite directions, for whereas O'Keeffe is able to see an equal power and beauty in the reality of the nearby skull, this is not so for the character in the story. Lawrence describes her experience as a 'fight with the immediate object', and a little later we read that:

> ... her love for her ranch turned sometimes into a certain repulsion. The underlying rat-dirt, the everlasting bristling tussle of the wild life, with the tangle and the bones strewing. Bones of horses struck by lightning, bones of dead cattle, skulls of goats with little horns: bleached, unburied bones. Then the cruel electricity of the mountains. And then, most mysterious but worst of all, the animosity of the spirit of place: the crude, half-created spirit of place, like some serpent-bird for ever attacking man, in a hatred of man's onward-struggle towards further creation.[53]

This is a quite different perspective. Instead of being objects of beauty that are at one with the beauty and spirit of the wilderness, the bones are seen as unwanted signs of harsh decay that threaten to destroy the mystery and wonder of the place. Lawrence has pictured the near as the enemy of the faraway, unlike O'Keeffe who strives in her painting to bring them together in a startling unity.

In this lies the majestic greatness of *From the Faraway Nearby*, not least because it provides a vision of the world that offers wisdom and truth for the spiritual journey. Here is an artist who sees the natural landscape laid bare and is unafraid to embrace what is distant with a tenderness that brings it near, and to gaze at the particular object nearby in order to give it a faraway depth. O'Keeffe lives in a multi-dimensional world, where at every level she finds a mysterious beauty that transcends the barriers of time and space, and it is this sense of the eternal as both distant and near that is such a wonderful gift. As well as the vast vistas that give freedom to the spirit, she dares to embrace the solid reality of the desert seen in the intricate patterns created by dry bones, wanting the skull to become as much a conveyor of the meaning and glory of the desert as the infinite landscape. Both together, in unity, capture the essence of an encounter with the wilderness, and both together become purveyors of the eternal.

We are reminded that there are those things we can grasp and hold in our hands and there is also that which lies far beyond our reach; that at each moment we are called to give attention to what is immediate, and to lift our eyes to distant horizons. But the way of wholeness requires that we learn to live with both the near and the far. The place where we encounter the mysterious presence of God is to be found as much in the earthly reality of what lies at our feet, as in the distant possibilities that stretch away into the future.

A sense of place

Our exploration of *From the Faraway Nearby* has already revealed O'Keeffe's deep sense of attachment to place, and to the desert landscape of the southwest in particular. It is a relationship of fundamental importance to this painting and others, and indeed to O'Keeffe's own life journey. Thus it is one that needs our further reflection.

American art has a history of landscape painting. During the course of the nineteenth century, artists used images of the land in an effort to express what it meant to be American, most notably those belonging to the 'Hudson River School'. They sought to portray an unspoilt environment threatened by rampant civilization, and voiced an unashamed romantic attachment to creation as that which is solid and lasting. The transcendentalists such as Ralph Waldo Emerson echoed this fervent commitment to nature, expressing the American belief that the land is sacred. To paint landscapes was to participate in a spiritual quest.

O'Keeffe grew up with such an understanding. She, too, was attuned to the natural world with its continuous cycle of growth and decay, finding pleasure in the changes of the seasons, and it was partly this that led her to seek a home away from New York. But perhaps what marked her out as different from many was her attraction to the wilderness place and her determination to explore this very distinctive landscape. It led her to take the tradition of landscape painting in new directions as is evidenced by *From the Faraway Nearby*. It is quite clearly neither a conventional landscape nor a still life painting but combines both, and so becomes O'Keeffe's unique and powerful attempt to evoke a sense of the place she had discovered.

So why was O'Keeffe so deeply attuned to this place? What was so important about the wilderness landscape for her? I sense that the answer must lie in the unique ability of the desert place to nourish and nurture the life of the spirit.

It is worth noting three parallel influences on O'Keeffe during the years she spent in New Mexico. First, there was the influence of western writers such as D. H. Lawrence and Walt Whitman. Favourites such as these gave voice not only to a developed sense of the vitality of place, but also to the enduring presence of mystery in the world. So, as we have seen, Lawrence had a profound connection with the same piece of land-scape, and his emphasis on the intuitive nature of the individual led to an intense mystical approach to life and where it is lived. With America par-ticularly in mind, he wrote:

> . . . every continent has its own great spirit of place. Every people is polarized in some particular locality, which is home, the homeland . . . . the spirit of place is a great reality.[54]

At the root of Whitman's poetry is a similar commitment to place, to cre-ation, and to the sense of the eternal found there. In his *Song of the Rolling Earth*, he pictures what he has written in terms of landscape and spirit:

> Were you thinking that those were words, those upright lines?
> Those curves, angles, dots?
> No, those are not the words, the substantial words are in the
> ground and sea,
> They are in the air, they are in you.[55]

Others too, such as James Joyce, were read and admired by O'Keeffe. Together they became companions for her own journey, using words where she used colour, but expressing the same depth of feeling for place.

Second, there was the continuing influence of Eastern thought and techniques referred to at the beginning of this chapter. Asian art taught O'Keeffe ways of manipulating scale and perspective that opened up all kinds of possibilities. It allowed her to magnify objects such as the skull in *From the Faraway Nearby* so that they attained a monumental, tran-scendent status. It enabled her to paint in ways that removed the anchors that normally control how we see things, so opening us up to the possibility of infinity (the painting *Ladder to the Moon*, 1958, is one example, where we are invited to climb from the earth into the depths of infinite space). It also gave her the idea that space was not merely emptiness, but a way of communicating depth.

It is not difficult to see the attraction of the desert for someone influenced in this way. The sense of a refined and uncluttered landscape, of space for the contemplative spirit to breathe, of a place marked by clarity and serenity, would all have grown with O'Keeffe's study of Japanese and Chinese art and her reading of Eastern mystical writers. She spoke of how:

> The desert is the last place you can see all around you. The light out here makes everything close, and it is never, never the same. Sometimes the light hits the mountain from behind and front at the same time, and gives them the look of Japanese prints, you know, distance in layers.[56]

Third, there was the influence of the Christian monk Thomas Merton. In the 1960s the two met one another, suggesting that each had an interest in the other, and though I have no knowledge of how significant that encounter might have been for either of them, it is easy to discern how much they had in common. Merton, like O'Keeffe, had developed a fascination for the East, reading and writing about Zen Buddhism in particular. But behind such common interests, there were also common experiences — of the desert, of solitude, of a sense of ultimate mystery. As a monk, living the life of a hermit, committed to being in one place, and deeply aware of the rhythms of nature, Merton would have known exactly why O'Keeffe had gone to live in the desert.

For Christians the desert has always been a place where the spiritual journey attains new depths. Monks went to the desert as a way of leaving behind the attractions and distractions of one world, in order to enter another world that was shaped and determined by the quest for God. The place they went was carefully chosen. After all, they would make promises of stability that would keep them there for the rest of their lives, and they believed that the place would in some way be an anticipation of paradise itself. Most important of all, they sought out the desert to make room for silence, believing that in the quiet wildness and emptiness of the landscape, there would be the opportunity to come face to face with the inner self and the God who has made us.

This linking of the desert with spiritual journeying has imbued it with a sense of the eternal. The history is part of the place, giving it power and meaning, and O'Keeffe has in her turn become part of that continuing story. She, too, has made it a place of the spirit, finding a harmony and simplicity there that enabled her to discover new paths of creativity. Paintings such as *From the Faraway Nearby* witness to the mystery she felt and experienced, and remind us of our need of such places where new visions can be glimpsed.

As she looked towards the end of her life, O'Keeffe said, 'When I think of death, I only regret that I will not be able to see this beautiful country anymore . . . unless the Indians are right and my spirit will walk here after I'm gone.'[57] We are reminded that, whether or not we would want to express things as the Indians do, we need a sense of place in order to continue the journey onwards.

Artist and mystic

It is time to draw together the threads that have been woven in this chapter, and to see the path that O'Keeffe has enabled us to travel.

As we noted right at the beginning, O'Keeffe showed no commitment to the Christian faith at any stage in her life. She would certainly be one person who makes it clear that formal religious practices, such as attending church, are no necessary indicators of spiritual depth. As we have looked at her life, the influences upon her, and most of all her paintings, we have discovered someone in touch with the life of the spirit. Indeed, a number of those who know most about her have described O'Keeffe as a mystic. Sharyn Udall gives particular attention to this theme, declaring that 'the impulses to mysticism expressed visually . . . are all there in O'Keeffe's work',[58] while Barbara Rose speaks of the way O'Keeffe is located correctly 'within the context of a mysticism firmly grounded in the direct experience of the here and now.'[59]

Of course, a word like 'mysticism' is slippery and has changed its meaning over the centuries. But if we satisfy ourselves with a very basic definition as having to do with a search for a depth or mystery at the heart of life, then I believe we have seen enough to know that this was the journey taken by O'Keeffe.

Throughout the ages mystics have always faced something of a dilemma, and it has to do with the question of how we know God. The apophatic tradition emphasizes the truth that God is always beyond knowing, and so every word or image we care to use is inadequate. It is a spirituality that takes us towards silence and darkness, for 'not knowing' is recognized as the only authentic response to the God who is utterly beyond us. By contrast, the cataphatic tradition emphasizes the truth of God's revelation, and invites us to engage with images and ideas that will lead us towards an encounter with the reality of God. This spiritual path affirms that all creation reflects the glory of God and that our calling is to seek to know and love God.

It would be easy to place these two traditions in opposition to one another as mutually exclusive alternatives. But perhaps the greatest mystics have always recognized that the two need to be held together in mutual tension, the one enriching the other. Our sense that God cannot ultimately be known has to be balanced with our belief that something can be known of the God revealed in creation. Our embodied humanity means that we cannot avoid the use of images, but this must be balanced against a recognition that God cannot be reduced to any one image. Both apophatic and cataphatic traditions say something important about the spiritual journey.

Though O'Keeffe would not have used this kind of language, I believe the same dilemma has come through in our study of her art. As an artist she worked with shape, form and colour; she was concerned to produce images. But throughout her life O'Keeffe used these images to try to portray hidden depths, always pushing back boundaries and struggling to express the infinite wonder of the world that ultimately defies expression.

She painted close-ups of flowers giving them the kind of loving attention that affirmed the sacredness of ordinary common things. They revealed the eternal at the heart of creation. Then as she moved towards abstraction O'Keeffe tried to allow the very essence of the flower to emerge, so searching for deeper and richer ways of seeing and knowing the world that go beyond conventional imaging. The fact that, as part of this process, O'Keeffe gave a distinctive feminine reading of the world, serves to bring us back to the truth that in the end we cannot transcend our embodied humanity, but must find God in our midst.

The desert experiences of New Mexico continued the mystic's journey. Here she brought together the faraway and the nearby in dynamic relationship, offering a multi-dimensional vision of the world and helping us recognize that the God who is distant and unknowable is also the God who is close enough to touch. Again, through using bleached bones, O'Keeffe reminds us that what some would discard as worthless are in fact ways of imaging the depths of divine glory. The desert was to prove her home, just as it has been for so many mystics, and as she continued to paint she wrestled with the contradictions. On the one hand, it is a landscape so empty and barren, speaking through its silence of the eternal that cannot be named or contained. On the other hand, its light and glory filled O'Keeffe with new visual possibilities, for she found beauty rising up out of the ground. For her as for others, the spirit was nourished by the mystery of the place.

To the end of her life, O'Keeffe explored the depths of what it means to live in this world. Those who knew her have spoken of the remarkable sense of peace and oneness she gained, as she went on working at the images that were an expression of her continuing spiritual quest. As artist and mystic, she can be a guide to all of us committed to the spiritual journey.

Selected (and annotated) Biography

A number of paintings by Georgia O'Keeffe have gained popularity over the years, and prints of these are often to be seen. This, no doubt, has stimulated a more general interest, and there are many books available that provide excellent reproductions of her paintings and helpful commentary on her life and work. There are two standard introductions that fulfil this description in a clear and concise way: Lisa Mintz Messinger, *Georgia O'Keeffe* (London: Thames and Hudson, 2001); and Britta Benke, *Georgia O'Keeffe 1887–1986: Flowers in the Desert* (Cologne: Benedikt Taschen, 2000). Messinger's biography is longer; both are well illustrated and readily available.

Having taken these first steps, it is well worth going on to look at the studies that reproduce a wide selection of O'Keeffe's paintings and contain some stimulating essays: Elizabeth Hutton Turner, *Georgia O'Keeffe: the poetry of things* (Washington DC: The Phillips Collection, 1999); Barbara Buhler Lynes,

O'Keeffe's O'Keeffes (London: The Artist's Collection, Thames and Hudson, 2001); Charles Eldredge, *Georgia O'Keeffe: American and Modern* (New Haven: Yale University Press, 1993); Peter Hassrick (ed.), *The Georgia O'Keeffe Museum* (New York: Harry N. Abrams, 1997); and Georgia O'Keeffe, *Art and Letters* (Washington DC: National Gallery of Art, 1987).

All these deserve recommendation. The first three on this list are beautiful books to look at and use, with particularly excellent reproductions. Turner's book has two fascinating essays that may be a little beyond those of us who are not art specialists, but without doubt repay careful and repeated reading, and similarly the text in Eldredge's book deserves close attention. The last on the list above contains three very brief essays, together with pictures and letters. For a comprehensive, straightforward biography, there is one obvious choice. It is over six hundred pages long, but very readable: Roxana Robinson, *Georgia O'Keeffe* (London: Bloomsbury Publishing, 1997).

One other illustrated biography can be listed, though this is not readily available, and the reproductions are poor quality and only black and white: Katherine Hoffman, *An Enduring Spirit: The Art of Georgia O'Keeffe* (Metuchen: Scarecrow Press, 1984).

There are several books that explore in greater depth particular aspects of O'Keeffe's life and work: Sarah Whitaker Peters, *Becoming O'Keeffe. The Early Years* (Abbeville Press, 2001); Sharyn Rohlfsen Udall, *O'Keeffe and Texas* (San Antonio: The Marion Koogler McNay Art Museum, 1998); Bram Dijkstra, *Georgia O'Keeffe and the Eros of Place* (Princeton University Press, 1998); and Sharyn Rohlfsen Udall, *Carr, O'Keeffe, Kahlo: Places of Their Own* (New Haven: Yale University Press, 2000).

The first two listed here concentrate on O'Keeffe's early years. Peters provides a very detailed account indeed and is definitely a book for the enthusiast. Udall's is lavishly illustrated, and is particularly interesting for its exploration of O'Keeffe's use of light. The remaining two are also detailed studies, with much of interest for those with the time and commitment to go deeper.

Finally, there is a collection of essays to mention. Despite the title, there is little reference to the actual painting in any of them, and while the quality and content is mixed, a number provide interesting insights into aspects of O'Keeffe's long life: Christopher Merrill and Ellen Bradbury (eds.), *From the Faraway Nearby. Georgia O'Keeffe as Icon* (Albuquerque: University of New Mexico Press, 1998).

The book by Wassily Kandinsky that had such an influence on O'Keeffe appears in many different editions. The one quoted in this chapter is Wassily

Kandinsky, *Concerning the Spiritual in Art*, trans. with an introduction by M. Sadler (New York: Dover Publications, 1977). Reference is also made to Peter Berger, *Ways of Seeing* (London: BBC & Penguin, 1972).

The writings of Julian of Norwich and Thomas Merton are spiritual classics: Julian of Norwich, *Showings* (London: SPCK, 1978); Thomas Merton, *Seeds of Contemplation* (Hertfordshire: Anthony Clarke Books, 1972).

In addition, the following book includes a number of photographs taken by Merton: Esther de Waal, *A Seven Day Journey with Thomas Merton* (Guildford: Eagle, 1992).

The writer D. H. Lawrence is quoted. His short story, *St. Mawr*, can be read as part of a collection: D. H. Lawrence, *Short Novels* (London: Penguin, 2000).

Walt Whitman is quoted from Walt Whitman, *The Complete Poems* (London: Penguin Books, 1975).

The feminist theologian Mary Grey has written a number of stimulating books and the one particularly referred to in this chapter is Mary Grey, *Redeeming the Dream* (London: SPCK, 1989).

Notes

This chapter is primarily the work of Graham Sparkes.

[1] O'Keeffe, statement in University of Illinois College of Fine and Applied Arts, *Contemporary American Painting and Sculpture* (Urbana: University of Illinois, 1955), p. 226; cited in Lisa Mintz Messinger, *Georgia O'Keeffe* (London: Thames and Hudson, 2001), p. 7.

[2] Quoted in Barbara Buhler Lynes, *O'Keeffe's O'Keeffes: The Artist's Collection* (London: Thames and Hudson, 2001), p. 14.

[3] O'Keeffe, recorded in Katharine Kuh, *The Artist's Voice: Talks with Seventeen Artists* (New York: Harper and Row, 1962), p. 190; cited in Messinger, *Georgia O'Keeffe*, p. 20.

[4] Wassily Kandinsky, *Concerning the Spiritual in Art*, trans. M. Sadler (New York: Dover Publications, 1977), p. 2.

[5] Ibid., p. 55.

[6] Ibid., p. 35.

[7] Ibid., pp. 37-8.

[8] Ibid., p. 47.

[9] O'Keeffe, recorded in Mary Lynn Kotz, 'A Day with Georgia O'Keeffe,' *ARTnews* 76/10 (Dec 1977), p. 43; cited in Sharyn Rohlfsen Udall, *O'Keeffe and Texas* (San Antonio: The Marion Koogler McNay Art Museum, 1998), p. 19.

[10] O'Keeffe, letter to Paul Strand, 3 June 1917, printed in Jack Cowart, Juan Hamilton and Sarah Greenough, *Georgia O'Keeffe: Art and Letters*. Exhibition catalogue (Washington DC: National Gallery of Art, 1987), p. 161 n.17; cited in Messinger, *Georgia O'Keeffe*, p. 44.

[11] Georgia O'Keeffe, *Georgia O'Keeffe* (New York: Viking Press, 1976), n.p., facing plate 71.

[12] O'Keeffe, letter to Anita Pollitzer, October 1915, printed in Anita Pollitzer, *A Woman on Paper: Georgia O'Keeffe* (New York: Simon and Schuster, 1988), p. 29; cited in Sarah Whitaker Peters, *Becoming O'Keeffe: The Early Years* (New York: Abbeville Press, 2001), p. 31.

[13] O'Keeffe, statement in *Alfred Stieglitz Presents One Hundred Pictures, Oils, Water-colours, Pastels, Drawings by Georgia O'Keeffe, American* (New York: Anderson Galleries, 1923) n.p.; cited in Peters, *Becoming O'Keeffe*, p. 31.

[14] Charles Eldredge, *Georgia O'Keeffe: American and Modern* (New York: Yale University Press, 1993), pp. 160-3.

[15] O'Keeffe, *Georgia O'Keeffe*, n.p., introduction.

[16] Quoted in Katherine Hoffman, *An Enduring Spirit: The Art of Georgia O'Keeffe* (Metuchen: Scarecrow Press, 1984), p. 104.

[17] Russell Bowman, 'Georgia O'Keeffe: an Introduction', in Lynes, *O'Keeffe's O'Keeffes: The Artist's Collection*, p. 15.

[18] Roxana Robinson, *Georgia O'Keeffe* (London: Bloomsbury Publishing, 1997), p. 354.

[19] Quoted in Britta Benke, *O'Keeffe 1887–1986: Flowers in the Desert* (Cologne: Benedikt Taschen, 2000), p. 32.

[20] Marjorie Welish, 'House Beautiful', in Christopher Merrill & Ellen Bradbury (eds.) *From the Faraway Nearby: Georgia O'Keeffe as Icon* (Alburquerque: University of New Mexico Press, 1998), p. 131.

[21] Messinger, *Georgia O'Keeffe*, p. 101.

[22] Recorded in Kuh, *The Artist's Voice*, pp. 190-1; cited in Marjorie Balge-Crozier, 'Still Life Redefined', in Elizabeth Hutton Turner, *Georgia O'Keeffe: the poetry of things* (Washington DC: The Phillips Collection, 1999), p. 48.

[23] Robinson, *Georgia O'Keeffe*, p. 278.

[24] O'Keeffe, *Georgia O'Keeffe*, n.p., facing plate 23.

[25] Barbara Novak, 'Georgia O'Keeffe and American Intellectual and Visual Traditions', in Peter Hassrick (ed.), *The Georgia O'Keeffe Museum* (New York: Harry N. Abrams, 1997), pp. 77f.

26 *Leaves of Grass* in Walt Whitman, *The Complete Poems* (London: Penguin Books, 1975), p. 93, line 663.

27 Julian of Norwich, *Showings* (London: SPCK, 1978), Long Text, 9.

28 Thomas Merton, *Seeds of Contemplation* (Hertfordshire: Anthony Clarke Books, 1972), p. 13.

29 See Jean-Pierre de Caussade, *The Sacrament of the Present Moment* (London: Fount, 1981).

30 Recorded in Kuh, *The Artist's Voice*, p. 200; cited in Messinger, *Georgia O'Keeffe*, p. 76.

31 Quoted in Turner, *Georgia O'Keeffe: the poetry of things*, n.p., facing page xvii.

32 John Berger, *Ways of Seeing* (London: BBC & Penguin, 1972).

33 Quoted in Benke, *O'Keeffe 1887-1986: Flowers in the Desert*, p. 28.

34 O'Keeffe, *Georgia O'Keeffe*, n.p., facing plate 88.

35 Balge-Crozier, 'Still Life Redefined', p. 60f.

36 O'Keeffe, letter to Sherwood Anderson, 11 February 1924, printed in Cowart, Hamilton and Greenough, *Georgia O'Keeffe*, p. 176; cited in Balge-Crozier, 'Still Life Redefined', p. 72.

37 O'Keeffe, quoted in Dorothy Seiberling, 'The Female View of Erotic,' *New York Magazine*, 11 February 1974, p. 54; cited in Messinger, *Georgia O'Keeffe*, p. 30.

38 O'Keeffe, letter of 1925 [?], printed in Cowart, Hamilton and Greenough, *Georgia O'Keeffe*, p. 180; cited in Anna Chave, 'O'Keeffe and the Masculine Gaze', in Merrill & Bradbury (eds.), *From the Faraway Nearby: Georgia O'Keeffe as Icon*, p. 37.

39 Chave, 'O'Keeffe and the Masculine Gaze', p. 34.

40 Mary Grey, *Redeeming the Dream. Feminism, Redemption and Christian Tradition* (London: SPCK, 1989), p. 24.

41 Ibid., p. 27.

42 Robinson, *Georgia O'Keeffe*, p. 283.

43 O'Keeffe, *Georgia O'Keeffe*, n.p., facing plates 26 and 27.

44 O'Keeffe, recorded in Calvin Tomkins, 'The Rose in the Eye Looked Pretty Fine,' *The New Yorker*, 4 March 1974, p. 54; cited in Messinger, *Georgia O'Keeffe*, p. 116.

45 O'Keeffe, letter to Stieglitz, 25 August 1937, printed in *Georgia O'Keeffe: Catalogue of the Fourteenth Annual Exhibition of Paintings, With*

Some Recent O'Keeffe Letters (New York: 1937), p. 8; cited in Elsa Mezvinsky Smithgall, 'Georgia O'Keeffe's Life and Influences: an Illustrated Chronology', in Turner, *Georgia O'Keeffe: the poetry of things*, p. 112.

[46] O'Keeffe, recorded in *Georgia O'Keeffe: Selected Paintings and Works on Paper. Dallas June 14 through July 14, 1986* (Dallas: Gerald Peters Gallery, 1986), p. 21; cited in Balge-Crozier, 'Still Life Redefined', p. 62.

[47] Balge-Crozier, 'Still Life Redefined', p. 65.

[48] O'Keeffe, *Georgia O'Keeffe*, n.p., facing plate 71.

[49] D. H. Lawrence, *St. Mawr*, in *Short Novels* (Harmondsworth: Penguin, 2000), p. 403.

[50] Ibid. 409.

[51] Ibid., p. 417.

[52] O'Keeffe, *Georgia O'Keeffe*, n.p., facing plate 60.

[53] Lawrence, *St. Mawr*, p. 421.

[54] Quoted in Hoffman, *An Enduring Spirit: The Art of Georgia O'Keeffe*, p. 26.

[55] 'Song of the Rolling Earth' in Walt Whitman, *The Complete Poems* (London: Penguin Books, 1975), p. 248, lines 2-4.

[56] Quoted in Hoffman, *An Enduring Spirit: The Art of Georgia O'Keeffe*, p. 110.

[57] O'Keeffe, recorded in Henry Seldis, 'Georgia O'Keeffe at 78: Tough Minded Romantic,' *Los Angeles Times West Magazine*, 22 January 1967, p. 22; cited in Messinger, *Georgia O'Keeffe*, p. 182.

[58] Sharyn Udall, 'Beholding the Epiphanies', in Merrill & Bradbury (eds.), *From the Faraway Nearby: Georgia O'Keeffe as Icon*, p. 112.

[59] Barbara Rose, 'O'Keeffe's Originality', in Hassrick (ed.), *The Georgia O'Keeffe Museum*, p. 108.

5
Jacob Lawrence:
The Beauty of Struggle

It is often said that history is written by the winners. Both what we know and how we know what we know tend to be shaped and formed by the controlling forces in society. Our patterns of learning together with our responses to particular events are dictated, to a lesser or greater extent, by those who have succeeded in occupying the positions of power and influence, whether in the past or in the present. Thus, any telling of the story of the twentieth century revolves around talk about empires and superpowers, dictators and generals, prime ministers and presidents. These are the loudest voices, and they provide the interpretive framework that guides our understanding.

No doubt there is a certain inevitability about this, but it is also dangerous. Too easily the way events are recounted ignores the voices of powerless participants, the marginalized, the minorities and the victims; because they have no means to make themselves heard; it is as if history had passed them by. This presents a particular challenge for Christians, who have been reminded by liberation theologians about God's 'preferential option for the poor' and of our need to share in the continuing struggle of those who are this world's losers. Faithfulness to the spiritual journey calls for our engagement in the politics of oppression.

One artist who inspires and guides us on this journey is Jacob Lawrence (1917–2000). Lawrence was an African American born into a society divided by racism, who used his art to give a voice to his people. As we shall see, he did not take on the role of an aggressive campaigner for civil rights, but in a gentle and persuasive way he employed his gift of creating vivid images accompanied by simple text to confront the terrible poverty, violence and discrimination faced by black people in America. Above all, Lawrence was a storyteller — a narrative painter. His most famous work consists of series of panels and pictures that tell some of the important stories from the history of his community, stories that might otherwise go neglected and forgotten. We will look at two in particular: a sixty-panel series painted on hardboard in 1941 titled *The Migration of the Negro*, and a seventeen-picture series painted on paper in 1967 titled *Harriet and the Promised Land*. The latter of these was, in fact, a return to a theme that he had first explored in 1939.

Both these narratives have to do with journeys. Most obviously they give an account of historic journeys made by African Americans, but they also work at deeper levels, echoing Lawrence's personal experience of journey and the ancient biblical journey of the exodus. We will want to link these in turn with our overarching theme of spiritual journeying, and to see how Lawrence helps us towards a recognition of the vital role played by storytelling.

The stories told by Lawrence are rooted in one particular country and community. At the same time, like all good stories they have wider resonance expressing basic human hopes and struggles, helping us to see ways in which stories of themselves educate, nurture and sustain a community's identity. Despite the fact that his work seems to be so little known or appreciated outside of America, Lawrence's deep commitment to narrate something of the history of his people invites us to recognize the universal power of art to address and challenge social context.

The Migration of the Negro (1941)

The early years of Lawrence's life were bound up with the history he was to recount through this series of pictures. He was born in Atlantic City, New Jersey, to parents who had independently moved north as part of the Great Migration that took place around the time of World War One, and from the age of two he was also on the move, living in Easton, Pennsylvania and Philadelphia, before settling with his mother and siblings in New York in 1930. He wrote:

> The great migration is part of my life. I grew up knowing about people on the move from the time I could understand what words meant. There was always talk in my house of other families arriving from the South.[1]

Though slavery had been brought to an end in 1863 following the defeat of the Confederate forces in the Civil War, the South remained a prison for vast numbers of black people. They were confined to the plantations and the sharecropping system, subject to a growing system of laws and customs designed to keep them economically poor and educationally illiterate. A policy of segregation was vigorously pursued, known as 'Jim Crow' statutes, and the opening years of the twentieth century saw yet further legal devices employed to disenfranchise African Americans.

Internally, however, the black community was making progress and the historian Lerone Bennett Jr. identifies the churches as key to this. Together with fraternal organizations and a growing number of black colleges, the black churches provided the community with institutions of their own, the opportunity to learn political economy, a sense of heritage and identity, and 'the dangerous idea that there was something higher than the white man at work in history.'[2] This helped sow the seeds for a mass movement of people that radically changed the face of America and shaped Lawrence's own life.

The Great Migration was a form of revolt. The need for additional labour in the rapidly expanding wartime industries certainly meant that the black workers were encouraged to leave the rural South for the large urban cities in the North, but the more basic reason for moving was simply to escape the discrimination, poverty and violence. They had had enough, and hundreds of thousands uprooted and began a mass exodus in search of freedom and opportunity, sending word back for others to join them. Between 1910 and 1930, the percentage of the black population in places like Chicago, Detroit and New York tripled.

As a young artist living in Harlem, New York, Lawrence was helped to link his own experiences with the larger story of the Great Migration until 'it seemed almost inevitable that I would tell this story in my art.'[3] The opportunity came in 1940 when he received a fellowship from the Rosenwald Foundation that enabled him to rent a studio of his own and engage in the research and planning required to paint the *Migration* series. It is fascinating to learn how Lawrence went about the task. He began by writing the sparse text that would accompany each of the panels, basing this careful account of the story on extensive reading and note-taking. Then, in order to ensure that the whole series formed a single work, the sixty hardboard panels of identical size were prepared together and Lawrence proceeded to work on all the paintings at the same time. He explained that he wanted 'to hold it together, to unify it, because if I did one panel and completed it, the next panel would probably be different, you see.'[4]

Lawrence worked from underdrawings, appearing as faint lines on the boards, and he systematically went through all the panels filling in one colour at a time, beginning with black and moving through the spectrum to the lighter colours. Unmixed pigments were generally used to ensure that the colour remained uniform throughout the series, and detailing was added as the work progressed.

Such a process might be thought of as very mechanical, perhaps reminiscent of a child filling in a primitive picture according to a given colour-code, and it is certainly true that Lawrence's style is not that of an Impressionist painter. His art does have a lot to do with pattern, as he himself recognized when reflecting on his formative years:

> Our homes were very decorative, full of a lot of pattern, like inexpensive throw rugs, all around the house. It must have had some influence, all this colour and everything . . . I got ideas from them . . .[5]

Lawrence's paintings always show a deep interest in abstract shapes and colours placed side by side, and the influence of Cubism on his work is often noted. Yet the result of adopting such a disciplined process, working with patterns of colour, is certainly not a rigid, formalized, mechanistic series of paintings. Lawrence succeeds in producing paintings full of life and movement and emotion. They are dynamic, allowing the story he tells to live and breathe.

The painting from the *Migration* series reproduced in this book is panel 15 in the series (Plate 9). Earlier panels have set the scene, introducing the history of the Great Migration and narrating some of the reasons why it took place, including the need for labour in the North, the struggle to produce crops due to floods and pests, and the resulting poverty. Now, in this picture, Lawrence adds a further reason as to why African Americans were prepared to uproot and leave the South. The text accompanying the image, as revised by Lawrence for a special exhibition of the series in 1993, reads: 'Another cause was lynching. It was found that where there had been a lynching, the people who were reluctant to leave at first left immediately after this.'

What makes this such a powerful and moving image? What gives it authority and meaning? Let us explore a number of interrelated answers, both to help us understand and appreciate this particular painting and to begin to identify the features of Lawrence's work that characterize the *Migration* series as a whole.

The first thing that strikes us is the simplicity of this painting. It is straightforward and easy to 'read'. Both background and foreground contain almost no detail. The colours are few and applied very directly in a way that corresponds with the process already described. We can also see the way Lawrence plays with abstract shapes and patterns. The branch on which the noose hangs echoes the shapes of crop stems portrayed in panel 13 and cloud formations seen in panel 8, and the fact that it extends across almost the entire width of the painting makes it a design feature rather than a real object. Yet at the same time the branch is clearly a human reality. As Lawrence explained, 'My work is abstract in the sense of having been designed and composed, but it is not abstract in the sense of having no human contact.'[6] The noose placed in the exact centre of the painting fulfils a similar function. Like the branch it lacks realism, and yet there is no doubting what it is and what it means.

It is true that this painting is simpler than most of his paintings in the sense that it is far more stark, but the style is typical. He paints bold images; people are multi-coloured shapes; broad bands of colour provide the backdrop; representation is flat; angles and perspectives play key roles. Such simplicity makes it tempting to describe Lawrence's work as 'naïve' or 'primitive' (a word we have already used in trying to understand his way of painting), but care is needed. These terms can imply a lack of any kind of training, such that the art depends on intuition and lacks any sophistication, yet this would certainly not be true of Lawrence. One early critic noted:

A style which it is easy to call primitive marks his (paintings), but closer inspection reveals draughtsmanship too accomplished to be called naïve. The bright colours in flat areas and the literal view of the world

turn out to be just his manner of expressing his very sensitive reactions
to a kaleidoscope, animated world.[7]

Lawrence learned at art classes taught by Charles Alston, a man who was
part of the great surge in African-American artistic endeavour during the
1920s known as the Harlem Renaissance. Alston provided the kind of
education that enabled Lawrence to build upon his innate abilities and
develop the skills for self-expression, and over subsequent years others
also contributed to his formation as a mature artist. He became part of a
community-based network of artists and writers meeting at Studio 306,
who worked together and in the process learned from one another.

So as we look at the *Migration* series, behind the simplicity is a
highly developed way of seeing. There is the very clever use of empty
and occupied space, the subtle relationship between human figures and
objects, and the ability to compose and organize a painting in ways that
inject life and feeling.

All this is true of panel 15. We have a painting where everything is
pared back to essentials, such that our eyes are drawn to nothing else but
the hanging noose and the bent-over figure. Nothing else matters! At this
place and this time, all that has significance is to be found in the relationship between the two, and by removing everything else Lawrence
accentuates the deep emotional intensity within the image. The emptiness
all around mirrors the emptiness created by such an act of injustice, and
we feel the anguish and despair in the hunched shoulders of the figure.

Alongside Lawrence's simplicity is also his restraint, and this, too, is
key to the power of the painting. It is worth pausing to ask: how would
we choose to portray a lynching, particularly if we were as intimately
connected as Lawrence was to such events? Almost certainly, the temptation would be to paint its full horror — a man hanging from the rope, his
face contorted and his head bent sideways, perhaps with the perpetrators
nearby. We would want viewers to see what it is like to hang helplessly
from a rope, and be brought face to face with the cruelty and violence
behind such an act. Indeed, as Ellen Harkins Wheat illustrates in her book
Jacob Lawrence: American Painter, Lawrence almost certainly knew of
two paintings that offer a more graphic portrayal of a lynching. One in
particular is contained in a series of paintings by Francisco Goya, titled

The Disasters of War, which made a notable impression on Lawrence when he first came across it during the art workshops he attended. The other is *Ahorcado* by a Mexican artist, Jose Clemente Orozco, whom we will mention again shortly.

Yet the way Lawrence chooses to paint panel 15 is with an enormous amount of restraint. The actual event goes unseen, and what is left is the silent aftermath. We are invited to imagine who was murdered, who the hunched-up figure might be, when the killing took place; we are led very gently into a scene of grief in a way that captures the heart as well as the eyes. Notice the economy with which Lawrence paints the bent-over figure, while perfectly capturing the sense of loss and loneliness. Notice the anonymity of the figure, in keeping with the way Lawrence normally portrayed the people in his paintings. He or she is one of the nameless masses who make up the story. Notice, too, the size of the noose, dwarfing that of the figure, so emphasizing the shrivelled nature of the one who is left helpless in the face of injustice and violence.

This willingness to hold back, to paint an image that appears to contain so little, is what actually gives panel 15 force and intensity. It allows space for the mind and heart to engage, and so it becomes a painting charged with meaning, as do many others in the *Migration* series. Panel 46 would be just one further example, where simplicity and restraint combine in a powerful painting that attracted particular attention when the series was first exhibited, and indeed led to its purchase (together with the other even-numbered panels) by the Museum of Modern Art, New York. It is about the unhealthy living conditions faced by many who migrated north, and their experience of having to live in labour camps. What we are shown, however, is nothing more than a rough wooden stairway, inside a prison-like building, leading upwards to a doorway with a yellow knob. It is bare, bleak and stark, and almost the entire image is painted brown. But the doorway is the exception and it is this that gives the painting life and meaning, for looked at another way the shut door might be an opening onto the sky and the yellow knob the moon, so offering the possibility of climbing out of the prison and finding a new future.

We could look at other panels in the same way. Lawrence knew how to construct a painting such that it would grip the viewers' attention and challenge them with the story that he wanted to tell. As Walker Evans said when reviewing the *Migration* series, 'They were daring pictures, done with a deliberately shocking economy of artistic method.'[8]

The development of African-American art

Art never happens in a vacuum. It always involves the coming together of a number of elements, notably the work of art, the artist, the viewer, and the act of viewing. These elements interact to provide a process and a context within which the art can grow in meaning. This is never more true than of a painter such as Lawrence, whose narrative work was firmly rooted in the political and social history of his people. This context also plays a vital part in giving power and meaning to the particular painting we are looking at, as well as the whole *Migration* series, and in order to help understand this more fully, it is worth pausing briefly to consider the way African-American art in general developed.

During the nineteenth century, achievement by any American in the field of the fine arts was measured by how well it imitated the European traditions. This was especially true of African Americans, who craved success as a sign that discrimination might be overcome and that they could occupy a respected place within society, and so sought to produce the kind of work that would transcend racial specificity. Moreover, the viewing public who paid to see and buy paintings, and thus provided an artist with a living, largely dictated aesthetic taste. The result was that almost all African-American painters of this period produced portraits, still life, and landscapes. Not only was such art popular, it was also safe!

There were certainly abolitionists who offered patronage to African-American artists as part of the fight against slavery, and this allowed for the production in books and periodicals of images that portrayed black people sympathetically. But the only African-American artists truly to succeed were those who gained universal appeal because they painted in ways that affirmed the dominant understanding of what it meant to be American: those such as Edward Mitchell Bannister, who produced land-scapes depicting the glorious harmony of the natural world and the seasons of the year. Such paintings could not offend and so were widely accepted, whereas to tackle themes that might be central to black experience would have been far too dangerous.

By the beginning of the twentieth century, however, perspectives were beginning to change in all kinds of ways, not least amongst African Americans. The Great Migration was a key event in transforming the black community, as so many seized the opportunity to make a new start in the North, and in the process brought new life and vigour to the urban ghettos. The birth of the New Negro movement affirmed this growing sense of black identity that expressed itself in political, economic, social and cultural terms.

In the development of African-American art, a key figure was Alain Locke. A Professor at Howard University and a leader of the New Negro movement, he believed that art had redemptive power and could play a crucial role in helping black people discover both their history and their future. He urged African-American artists to return to their own roots and tradition for inspiration rather than merely copying white artists, and promoted a rediscovery of the African legacy as a vital inheritance that could inspire this move, drawing particular attention to its abstract designs and decorations. Many New Negro artists were influenced by Locke and received help and support from him, such as Aaron Douglas and Palmer Hayden. Slowly but surely artists such as these began to portray black life and culture, finding ways of affirming the real experiences of the black community, and in 1939 Locke declared:

> The recent advances in contemporary Negro art remind me of nothing so much as a courageous cavalry move over difficult ground in the face of obstacles worse than powder and shell — silence and uncertainty.[9]

It was Lawrence who did as much as anyone to break through the wall of silence. In the *Migration* series, he dealt directly with the disturbing reality of racism and the oppression it engendered, offering a way of understanding and interpreting the events of the past. He portrayed the life-story of an earlier generation with all its hopes and its struggles, and so allowed that drama to illuminate the life of the existing community to which he belonged. Perhaps most important of all, through his art Lawrence gave voice to black history as a significant part of the American story — a part that could not and should not be forgotten.

The power of stories

This, then, is the context that helps define Lawrence's achievement as an artist, and it leads us back to a further consideration of panel 15 as well as the other images in the *Migration* series. Despite its restraint, panel 15 is a direct, forthright painting. It shines with a sincerity and honesty, refusing to ignore the fact that lynching took place, and inviting the viewers to face this dark and horrific reality. Here, Lawrence believed, was a story that had to be told.

Bennett indicates that towards the end of the nineteenth century, 'lynching became more barbarous, and lynchers became more sadistic.'[10] Of the 1217 persons lynched between 1890 and 1900, the vast majority 'were charged with the "crimes" of testifying against whites in court, seeking another job, using offensive language, failing to say "mister" to whites, disputing the price of blackberries, attempting to vote and accepting the job of postmaster.'[11] The record of the reported number of lynchings for the first quarter of the twentieth century indicates that between fifty and one hundred each year was the norm. It is no wonder, then, that this was a crucial factor in the decision of many to head North, and it was one Lawrence could not ignore as he sought to portray and define the migration experience. He wanted this story to be made known, and the style of art he adopted to make this possible was known as Social Realism.

One of those who influenced him in this direction was Orozco. Orozco was part of a group of Mexican artists who painted large murals in public places with the specific aim of expressing social and moral convictions. His bold and dramatic paintings made a deep impression on Lawrence, who explained in an interview that 'Painters like Orozco . . . People of this sort and the type of content that they were doing was very important to the people of the time. They were working in a social realist philosophy.'[12] Indeed, during the painting of the *Migration* series Lawrence had a brief meeting with Orozco during which he watched the Mexican work quietly and spontaneously, and described the encounter as having 'great meaning to me.'[13] Like Orozco, Lawrence believed in giving his art social content. He dealt with history, the reality of life for those who were black and poor, so that their struggle could be recalled and understood. And lynching was a fearful part of this reality.

There are many reasons for engaging in this kind of storytelling, and Lawrence points us in the direction of at least three, all interrelated. First, stories are a means of education; in a poor community, subject to movement and change, where not all can read and write, stories prove a vital tool for the task of teaching and learning, remembering and interpreting. In an essay on Lawrence and the community in which he grew up, Leslie King-Hammond declares:

> Lawrence's intent for the series was nothing less than educational in the most profound sense. Pivotal to the success of the series were the complementary texts that accompanied each panel. Because looking at art was new to the New Negroes, Lawrence tried, through the text panels, to underscore the message of his art and to validate his viewers' newly found sense of literacy.[14]

Lawrence could easily have produced crude propaganda, painting and annotating panel 15 in a way that was designed to condemn the perpetrators of lynching. But as we have seen, he chose instead to present the facts as objectively as possible, and so as I look and read, it is impossible for me to dismiss what I encounter as biased or exaggerated. The disturbing social message is found in the truthful simplicity of the storytelling.

In offering his own explanation of what led him to paint the *Migration* series, Lawrence comments:

> I was very involved with Negro history at the time . . . To me it was a very dramatic thing of people moving, this great trek, you know. This is the historical thing I think which fascinates us all . . . This may have fascinated me greatly. And this is how the Negro Migration theme came into being.[15]

In other words, this is an epic event with far-reaching consequences; it is a story of powerful significance. By contrast, on a further occasion, when commenting on the series of paintings we will turn to shortly, Lawrence made another very revealing observation:

> I've always been interested in history, but they never taught Negro his-
> tory in the public schools . . . I don't see how a history of the United
> States can be written honestly without including the Negro.[16]

So despite the fact that the Great Migration was of epic proportions, it
was largely lost to view. A process of education was needed for sight to be
restored, and narrative is one of the most powerful ways of learning.

Second, stories nurture a community's sense of identity. In the
Migration series, Lawrence participated in the crucial task of document-
ing the story of his people, depicting events, concerns and issues that
made them who they were.

There was, as we have already noted, a two-way process at work.
Lawrence himself was influenced and shaped by the Harlem community
— by poets such as Langston Hughes who were bringing new vitality to
black writing. Clearly the two were of one mind when Lawrence said that
he could well understand Hughes' comment that 'he would never live outside the Negro community . . . this was his life . . . his sustenance.'[17] In
1948 Hughes wrote a poem titled 'One-Way Ticket', telling of the experience of migration, and this prompted Lawrence to make a drawing with
the same title. The third stanza, however, could have used panel 15 as its
own source of inspiration:

> I am fed up
> With Jim Crow laws,
> People who are cruel
> And afraid,
> Who lynch and run,
> Who are scared of me
> And me of them.[18]

Life and creativity was nurtured in this time of renaissance, and the narrative work of Lawrence with its historical focus and its social conscience
made a very special contribution. He depicted the struggles of the black
community, not in a way that reduced them to the role of helpless victims,
but so as to lift them up and affirm them in the journey they were on. As
Juanita Marie Holland says:

Jacob Lawrence has documented, throughout his career, the trials of African Americans under the yoke of slavery and racism and helped promote a collective public identity of pride, place, and dignity in his depictions of historical figures and moments.[19]

It is not surprising, therefore, that Lawrence should often be described as taking on the role of the *griot* in his community — the professional story-teller belonging within the traditions of West Africa who would keep the past alive by retelling events in ways that had meaning for the present and the future.

This leads us to a third reason for telling stories: to bring about change. Storytelling is a dynamic activity inviting participation. When done well it allows room for the imagination to work, and so initiates a process that can provide healing and transformation, and the envisioning of new realities. This was certainly part of Lawrence's achievement in painting the *Migration* series, as he confronted the disturbing memories of the past, including the violence and the lynchings, and so empowered African Americans in the struggle to create a new future free of racism.

Yet we must be careful not to make assumptions. As we have already seen, Lawrence did not produce propaganda, and it would be a mistake to see him as a protest painter promoting a particular social and political agenda for change on behalf of the black community. The way Lawrence told stories was more subtle and powerful than this. He said:

> I've expanded my interest to include not just the Negro theme but man generally and maybe if this speaks through the Negro I think this is valid also. I don't like to think of myself as just confined to this. I'll put it this way, although my themes may deal with the Negro but I would like to think of it as dealing with all people, the struggle of man to always better his condition and to move forward, you see, in a social manner however you may interpret this.[20]

In other words, the aims Lawrence had in his work as an artist were universal in scope. Using his own experience as the starting point, he told history that never ignored the injustices faced by his own people and never refused to speak on their behalf. He continually gave his art social and moral content. But at the same time, he retained the independence of any great artist, who saw beyond his immediate community and sought to express basic human hopes for change. 'For me', he said, 'a painting should have three things: universality, clarity and strength.'[21]

Much of the story Lawrence has to tell in the *Migration* series is about struggle. Panel 15 is illustrative of the kind of oppression faced by African Americans in the South, but Lawrence refuses to suggest that all was well after taking the journey to the North; panels 46 through to 53 highlight the poor conditions faced by factory workers, the race riots that took place, and the division between the well-established Negroes and those who were newcomers. Yet in the midst of the struggles, Lawrence had something else to say:

> Uprooting yourself from one way of life to make your way in another involves conflict and struggle. But out of the struggle comes a kind of power, and even beauty. I tried to convey this in the rhythm of the pictures, and in the repetition of certain images.[22]

Again, in an interview with Charlayne Hunter-Gault in 1995, he said of the *Migration* series, 'I'd like (the audience) to experience the beauty of life, the struggle, how people can overcome certain things that could be very frustrating or demeaning.'[23] This is surely the secret of Lawrence's power as a storyteller. Even amidst the pain and anguish that is portrayed in panel 15, there is the almost defiant red of the hunched figure that will reappear again in the final panel with its assertive, triumphant message: 'And the migrants kept coming.' Lawrence's art testifies to the strength of the human spirit to bring light out of darkness, and hope out of pain, and to find the beauty of colour in the midst of struggle and suffering. It is beyond doubt a gospel message — one that does indeed have the power to transform lives and communities.

The story of Harriet Tubman

While the *Migration* series was the first to be featured in the Downtown Gallery of New York and to win him wide acclaim, Lawrence had already completed several other series of paintings that narrated the lives of heroic figures in black history. *The Life of Toussaint L'Ouverture* (1938)

consists of forty-one panels and tells the story of the black Haitian revolutionary who led his country to freedom, while *The Life of Frederick
Douglass* (1939) recounts in thirty-two panels how this former slave
became a leading public figure and abolitionist.

There was one story, however, that seems to have particularly
attracted Lawrence — the story of Harriet Tubman. Of this he said, 'if
you're involved in history and in Negro history I think it's inevitable that
you would be fascinated by the life of Harriet Tubman.'[24] That fascination
would lead to two series of paintings based on the life of this remarkable
woman. The first was completed in 1940, shortly before Lawrence began
work on the *Migration* series; the second was painted much later in 1967
for use in a children's book. They provide us with a further example of
the significance of storytelling, and of Lawrence's skill in using images to
give the story power and meaning.

No one is quite sure when Harriet was born. It was probably in 1820,
in Maryland, as a slave. From a very early age she was forced into hard
labour, and at some point during her childhood years the brutality of her
overseer resulted in a severe head injury; it is likely that this caused nar-
colepsy and meant that for the rest of her life she suffered from short
bouts of sleepiness. In 1844 she married John Tubman, a free African
American. Then five years later, under threat of being sold South, Harriet
made the decision to escape to freedom leaving behind her husband, parents, brothers and sisters. Walking by night and hiding by day, with only
the North Star as her guide, she made her way to safety in Pennsylvania,
where she took on domestic work with the aim of saving enough money
to enable her to return to rescue other slaves.

Harriet began her return journeys to the South in 1850, and over the
following ten years she went at least nineteen times and rescued over
three hundred slaves, including members of her own family, leading them
up to and across the Canadian border as that had become the only guarantee of safety. She used what was known as the Underground Railroad, a
secret network of routes along which slaves were led to freedom by 'conductors', and which linked safe-houses together. Harriet became one of
these 'conductors' and rapidly gained a reputation for her fierce commitment and courage, her skill in never losing a 'passenger', and her
remarkable ability to avoid capture. The price on her head was reputed to

be $40,000, a sign of how desperately the slave owners wanted to be rid of her.

It is said that two things sustained Harriet in her dangerous work. The gun she carried (which she would not hesitate to use, either to defend herself and those in her charge, or to threaten any fugitive who thought of turning back), and her deep faith in God. In her biography written in 1869 to raise funds for Harriet, Sarah Bradford says:

> . . . she had never known the time, I imagine, when she did not trust (God), and cling to Him, with an all-abiding confidence . . . Hers was not the religion of a morning and evening prayer at stated times, but when she felt a need, she simply told God of it, and trusted Him to set the matter right.[25]

Despite her long-term illness and the constant travelling in fear of her life, Harriet's faith ensured she never lost her passion for freedom.

She was a friend to a number of famous abolitionists, including Frederick Douglass and John Brown, and often spoke at anti-slavery meetings to further the campaign for change. This work continued after the Civil War broke out, when she also served as a scout and spy for the Unionists, making use of her intimate knowledge of the territory and her friendship with black people in the South.

After the war ended in 1865, Harriet gave her time and energy to helping former slaves begin new lives and to speaking up for women's rights. Her first husband had remarried following her escape from slavery, and she herself married again in 1869 to Nelson Davis. She should have received an income in recognition of her wartime service but got nothing, and had to support herself by doing domestic work as well as relying on the donations of others. It was not until she was eighty years old that the Government finally paid her a small pension, so giving her some measure of security during her final years. Harriet died on 10 March 1913. Vast numbers turned up to a memorial service in her honour, recognizing her very special contribution to the African-American struggle for freedom.

It is easy to see why Lawrence was attracted to the figure of Harriet Tubman. Like the Great Migration, it provides a story of epic proportions, and Lawrence himself described it as 'one of the great American sagas.'[26]

The almost mythic status accorded to Harriet within the Harlem community had much to do with Lawrence's decision to paint the first series of thirty-one panels in 1939–1940, and though one of his earliest, it is a wonderful narrative sequence full of bold, striking images, telling the story with great warmth and understanding. As with the *Migration* series, Lawrence shows great skill in balancing the emotional forces at work in the images. Strength and vulnerability, fear and courage, tension and humour, struggle and beauty — all these are present and alive in both the paintings and the accompanying text.

When asked in 1967 to choose a subject to illustrate a children's book, Lawrence decided to return to the story of Harriet, describing it as 'a dramatic tale of flight and fugitives'[27] that would have natural appeal to a young audience. This later series contains just seventeen paintings, reproduced in colour on paper with verses alongside each, and while there were certain restrictions on content due to the age of those for whom it was intended, Lawrence seemed to like the results:

> I think if I can see the two series side by side I think I would say that this is the better of the two. I think it's more subtle; I guess it would be because I'm older, you know, and I have developed a degree of selectivity . . . And I think technically it's a better series . . . After working for twenty-five years you should be better technically.[28]

The painting reproduced here (Plate 10) is the fourth in the second series and is titled *A Mother tells the Story of Moses, Harriet and the Promised Land*.

Harriet and the Promised Land (1967)

I find this an immensely appealing image. It embodies so much that is typical of Lawrence as an artist and it is, of course, all about storytelling. Together with the title, the accompanying verses help us see its place within the whole series:

> Harriet, hear tell
> About 'The Promised Land':

How Moses led the slaves
Over Egypt's land,

How Pharaoh's heart
Was hard as stone.
How the Lord told Moses
He was not alone.[29]

Harriet is depicted as a young slave girl growing up. The woman — presumably Harriet's own mother — is recounting the great biblical story of the exodus, and her daughter sits at her feet listening. Form, colour, style and content all contribute to the painting. Lawrence's sense of pattern is certainly there, as we see beautifully contrasting shapes put together side by side. The 'seats' on which the two figures sit appear as abstract designs, while the lace patterning on the hem of the woman's dress is a delicate, human touch that cleverly breaks up the areas of bold colour. Two particular features contrast with Lawrence's earlier work. First, the faces are more fully drawn, though even here they remain simplified. Second, the design of the hands and feet is exaggerated in a very expressive manner. It is suggested by Wheat that this way of drawing human anatomy appears in Lawrence's art after visits to Nigeria in the early 1960s, suggesting a particular African influence.[30]

As we might expect, Lawrence chose strong colours for this and the other images in the series. The brightness of the sky and the warmth of the earth help remove any sense of threat from this painting, while the colour of the clothing worn draws attention to both mother and child. Indeed, when this later series is put alongside the earlier one, some interesting changes in his use of colour emerge. The paintings appear to use bolder colours in a more intricate way, while at the same time there are fewer images dominated by dark colours. One other change is the much deeper perspective achieved, no doubt part of his technical development.

Certain stylistic features are carried over from the first series, while others are added. The North Star is prominent in both as the guiding light for Harriet's dangerous journeying, but there is a far greater abundance of animals and insects in the second series — no doubt to appeal to children.

In this painting we can see several, adding to the gentle humour of the image.

It is a picture to make us smile! There is a joyful exuberance in the way the mother tells the story, with arms outstretched in a dramatic gesture, both fingers and toes accentuated, pulling the child into the wonder and glory of what is being recounted. Her movement is clearly the focus of attention. Harriet sits passively yet attentively, absorbing what is being said in just the way any child might listen to a good story. There is beauty in this scene from childhood.

Lawrence, however, did not want to idealize the story of Harriet's life — even for children. In picture 7, Harriet is depicted labouring on her knees, the fingers of both hands crab-like as she scrubs the floor; picture 9 then expresses something of the fear associated with the journey of escape, with its strange patterns, shapes and forms. Even in this fourth painting we see there are no shoes on the feet, one sign of the poverty experienced by both mother and child.

It is interesting that there were those who found all this far from suitable material for a children's book, despite the omission of such features as Harriet's gun. One complaint from a librarian concerned the fact that Harriet was made to look so ugly, to which Lawrence replied:

> If you had walked in the fields, stopping for short periods to be replenished by Underground stations; if you couldn't feel secure until you reached the Canadian border, you too, madam, would look grotesque and ugly. Isn't it sad that the oppressed often find themselves grotesque and ugly and find the oppressor refined and beautiful.[31]

The art of seeing requires us to go deeper than superficial appearances.

There is another sense in which both *Harriet Tubman* series, and picture 4 in particular, invite us to go deeper, for the storytelling is deliberately layered. Unlike the *Migration* series where Lawrence portrays history in a deliberately straightforward and literal manner, here he employs symbol and allusion linking Harriet's story with the biblical narratives. It is not just that Harriet as a child listens to her mother tell the ancient story of Moses and the journey to the promised land; it is that

Harriet becomes another Moses who leads her own people to the promised land of freedom.

This idea would certainly have come through in the research Lawrence carried out. The subtitle Bradford gave to her biography of Harriet was, 'The Moses of Her People', and she explains it by saying, 'I only give her here the name by which she was familiarly known, both at the North and the South, during the years of terror of the Fugitive Slave Law, and during our last Civil War.'[32] Later Bradford recounts how she led former slaves to freedom:

> Up and down the road she passes to see if the coast is clear, and then to make them certain that it is their leader who is coming, she breaks out into the plaintive strains of the song, forbidden to her people in the South, but which she and her followers delight to sing together:

> Oh go down, Moses,
> Way down into Egypt's land,
> Tell old Pharaoh,
> Let my people go.[33]

The comparison between the stories of the founding father of the nation of Israel and the nineteenth-century former slave girl is a powerful one. Both were liberators; both resisted oppression; both were leaders of their people; both journeyed in search of the promised land.

In his paintings Lawrence finds ways of making the links explicit. As the mother tells the story of Moses in picture 4, the backdrop is an open and rugged landscape reminding us of the wilderness that had to be crossed to reach the promised land; a similar empty and barren landscape reoccurs in a number of the other images. At the same time the small, silent figure of Harriet makes her as unlikely a candidate for greatness as Moses seems to have been, and yet by picture 8 she has clearly become the leader as her figure, dressed in white to emphasize the purity of her mission, dominates the group who are planning the escape.

Another particularly moving painting in this later *Harriet* series is picture 13, where a group of fugitives are taking refuge in one of the Underground Railroad safe-houses. They are gathered around a table, heads bowed, sharing a simple meal, while at the same time a man lovingly fits a new pair of shoes onto Harriet's feet. It is full of allusions to manna received in the wilderness, to food that is sacramental, to the significance of hospitality given and received, to humble service that cares for a person's feet. Put together, Lawrence has provided us with a sequence of paintings that demand close attention, for they reveal not only the details of a dramatic journey from slavery to freedom, but also the resources of faith that make such a journey possible.

Journey to liberation

What have we learned from a study of Lawrence's work, and where must we make the connections with our Christian faith? From all that might be said, let us try to draw together some of the main threads that have emerged during the course of this chapter.

After Lawrence arrived in Harlem, he went with his mother to the Abyssinian Baptist Church. The minister, Adam Clayton Powell Sr., was well known and Lawrence recalls:

> I can remember some of his sermons. One of his famous ones was the dry bones sermon. And he was called on to preach that sermon not only in his own church but as guest minister in other churches. And I heard him do that several times and he was very dramatic with it.[34]

It is, indeed, a powerful story of promise and hope using imagery not easily forgotten. The Bible is full of such stories, and the Christian faith often uses stories to help communicate its message. I would want to go further, however, and suggest that Christian faith needs to use 'story' as its fundamental means of expression.

There are two reasons for saying this. First, as we have seen in the work of Lawrence, storytelling provides a community with a sense of identity, and it can do so for the Christian community in a far more helpful way than is possible by using doctrinal statements and credal proclamations. Creeds are invariably used to set limits, to draw boundaries in their attempt to define identity. But the identity of a community is too complex and dynamic to be held captive by definitions, for it must constantly be rediscovered and reinterpreted. Stories allow this to happen.

The joy of a story is that it can be told and retold in different ways and yet still be the same story; it leaves room for development, for growth, and for the imagination to work, while continuing to provide the roots from which the community draws its identity.

Second, in a culture where the significance of story and storytelling is widely understood, this becomes the way by which the Christian community can engage in mission. Our calling is to tell the story of Jesus of Nazareth in ways that reveal it to be, for us Christians, *the* story that gives meaning and content to all our personal and collective stories. Through imaginative telling, this story has power to resonate with the whole of human experience, and so it invites people to participate by living out the story in their own lives. No amount of doctrine can achieve such involvement.

Lawrence's narrative art works in just this way — it invites participation. The *Migration* series told his own story as well as the story of many who first looked at it and this sense of involvement was key. The *Harriet* series recounted the past history of release from slavery, but in order that a new journey might be made. Lawrence wrote:

> I didn't do it just as a historical thing, but because I believe these things tie up with the Negro today. We don't have physical slavery, but an economic slavery. If these people, who were so much worse off than the people today, could conquer their slavery, we certainly can do the same thing.[35]

Stories have power to transform because they call for active participation, and for the Christian community this is true above all else of the story of Jesus.

But if we accept that learning to tell the story of Jesus is central to the nurture and discovery of Christian faith, Lawrence reminds us that there are further questions to ask about how this story is to be told. There are many possibilities; even within the first four books of the New Testament we have four different ways of recounting the story. As a result of paying close attention to the paintings of Lawrence, I have no doubt as to the direction he would take: he would want the story told in a way that brings liberation to the oppressed. In other words, his art has much in common with the writings of liberation theologians and the lived experience of the Christian communities who strive to be liberated.

I am struck by a number of parallels. The life of base ecclesial communities in areas such as Latin America are about people oppressed by violence and poverty gathering to tell their stories, to reflect on them in the light of scripture, and then to act. Sometimes the method is described as 'See-Judge-Act'; it begins with the need to open eyes to see so as then to be able to tell stories rooted in reality, in much the same way as Lawrence learned to do. Further, it is clear that in the task of biblical reflection, one story that became a rich source of inspiration was the story of the exodus. Pedro Casaldaliga and Jose Maria Vigil speak of 'ethical indignation' in the face of poverty, and say:

> This indignation, first described in Exodus 3, is the model for ours. God listened to the cry of his people and took a stance in relation to it; God decided to enter the struggle for historical liberation.[36]

It is no accident that Harriet becomes a nineteenth-century Moses, and that Lawrence calls his series of paintings *Harriet and the Promised Land*.

The task of liberation theology is to change the way things are, to lead people to act in order to bring freedom from injustice and oppression, guided by the story of Jesus Christ. So, just as oppression takes many forms, liberation theology develops in response to a number of different contexts, describing itself as, for example, 'black theology'. In this way, it is unashamed to root itself in the particular and to give its message of freedom social and political content.

As we have seen, Lawrence did the same, employing great subtlety in using his art to address the particular experiences of poverty, injustice and racism faced by the black community in America. He is a natural resource for black theology, but also for feminist theology. In commenting upon Lawrence's *Harriet* series, Wheat says:

> . . . the lack of historical material on Harriet Tubman is not only part of a long neglect of African-American history by mainstream American historians. It also may be related to a seemingly entrenched avoidance

of active interest in the achievement of women in America . . . The fact
that she was a black woman further enforced her obscurity.[37]

It has been Lawrence's achievement to change that, and so contribute to
the journey of liberation for black people and for women.

Perhaps, however, Lawrence has something further to say to all of us,
for, as we have seen, he was deeply committed to a universal message of
hope. Part of the greatness of his art is that he refused to allow it to be
held captive by one group, but constantly reiterated the belief that the
journey to freedom is one that embraces all humanity. With gentle wisdom, he would speak of the need for all in society who sought change to
work together: black and white, women and men. He painted an inclusive
picture and told a story that called for the involvement of everyone. Of
course, the journey to freedom is far from easy, and Lawrence's images
tell of the struggle to overcome the forces of oppression. But when I see
his paintings, there is an unmistakable beauty — a vibrancy of colour, a
strength of form, a joyous use of pattern, and a sense that amidst the pain
there is the birth of new hope. The art of seeing involves both struggle
and beauty, and Lawrence seemed to sum up the meaning of his work
when he said:

> If at times my productions do not express the conventionally beautiful,
> there is always an effort to express the universal beauty of man's con-
> tinuous struggle to lift his social position and to add dimension to his
> spiritual being.[38]

I want to draw attention to one final way in which I believe Lawrence
serves as a guide for the spiritual journey: he reminds us that all journeys
of any consequence require us to cross borders. We know that when we
embark on a physical journey, it is impossible to go very far before we
come up against some kind of border that has to be crossed — at an air-
port where passports must be shown, or overland where an invisible line
marks out the territory of one country from that of its neighbour. These
borders can be disturbing places if, for example, we do not know the language spoken or we fail to have the correct documentation to hand. They
will invariably be places of trauma for those who are the poorest —

refugees who are making the journey in order to escape violence, poverty and persecution.

In our spiritual journeying there are also borders to be crossed. Latin American liberation theologians have always used the term 'conversion' not only to describe the time when we make the initial decision to follow the way of Jesus Christ, but also for every other significant reorientation of our discipleship commitment — not least our decision to align ourselves with God's preferential option for the poor. In truth the spiritual journey requires us continually to go through the process of conversion, of border-crossings, that takes us from our past way of life into new and deeper ways of being in Christ.

These kinds of border-crossings can also be traumatic. They are moments that can stretch our minds, demanding of us new ways of understanding the Christian faith; or they can ask of us new depths of loving for which we feel unprepared; or they might call us to act in the name of justice whatever the cost involved.

It is noticeable how often the task of crossing borders features in Lawrence's art. In the *Migration* series, there is the physical crossing from South to North as well as from country to city. Lines are crossed in the struggle to escape discrimination, violence and poverty, and to find decent education, voting rights and enough money to live. In the *Harriet* series, the journey is up to and over the Canadian border. It is a crossing over from slavery to freedom, matching the border-crossing made by Moses and the Israelites as they also journeyed to the promised land. And in all his work, Lawrence offered the universal vision that requires a journey of reconciliation across the borders of race and culture that so easily divide. His paintings provide a rich and powerful resource for those engaged with issues of racism, confronting us with fearful stories that challenge prevailing cultural perceptions.

As we encounter these border-crossings in the art of Lawrence, we are invited to recognise the borders we must cross as part of our own spiritual journey. Whatever shape or form they take, we can be sure that they will be places of struggle; but we can be equally sure that they can become places of beauty.

Selected (and annotated) Bibliography

It is regrettable that readers in Britain will often look in vain on bookshelves for those books that contain Lawrence's work. It should be possible, however, to order a two-volume recent work prepared in association with a special exhibition of his work. They provide excellent reproductions of his work and contain some inspiring essays, though they are both substantial and costly: Peter T. Nesbett and Michelle DuBois (eds.), *Jacob Lawrence: Paintings, Drawings and Murals (1935–1999). A Catalogue Raisonné* (Seattle and London: University of Washington Press; in association with the Jacob and Gwendolyn Lawrence Foundation, Seattle and New York, 2000); Peter T. Nesbett and Michelle DuBois (eds.), *Over the Line: The Art and Life of Jacob Lawrence* (Seattle and London: University of Washington Press; in association with the Jacob and Gwendolyn Lawrence Foundation, Seattle and New York, 2000).

Other books may prove to be even less readily available, but deserve to be tracked down if at all possible. The book that continues to serve as an authoritative introduction to Lawrence's work is Ellen Harkins Wheat, *Jacob Lawrence: American Painter* (Seattle and London: University of Washington Press, 1986).

The particular series of paintings explored in this chapter are discussed in detail in Elizabeth Hutton Turner, *Jacob Lawrence: The Migration Series* (Washington DC: The Rappahannock Press, in association with the Phillips Collection, 1993); Ellen Harkins Wheat, *Jacob Lawrence: The Frederick Douglass and Harriet Tubman Series of 1938-40* (Hampton University Museum, 1991).

It is more possible to find books prepared for children that use Lawrence's paintings and tell his story. These are well worth having whatever age you happen to be! The following are superbly produced and certainly capture the beauty of his art: Deba Foxley Leach, *I See You. I See Myself: The Young Life of Jacob Lawrence* (Washington DC: The Phillips Collection, 2001); John Duggleby, *Story Painter: the Life of Jacob Lawrence* (San Francisco: Chronicle Books, 1998); Jacob Lawrence, *The Great Migration: an American Story* (New York: The Museum of Modern Art, The Phillips Collection/Harper Collins, 1993).

The original *Harriet and the Promised Land* series was published some years ago: Jacob Lawrence, *Harriet and the Promised Land* (New York: Simon and Schuster, 1968).

There are a number of resources that can provide further understanding of the history and context in which Lawrence was painting. These include Lerone Bennett Jr., *Before the Mayflower. A History of Black America* (New York:

Penguin Books, 1993); Sharon F. Patton, *African-American Art* (Oxford and New York: Oxford University Press, 1998).

The poet Langston Hughes has been referred to, and a representative selection of his work can be found in Langston Hughes, *Selected Poems* (New York: Vintage Classics, 1990).

There is a modern edition of the early biography of Harriet Tubman: Sarah Bradford, *Harriet Tubman. The Moses of Her People* (New York: Citadel Press/Kensington Publishing, 2001).

Much has been written about the liberation theology movement, and the following collection of essays provides a very helpful and comprehensive introduction: Christopher Rowland (ed.), *The Cambridge Companion to Liberation Theology* (Cambridge: Cambridge University Press, 1999)

Also available is Pedro Casaldaliga and Jose Maria Vigil, *The Spirituality of Liberation* (Tunbridge Wells: Burns and Oates, 1994).

These days it is not necessary to rely on printed material, and in view of the difficulty in gaining access to Lawrence's work, it is well worth making use of internet resources. The main website is www.jacoblawrence.org. This will provide much valuable introductory information about Lawrence, his life and his work, and provide images of a wide variety of his paintings. Reference has also been made in this chapter to two interviews with Lawrence. One is with Carroll Greene and is in the Smithsonian Archives of American Art. The other is with Charlayne Hunter-Gault and formed part of a NewsHour broadcast. Again, the transcripts of both these are available and can be found on the following websites by using the search functions: www.archivesofamericanart.si.edu; www.pbs.org/newshour.

Notes

This chapter is primarily the work of Graham Sparkes.

[1] Jacob Lawrence, *The Great Migration: an American Story* (New York: The Museum of Modern Art, The Phillips Collection/Harper Collins, 1993), introduction.

[2] Lerone Bennett Jr., *Before the Mayflower. A History of Black America* (New York: Penguin Books, 1993), p. 287.

[3] Lawrence, *The Great Migration*, introduction.

[4] Quoted (interview, 4 July 1992) in Elizabeth Steele, 'The Materials and Techniques of Jacob Lawrence', in Peter T. Nesbett and Michelle DuBois (eds.), *Over the Line: The Art and Life of Jacob Lawrence* (Seattle and London:

University of Washington Press; in association with the Jacob and Gwendolyn Lawrence Foundation, Seattle and New York, 2000), p. 250.

[5] Quoted (from conversation with the author, 15 February 1983) in Ellen Harkins Wheat, *Jacob Lawrence: American Painter* (Seattle and London: University of Washington Press, 1986), p. 29.

[6] Elizabeth McCausland, 'Jacob Lawrence', *Magazine of Art* (Washington DC), November 1945, p. 251.

[7] 'The Negro Sympathetically Rendered by Lawrence', *Art News* (37), 18 February 1939.

[8] Walker Evans, 'In the Heart of the Black Belt', *Fortune* (37), August 1948.

[9] Alain Locke, 'Advance on the Art Front', *Opportunity* (17), February 1939, p. 132.

[10] Bennett, *Before the Mayflower*, p. 271.

[11] Ibid.

[12] Carroll Greene, 'Oral History Interview with Jacob Lawrence', *Smithsonian Archives of American Art*, 26 October 1968, p. 6.

[13] Quoted in Elton C. Fax, *Seventeen Black Artists* (New York: Dodd, Mead & Co., 1971), p. 158; cited in Wheat, *Jacob Lawrence: American Painter*, p. 61.

[14] Leslie King Hammond, 'Inside-Outside, Uptown-Downtown', in Nesbett and DuBois (eds.), *Over the Line: The Art and Life of Jacob Lawrence*, p. 78.

[15] Greene, 'Oral History Interview with Jacob Lawrence', p. 34.

[16] Quoted in Ellen Harkins Wheat, *Jacob Lawrence: The Frederick Douglass and Harriet Tubman Series of 1938-40* (Hampton University Museum, 1991), p. 14.

[17] Greene, 'Oral History Interview with Jacob Lawrence', p. 40.

[18] Langston Hughes, *Selected Poems* (New York: Vintage Classics, 1990), p. 177.

[19] Juanita Marie Holland, 'The Colour of Art: African American Artistic Identities in the Twentieth Century', in Terry Gips (ed.), *Narratives of African American Art and Identity: The David C. Driskell Collection* (College Park Art Gallery, University of Maryland, 1998), p. 44.

[20] Greene, 'Oral History Interview with Jacob Lawrence', p. 34.

[21] From a statement by Jacob Lawrence, 'Philosophy of Art' (30 May 1951), in the Jacob Lawrence Artist File in the Whitney Museum Library; cited in Wheat, *Jacob Lawrence: American Painter*, p. 192.

[22] Lawrence, *The Great Migration*, introduction.

[23] Charlayne Hunter-Gault, 'Remembering Jacob Lawrence', *NewsHour* 13 June 2000, first broadcast in 1995; text published online, www.pbs.org/newshour.

[24] Greene, 'Oral History Interview with Jacob Lawrence', p. 36.

[25] Sarah Bradford, *Harriet Tubman. The Moses of Her People* (New York: Citadel Press/Kensington Publishing, 2001), p. 23.

[26] From a lecture by Lawrence at the University of Washington, Seattle, 15 November 1982; quoted in Wheat, *Jacob Lawrence: American Painter*, p. 47.

[27] From a lecture by Lawrence at the University of Washington, Seattle, 15 November 1982; quoted in Wheat, *Jacob Lawrence: The Frederick Douglass and Harriet Tubman Series*, p. 40.

[28] Carroll Greene, 'Oral History Interview with Jacob Lawrence', p. 37.

[29] Jacob Lawrence, *Harriet and the Promised Land* (New York: Simon and Schuster, 1968).

[30] Wheat, *Jacob Lawrence: The Frederick Douglass and Harriet Tubman Series*, pp. 40-41.

[31] Quoted in Barbara Seese, 'The Black Experience — pictures Tell the Story', University of Washington Daily, 10 October 1978; cited in Wheat, *Jacob Lawrence: American Painter*, p. 116.

[32] Bradford, *Harriet Tubman. The Moses of Her People*, p. 3.

[33] Ibid., p. 37.

[34] Greene, 'Oral History Interview with Jacob Lawrence', p. 2.

[35] Quoted in Wheat, *Jacob Lawrence: The Frederick Douglass and Harriet Tubman Series*, p. 14.

[36] Pedro Casaldaliga and Jose Maria Vigil, *The Spirituality of Liberation*, trans. P. Burns and F. McDonagh (Tunbridge Wells: Burns and Oates, 1994), p. 26.

[37] Wheat, *Jacob Lawrence: The Frederick Douglass and Harriet Tubman Series*, p. 40.

[38] Quoted in Wheat, *Jacob Lawrence: The Frederick Douglass and Harriet Tubman Series*, p. 45.

6
Vincent van Gogh:
The Colours of Darkness

Into a single decade in the 1880s, Vincent van Gogh (1853–1890) packed more creative living than others would achieve given an entire century. Between 1882, when first he laid oil on canvas, and 1890, when he died from the effects of a self-inflicted wound, van Gogh produced more than eight hundred canvases, no less than twenty-five in the twenty-seven days of July before the gunshot which eventually killed him. In style, he had ventured from the tired conventions of his native Dutch predecessors to that unique and innovative form of expression that today people the world over recognize as distinctively 'van Gogh'. In technique, he had moved from the use of dark and sombre tones to the brilliant and colourful palette that marked his final years. In health, he had strayed far and deep into sickness of body and mind. In religious commitment, he had journeyed from zealous evangelical preacher to mature and reflective 'modernist' Christian.

Few words could capture the spirit of this extraordinary journey better than that phrase in the Prayer Book's Order for Evening Prayer, 'Lighten our darkness . . . .' This simple petition resonates with van Gogh's lasting understanding of God's presence in the world as bringer of light and love; it reflects the steady transformation of his own artistic style, from darkness into light; and it effectively describes the proven power of his art to illumine the lives of others, like us, who take time to give it our attention.

As in other chapters, we begin by looking at pictures, gradually identifying key motifs that then become resources for the journey of faith.

The Potato Eaters (1885)
June 1885 marked a crucial turning point in van Gogh's life as a painter. *The Potato Eaters* (Plate 11) was the last in a long series of studies illustrating the life and work of people in peasant communities and, from that

time on, his painting was to take a number of new and revolutionary turns.

It is hard to believe that before 1880, already aged twenty-seven, van Gogh had showed little or no inclination to draw or paint. There is no suggestion, for example, that he showed any unusual flair for art through the years of his schooling. From time to time, letters that he wrote in the 1870s suggest periods when he gave some limited attention to drawing, but never in a formal or structured way. The years 1869 to 1876, working for Messrs Goupil & Co, a firm of art dealers — first in The Hague, then in London and finally in Paris — were certainly significant for his future as an artist. They awakened his interest in, and deepened his knowledge of, many of the great artists of his day; but there is no indication, even at this time, that these were accompanied by an urge to paint.

His first aspiration was to follow in the steps of his father, his grandfather and his Uncle Stricker and to pursue a vocation to Christian ministry. Van Gogh had grown up in the various homes of his parents Theodorus and Anna van Gogh, deeply imbibing their religious values and the ethos of the communities in which they worked. Theodorus was himself a strong and distinctive figure. His allegiance to the so-called Groningen School within the Reformed Church furnished him with a creative blend of beliefs ranging from those of the most orthodox to the most liberal thinkers of his day. On the one hand, he held to the verbal inspiration of scripture; on the other, his ministry had social and ecumenical dimensions that still looked significantly prophetic a hundred years on. His reputation for work amongst the poor, including Catholic peasants, was a source both of admiration and intense suspicion.

The lamp hanging above the table of *The Potato Eaters* is surely reminiscent of Theodorus' ministry. Van Gogh described his father as one:

> . . . who so often goes long distances, even in the night with a lantern, to visit a sick or dying man, to speak with him about One whose word is light, even in the night of suffering and agony . . .[1]

Light, as we shall see, becomes a central motif in van Gogh's work, the burning lamp being a symbol of love: sometimes his own, sometimes the love of his friends and, occasionally, quite clearly the love of God.

Above is the first of many quotations we shall glean from the immense written correspondence between van Gogh and his younger brother, Theo. This provides a rich commentary on his life as a painter and has become an invaluable lens through which to interpret his work. Vincent and Theo became and remained intimate companions, and their relationship will emerge as this chapter unfolds.

Returning to van Gogh's own development, it seems that between 1874 and 1875 he experienced what many have interpreted in terms of an evangelical conversion. With all the arrogance of a new convert his letters home begin to include numerous biblical quotations and injunctions addressed to (or at!) the family. Notably he argued for the rejection of all secular literature in favour of the Bible and a somewhat unusual combination of John Bunyan's *The Pilgrim's Progress* and Thomas à Kempis' *The Imitation of Christ*, to which he had already become very much attached. The rejection of other literary works, significantly Victor Hugo, Jules Michelet and Emile Zola, was no small sacrifice; but it was one that he clearly felt to be incumbent upon him as an adjunct to his newfound faith. This 'fanatical' form of evangelicalism did not go down well with Theodorus or, for that matter, with other members of van Gogh's family.

This moment in van Gogh's story is relevant to *The Potato Eaters* because it marks the start of a process that rapidly propelled him into new dimensions of contact with peasant communities. By April 1876 enthusiasm for religion had become incompatible with serious attention to work at Goupil's, and from that point on van Gogh's mind was firmly set on a vocation to ministry. By May he was in England teaching at a boys' school in Ramsgate and soon after, when the school moved to Isleworth, he began to work as assistant to a Methodist minister, the Revd T. Slade Jones, an arrangement that enabled him to preach his earliest sermons at Richmond, Petersham and Turnham Green on the outskirts of London. Describing his first experience as a preacher, it is images of light to which he intuitively turned. In a letter to Theo he wrote:

When I was standing in the pulpit, I felt like somebody who, emerging from a dark cave underground, comes back to the friendly daylight. It is a delightful thought that in the future wherever I go, I shall preach the Gospel . . .[2]

The path ahead, however, was never as straight or free from obstructions as the zealous van Gogh might have hoped. The months through to July 1878 saw him return to Holland, where the family had secured for him better paid work as a book dealer. This was followed by a period living with his Uncle Jan during which he was tutored in theology and ancient languages by his Uncle Stricker and Mendes da Costa, anticipating an entry examination into the Faculty of Theology at the University of Amsterdam. Van Gogh was unable, however, to sustain sufficient enthusiasm for academic studies, and instead determined at all costs to be found actively preaching the gospel. By late August, therefore, he was enrolled in a missionary school for lay evangelists at Laeken, near Brussels; but after only three months, following an exam at the end of his probationary period, the arrangement was abruptly terminated.

Undeterred from his calling, van Gogh took an independent initiative, moving in December 1878 to the Belgian mining district of the Borinage. There he took a room and threw himself into the work of ministry, visiting the sick and reading the Bible to miners. At the turn of a new year, the evangelical college in Brussels assigned him for a six-month trial as lay preacher at Wasmes in the Borinage. In his characteristic 'all or nothing' style, van Gogh placed himself on the same level of poverty as the peasant miners amongst whom he was called to preach. His commitment to self-denial and his lack of attention to his own needs were so extreme that at the end of the trial period his assignment was simply allowed to lapse. It seems that van Gogh's ascetic zeal was more than the Committee could cope with; publicly, the message was that van Gogh lacked the oratorical skills required for an evangelistic ministry. Van Gogh continued the work unsupported at Cuesme, but soon he was sleeping on straw and had given away all his money and his clothes. By the end of 1879, all external support withdrawn, he was physically, emotionally and spiritually exhausted — 'burned out' we would say today.

In retrospect van Gogh referred to the years 1875–1879 as a miserable time in his life; but they were more than a little formative for the creative decade which lay immediately ahead. Increasingly van Gogh had dedicated himself to drawing, mainly amongst the mining and weaving communities in which he had lived. As the starkness of his evangelical commitment waned, gradually replaced by influences carried over from his years in the Groningen ethos of the family home, van Gogh rediscovered the joy of literature, now adding William Shakespeare and Harriet Beecher-Stowe to his shortlist of favourites. By August of 1880, with Theo providing a small but crucial share of his own income at Goupil's in the form of an allowance, van Gogh was able to make the monumental decision to become an artist.

In the years through to 1885 when he painted the finished canvas of *The Potato Eaters,* the majority of his drawings (and from 1882 his paintings) in some way reflect his continuing concern for peasant communities. His formal education as artist was at best fragmentary. At various times, van Gogh attended the Brussels Academy, received personal tuition from the painter Anton Mauve in The Hague, developed relationships with other artists including Ridder van Rappard; but invariably he was soon at odds with teachers and companions alike, and it is probably more appropriate to describe him as essentially self-taught. During this time, first at the prompting of Mauve, van Gogh began to consider the possibilities of colour, and a conviction that colour and music are closely related, specially focused in the music of Wagner, briefly attracted him to take lessons in music and singing. All that he had learned by 1885, not far from the midpoint of his short career as a painter, can be found in *The Potato Eaters.*

First impressions can be deceptive. It would be easy to be put off by the sheer drabness of this picture, as also by the almost unreal ugliness of the characters gathered around the table. Some viewers also react to the extreme lack of connection between the grouped figures, their isolation one from another suggesting an acute lack of compositional skills on the part of the artist. We know, however, that van Gogh planned this painting very carefully as his first 'set-piece', something which would become a marker on his journey as a painter and, quite specifically, launch him into the world of publicly recognized art. We also know that he continued to rate this painting very highly amongst his own output. As late as 1887 in a letter to his sister Willemien he wrote, 'What I think of my own work is this — that that picture I did at Nuenen of those peasants eating potatoes is the best one of all.'[3] All this suggests that we are advised to look at this painting much more carefully than we might have guessed.

It is not, for example, anything like as drab as at first it seems; indeed it is immensely colourful, even if the colours are defined within a restricted range of hue and tone. Look again at the vitality of the light as it plays from the lamp onto the various surfaces that make up this simple scene. It is true that the picture is very dark, muddy even. Van Gogh himself wrote:

> ... the colour they are painted in now is like the colour of a very dusty potato, unpeeled of course.
> While doing this I thought how perfect that saying of Millet's about the peasants is: Ses paysans semblant peints avec la terre qu'ils ensemencent [His peasants look as if they have been painted with the mud that they work].[4]

What an achievement: to paint these figures as if with the mud that they work as they plant and, at the very same time, to convey such vitality and such deep human concern.

The crux was, as it was always to be, in van Gogh's remarkable handling of colour; in particular, there was his growing understanding of tonal painting, tone taking precedence over colour, and his rendering of 'chairoscuro', the contrast between light and dark. Van Gogh's accelerating understanding of colour theory had been fired by his reading of Charles Blanc: first, *Les Artistes de mon Temps* and, then, *Grammaire des Arts du Dessin, Architecture, Sculpture, Peinture*. Once hooked, van Gogh never lost his fascination for colour theory and, through the remainder of his short life, he used his unique insights to unparalleled artistic advantage.

At the core of Blanc's theory had been the idea of 'complementaries' or, as van Gogh called them, 'opposites'. Starting from the triangle of primary colours — red, yellow and blue — the complementaries are the colours obtained by mixing the colours at the opposite two corners of the triangle. So, orange complements blue, green complements red, and violet complements yellow. There are two particular effects associated with complementaries which van Gogh learned to exploit with unprecedented subtlety. First, there is the way in which colours mixed with their complementaries create an unlimited array of interesting greys; second, there is the way in which, when complementaries are juxtaposed, the visual impact of each is so radically enhanced. A third effect which van Gogh uses relies on the concept of tonal value, the intensity of light that is associated with each particular colour. It is not immediately obvious to the untrained eye that the creation of light and dark does not depend on white and black alone; since tone is a relative measure, sharp contrast can be effected by any pair of tonally disparate values.

The Potato Eaters was a result of van Gogh's detailed experimentation with all these crucial insights into the dynamics of colour. The darkness of the picture, for example, is not created by the use of black at all; indeed, black pigment is almost entirely absent. Often it is generated by deep Prussian blues, whose low tonal values read black alongside high value yellows. Sometimes heightened contrasts are created by the juxtaposition of colourful greys arising out of the skilful mixing of complementaries. So, using van Gogh's own example, in a letter to his brother he explains that:

> . . . in the white, for instance, hardly any white has been used, but simply the neutral colour, which is made by mixing red, blue, yellow, for instance vermilion, Paris blue and Naples yellow.
> Therefore that colour is itself a pretty dark gray, but in the picture it looks white.[5]

Yet another effect relies on 'breaking' the colours with an optical mix, such as the application of the complementary colour in the form of dots — as on the dress of the girl who is standing with her back to the painter.

It is not that all these ideas had been totally unknown in the past. Painters from Titian to Delacroix were also famous for their innovative use of colour. Indeed, these are two painters whom van Gogh admired and studied in considerable detail. The point is that, as van Gogh began to grasp some of the newly defined theory underlying their practice, he was able to take the application of colour another step, a step that contributed more than any other to the unique colour-signature we now associate with his work.

But there is another dimension to this painting's vitality that concerns the method of composition rather than the application of colour. In painting *The Potato Eaters* van Gogh was concerned to avoid what he experienced as the deadening effect that can arise when a painting originates as a study from real life or as a carefully crafted sketch. Instead he struggled to achieve the enhanced vitality that is more commonly found when paint is applied direct on the canvas, taking its form from a combination of memory and imagination. This is a difficult task, and not one to which van Gogh took easily. All his earlier studies — and there were an enormous number of them — had begun with sketches of real figures. We know, for example, the precise location of the kitchen on which *The Potato Eaters* is based. It could be found in the home of the De Groot-Van Rooij family, and it can be seen from the outside in a picture titled *The Cottage* which van Gogh painted shortly afterwards. As well as a plethora of pencil and oil sketches, mainly of faces and hands, there are also two 'drafts' of the finished work, the first with only four characters, lacking the woman furthest to the left. It was only in the final version that van Gogh set about his task direct onto the fresh canvas. Later, the monumental effort of *The Potato Eaters* behind him, he would revert more and more to painting from real life — though one price to be paid was the relentless criticism of his friend and companion Paul Gauguin, who always pushed him to paint again more freely out of his imagination.

In producing *The Potato Eaters* van Gogh set himself his own challenge to work directly onto the canvas and, though constantly worried that he would fail in the process, he saw it through to a finished result. The constant temptation is, of course, to continue retouching the details and to take a picture beyond its optimum moment of vitality. Even after sending the painting to a friend, van Gogh could not resist retouching it several more times with a small brush and, after that, returned to the original cottage yet again so that he could retouch the canvas from a detailed observation of real life. On 6th May 1885, however, he hurriedly packed the barely dry canvas in a flat crate and sent it to his brother Theo, suggesting that it should now be displayed against a colour such as gold or copper. *The Potato Eaters* was finally complete.

We now return to consider further the content of the painting as well as its colour and mode of production. The subject matter, peasant life, was by no means accidental. Following his return to the parental home, van Gogh never discovered a way to live comfortably in their world. Out of his restlessness, van Gogh continued to spend a great deal of time sketching amongst rural peasant communities, as he had done in the Borinage. In his letters he repeatedly described himself as being more at ease with peasants and weavers than with 'educated' people.

The portrayal of peasant life, even labourers taking their daily meal, was not unknown elsewhere in European art at this time. *Labourer's Family at Table* by Jozef Israëls, *Saying Grace* by Max Liebermann and *The Meal* by Albert Neuhuys, were also painted around the same decade of the 1880s, show striking thematic similarities. More directly, van Gogh consciously connected his depiction of peasants back into the work of his immediate predecessor and evident mentor Jean-Francois Millet.

Why had the peasant lifestyle become so significant for van Gogh and his work as an artist? An exploration of this question takes us back into his continuing journey of faith. Many commentators on van Gogh's work, the majority even, choose to equate the end of his evangelistic missionary career with a definitive end to his Christian faith — even to his belief in God. Tsukasa Kōdera, for example, in his book *Vincent van Gogh: Christianity versus Nature,* argues that from the time van Gogh began to work as an artist, the really significant source of spiritual energy inspiring his work is 'Nature' — rather, that is, than any appreciatively Christian understanding of God.[6] I find this an extraordinary argument, and suspect that it reflects more on the writer's lack of spiritual empathy with the painter than it does on the reality of van Gogh's actual experience and spirituality. There are, happily, a smaller number of commentators who, arguing both from the letters and the paintings, find no difficulty at all in mapping van Gogh's continuing journey of faith. There they find both continuity with his earlier experience as well as fresh insight associated with his increasing spiritual maturity. So, for example, Kathleen Powers Erickson argues that van Gogh remained deeply religious throughout his life, and that ideas formed during his years as an evangelical missionary were of lasting significance for his work as an artist. She writes:

> While he left the Church in 1880 because of his frustration with his perceived hypocrisy of the clergy, particularly that of his father and his uncle, van Gogh continued to hold to many aspects of his earlier

Christian faith: his respect for the Bible and the person of Jesus Christ, his concern for the poor and his belief in a revolution that would bring about the kingdom of God on earth, as well as his belief in the reward of an afterlife for those who had suffered the earthly journey of faith. He viewed his religious experience as an arduous pilgrimage through the woes and sorrows of temporal existence, with the hope of ultimate renewal and rebirth on the other side of life. This notion of the central and fundamental importance of religion pervades his artistic oeuvre.[7]

The remainder of this chapter explores the content of van Gogh's continuing faith journey, what sustained it and, importantly, how it came to be expressed in his art.

Van Gogh's commitment to understand and interpret peasant life was an essential component of his mature spirituality. Tsukasa Kōdera is right when he argues that van Gogh looked to nature and to the lives of those who, in contrast to city-dwellers, had not lost touch with the land and the cycle of seasons, for symbols of life's deepest meaning. This need not be viewed, however, as an alternative to looking to God; it can be profoundly complementary to it. The aspects of nature to which van Gogh was most attracted were precisely those that also provided the most powerful symbols for his continuing understanding of God. He was particularly drawn by images of the fertility of the land, especially when seen as a direct result of the effort of the workers portrayed in *The Potato Eaters*. Following the example of Millet, van Gogh painted numerous images titled *The Sower*, based on the well-known biblical parable. For van Gogh, both these kinds of images were in some way associated with the life-giving, resurrecting presence of God. The work of the sower is, after all, the pre-condition of those ripe fields of wheat which, glowing yellow, the colour of the divine presence, pervade so many of his later works. This is a theme to which we will return later in the chapter.

Van Gogh did not idealize the lives of the poor, as if theirs was a manifestation of the kingdom already present. He was clear about the fact that their lives are very miserable indeed, and he aimed through painting to expose the distasteful effects of their harsh and debilitating existence. His motives were twofold: to draw attention to their desperate need *and* to uncover what he perceived to be a peculiar richness in their lives, a richness rarely accessible to those who enjoy more tangible comforts. This same duality was evident from the earliest years of his ministry in the Borinage; on the one hand he was moved with compassion by the needs of those amongst whom he worked, while on the other he was attracted by their values which he measured favourably against the prevailing standards in the polite and religious society of his day. He wrote: 'I often think how peasants form a world apart, in many respects so much better than the civilized world.'[8] This is an experience still echoed in the testimony of contemporary Christian disciples who have the opportunity to minister in what we now call the Third World. The experience of those who live in a Brazilian *favela* must never be romanticized, and it is the responsibility of today's Christians to enact solidarity through their commitment to the transformation of societies where people live in the traps of poverty and oppression. Those who do work in the *favelas*, however, often share stories that deeply challenge the distorted values of the so-called First World.

As also emerges in the chapter on O'Keeffe, van Gogh sought to show that God's presence can be seen in everything and anything, no matter how lowly or simple. This is as true of the objects which feature in his pictures as it is of the people. It is no accident that the faces that appear in *The Potato Eaters* are striking for their ugliness. Inspired by the example of Millet, van Gogh actually sought out models whose physiognomy suggested to him associations with the faces of animals. His letters refer to one woman whose expression recalled 'a lowing cow', and to another whose face was 'a kind of cockerel type'. The figures in *The Potato Eaters* all have exaggerated lips and cheekbones. The man on the left has protruding ears and the woman has an extraordinarily flattened face. These were meant to shock his viewers; they were not intended, however, to insult his models. Van Gogh's intention, precisely the opposite, was to indicate their affinity with nature and to invite respect for them. Earlier in the letter quoted above, he wrote:

I have tried to emphasize that those people, eating their potatoes in the lamp-light, have dug the earth with those very hands they put in the dish, and so it speaks of manual labour, and how they have honestly earned their food.[9]

Van Gogh seeks to show us that these people are the salt of the earth.

The simplicity of the objects in the cottage where *The Potato Eaters* share their meal is as important as the earthiness of the people themselves in communicating the import of the mundane. At the back of the room is a box bed, and on the wall hangs a pendulum clock and a picture of the crucifixion with St. John and the Virgin. The woman on the right pours chicory from a copper kettle. Hanging near the rafters on the chimney wall it is just possible to identify a clog holding kitchen utensils. Van Gogh made minor adjustments to some details of the original room as we know it from later photographs — the lie of the roof beam, for example — and he played tricks with the perspective to bring everything into view that he wanted for his picture. True to local tradition, the family all eat from the single platter of hot potatoes, the rising steam from which brilliantly contributes to the 'chairoscuro' framing a profile of the girl standing at our side of the table.

The other striking feature of this painting, one alluded to earlier in this section, concerns the lack of connectedness between the characters within the composition. Real relationships between the figures in a painting are notoriously difficult to achieve, especially in compositions from memory and imagination, and there is continuing debate as to just how much this does or does not reflect a limitation on van Gogh's compositional skills at the time. Kinder critics have expressed the view that oppressed peasants are simply too weary from their labours to show any interest in one another; but this might be taking kindness just a little too far. Certainly the difficulty of composing a work with multiple characters is discussed by van Gogh in his letters, and is offered as a reason for delaying a start to the project as long as he did. Another approach sees in the isolation of the peasants a reflection of van Gogh's own experience of isolation within a family unit, something which features as another significant motif in his letters. My own guess is that both these factors are at play in some measure in this composition. The energy and determination necessary to see this difficult project through was eventually occasioned by the death of his father, a little over a month previous, and the theme of family and his own location within it were doubtless fresh in his mind. It might also be significant that he did not again attempt to paint a picture with more than two grouped figures at any time through the remainder of his short career.

Lastly we will look at how this picture was received by a viewing public. Initially it was not seen at all beyond a close circle of friends and colleagues. Theo did not feel confident to exhibit *The Potato Eaters* in Paris, as van Gogh had hoped, and those individuals who did see it were very much divided in their responses. A now infamous response came from van Gogh's teacher and so-called friend, Ridder van Rappard, who wrote as follows after seeing a lithograph of the picture:

> You will agree with me that such a work is not meant seriously. Fortunately, you can do better than that, but why then did you see and treat everything so superficially? Why didn't you study the movements? Now they are only posing. How far from true that coquettish little hand of the woman in the background is — and what connection is there between the coffeekettle, the table and the hand that is lying on top of the handle? What on earth is that kettle doing? — it isn't standing, it isn't being lifted up — so what then? And why isn't that man to the right allowed to have a knee, a belly and lungs? Or are they located in his back? And why must his arm be a yard too short? And why must he do without one half of his nose? And why must that woman on the left have some sort of little tobacco-pipe stem with a little cube at the end for a nose?
>
> And after that, while working in such a manner, you dare invoke the names of Millet and Breton? Come on! In my opinion art stands too sublime a thing to be treated so nonchalantly.[10]

He did not like it! And nor did van Gogh like receiving this letter. From this moment on their relationship was scheduled for a rapid end. Van Gogh made several written replies, their tone a blend of self-defence and spirited attack. From them we can learn much about how he felt about his own picture:

> As for my work, that scene of the potato eaters — you saw the lithograph of it — is a subject that I tried to paint, being inspired by the peculiar light effect in that grimy cottage . . .

Now you call the aggregate of my work utterly weak, and demonstrate
at great length that its deficiencies exceed its good qualities.
Thus about my work, thus about my person.
Well, I won't accept this, never.
The work in question, the painting of peasants, is such a hard job that
the utterly weak won't even attempt it . . .
And yet I believe that — even if I go on producing work in which people can point out errors — when they want to, if this is their special
purpose and point of view — it will have a certain vitality and raison
d'être of its own that will hurl the errors into the shade — in the eye of
those who appreciate character and the spiritual conception of things.
And it will not be so easy to confound me as they think, despite all my
faults. I know too well what my ultimate goal is, and I am too firmly
convinced of being on the right road after all, to pay too much attention
to what people say of me — when I want to paint what I feel and feel
what I paint. Nevertheless it makes life very difficult at times, and — I
think it quite possible that later on some fellows will regret either the
things they said of me or the opposition and indifference which they
pestered me with. The way I see it is this: I withdraw from people to
such an extent that I literally don't meet anybody except — the poor
peasants — with whom I am directly concerned because I paint them.
And this will remain my policy, and it is quite possible that I shall give
up my studio before long and go live in a peasant's cottage, so as not to
see or hear educated people — as they call themselves — any longer.[11]

How ironic that a century later people the world over would know the
name of Vincent van Gogh, and hardly anyone would have heard of
Ridder van Rappard.

It is a costly business being creative and innovative in any sphere of
life. Rarely can the contemporaries of those who are pioneers see what is
happening in their midst; and all too often the price for the innovator is
rejection and ridicule. The fact that this was also the experience of Jesus
of Nazareth undoubtedly brought comfort to van Gogh in his own
moment of need, and the way van Gogh drew on Gospel images of suffering will occupy our attention again before this chapter is complete.

The Starry Night (1889)

At this point we are about to take an enormous leap, brief when measured in time, but immense when measured in terms of achievement. In the four years between May 1885 and June 1889 van Gogh's work had evolved from *The Potato Eaters* to *The Starry Night*, and the artist had already painted several hundred pictures in the style we all now immediately recognize as 'van Gogh'. Why it has been chosen for the place of honour on the cover of this book should become clear as this chapter unfolds.

Let us look at it closely. It is utterly 'van Gogh'; all, that is, but for one thing, the darkness. Amongst dozens of brilliantly lit daylight pictures — of trees, of flowers and of corn — there are just a few night-time 'specials'. Its claim to total 'van Goghness' is fully justified, however, by the peculiar illumination of this night; even from the darkness an unparalleled radiance beams from this painting. It is the same radiance I remember on first seeing a van Gogh, 'in the canvas', as it were. It was hanging in the City Art Gallery in Zurich, at least ten years ago now, but the immediate impact on my retina has never been erased. The picture I saw on that occasion was one of van Gogh's many composite images of wheat fields and cypresses. Admittedly the Zurich gallery is beautifully lit, and the painting had probably received careful restorative attention, but the sheer radiance of light emitted from the oil's surface was peculiarly unforgettable. That this same radiance is also present in *The Starry Night*, even at dead of night, is extraordinary.

Much of the light, quite understandably, beams from the starry sky that fills two thirds of the visible canvas. Amongst several stars there is one huge 'droop'd' star (a phrase from Walt Whitman, of whom more later) hanging just above the horizon; it has to be a planet, a wandering star. High on the right is a sickle-shaped moon, its brilliance of that peculiar kind only seen on special nights. So great is its light that the whole of its orb is also visible — here so visible it might even be mistaken for the sun. And the moon is haloed, as sometimes seen on those nights with just the right amount of vapour in the atmosphere. The radiance belongs to the sky itself and not alone to the stars which pepper it. It bursts out from the wave-like swirls, following the curvature of an Einsteinian space, and a low blanket of light rests along the line of the hills. Was there ever such a night as this?

Painting darkness is horrendously difficult at the best of times. How can a painter hold to the low tonal values suggestive of darkness, and at the same time achieve the colourfulness and the relative brightness that is the truth about night vision? We have already explored some of the techniques which van Gogh developed and which, here, he employs with unparalleled genius. There is an interplay of complementary colours, yellow-orange against violet-blue. There is also precision control of tonal values. Taken out of their context in the picture, seen as it were in their true colours ('local' colours would be the technical name), the stars would look a dim and dingy yellow, almost obliterated by smudges of greens and blues (try isolating a single star by viewing it through a small hole in a scrap of paper). Seen as a whole, however, the sky shines as on the holiest of nights; the heavens are indeed telling the glory of God.

But the light comes not from the sky alone. Below the dark hills — relatively dark, that is — nestles a village. Even given its minimal representation, viewed from an angle that largely reduces it to an array of parallelogram rooftops, the dark blues communicate a deep sense of peacefulness and security. And there are lights in some of the houses, radiating the same yellow aura already seen in the moon and stars. Earlier in the chapter we interpreted the light hanging in a peasant home as van Gogh's symbol for the love of God. If the night sky radiates the love of God — and that of van Gogh's friends — perhaps it is love radiating from the houses that provides the village with its unmistakable feeling of peace.

The village is not actually true to the French region of St Rémy where this picture was painted. It is much more like the villages which van Gogh would have remembered from his childhood in Holland. Nowhere is this more evident than in the representation of the church, whose slightly crooked spire stands out against the hills behind, drawing our eye as we survey the village. This is a Dutch church, of the kind in which van Gogh's father had ministered; French churches in this region do not look like this at all. Most significant of all, there is no light emitted from the church; it stands in total darkness. In fact it is hard to keep our eye on it for long, because we are soon drawn to the immense cypress that runs parallel and so much more prominently to its immediate left. Here we see a recapitulation of the crooked spire, and begin to understand what demanded the distortion in its form. For the cypress tells the truth about the church. The cypress had already become for van Gogh a well-established symbol of foreboding, associated with impending disaster, even death. Here it has the unmistakable likeness of flames. These flames, however, contribute no light to the scene; they are fearsome in their darkness. The cypress, here on such a massive scale as to run right off the picture, declares the truth about the church — which has nothing to declare. The spire, conventionally the symbol of hope (in French *espérer* means 'to hope') is exposed for its utter hopelessness.

The whole image is conceived in patterns that balance with extraordinary beauty. The movement generated by hill and sky and tree traps our eye within the picture: creative energy, peace and foreboding are held together in dynamic tension. This is a remarkable picture, and it is not surprising that van Gogh took extreme pleasure in his finished work.

It is clear from his letters that the production of this and an earlier painting, completed in Arles the previous year and also titled *The Starry Night*, was for Van Gogh both an immense effort and a major achievement. In the build-up to painting the Arles version, he wrote 'for three nights running I sat up to paint and went to bed during the day. I often think that the night is much more alive and more richly coloured than the day.'[12] He worked at the picture outside at night by the light of a gas lamp, and he was thrilled at the result:

> Enclosed a little sketch of a square size 30 canvas, the starry sky actually painted at night under a gas jet. The sky is greenish-blue, the water is royal blue, the ground mauve. The town is blue and violet, the gas is yellow and the reflections are russet-gold down to greenish-bronze. On the blue-green expanse of sky, the Great Bear sparkles green and pink, its discreet pallor contrasts with the harsh gold of the gas.
> Two colourful little figures of lovers in the foreground . . .
> I go out at night to paint the stars, and I am always dreaming of a picture like this with a group of living figures of our comrades.[13]

The night sky at Arles was a much more literal painting than the later work at St Rémy. There is no doubting the lie of the bay at Arles or the actual constellations of stars in the sky. The 'comrades', however, had to wait for his more imaginative picture at St Rémy. This is a reference to his artist friends, whom we must deduce are represented by the twelve stars in the St Rémy sky. Art historians have entered contortions in their efforts to locate the elements that make up the later image. The cypress tree looks to be a quotation from an earlier painting, *Green Wheat Field with Cypress* (mid-June 1889), and the mountains look to originate in a picture called *Mountainous Landscape Behind Saint-Paul Hospital*, also painted earlier in the same month. The village and the church we have already identified to be Dutch; but the sky is almost certainly a dramatic figment of van Gogh's cosmic imagination, and any attempt to project actual constellations onto the stars is decidedly unproductive. The best reading of the stars seems to be to interpret the twelve 'comrades' as an imaginative fulfilment of his continuing dream to form a creative artistic community, bound together by strong commitments of loyalty and love. As we shall see, his recent attempt to earth this dream in the 'Yellow House' that he rented in Arles had been singularly unsuccessful. Here it is achieved, only in his mind and in oil, always to remain pie in the sky.

The interpretation of van Gogh's *The Starry Night* offered in these pages is, of course, my own and, whilst informed by the suggestions of many other writers, is only one of many ways it can be viewed. Just how it is read seems to depend primarily on how we view van Gogh's attitude towards his religion at this particular moment of his life. Whatever our own understanding — and we shall return to this issue again later — there is no doubting that some generations later *The Starry Night* was to become famous precisely as a religious work. At an exhibition in Chicago in 1954 it was chosen as *the* representative masterpiece of religious art in the nineteenth century. In a preface to the exhibition catalogue written by Paul Tillich and Theodore Green, titled 'Religious Art', there appears the following passage:

> If religion be defined as man's ultimate concern for Ultimate Reality, all art which reflects, however partially and distortedly, this ultimate concern is at least implicitly religious, even if it makes no use whatever of a recognisable religious subject matter or any traditional religious symbols.[14]

There are no prizes for recognizing the inimitable style of Paul Tillich, and it is clear why this picture, interpreted as a statement about 'God beyond the church' should find its moment at that particular juncture, immediately post-War, in western theological history. For Tillich, it symbolized all that he found so powerful in an alliance between Expressionism, which he had experienced with such intensity in the recent art and other cultural forms of his native Germany, and the possibility of a new era in Christian theology. Of this picture, on another occasion, Tillich also wrote:

> Van Gogh's Starry Night has the character of going below the surface. It is a description of the creative powers of nature. It goes into the depths of reality where the forms are dynamically created . . . those depths in which the tension of the forces creates nature.[15]

For Tillich and his contemporaries, overwhelmed by the inauthenticity and failure of a church that they saw to be hopelessly tied to middle-class moralistic values, the discovery of a painting that both symbolized 'God beyond the church' and demonstrated on canvas that God can be powerfully expressed in art free from explicitly 'churchy' content was a wonderful gift. It is also one that prophetic spirits in every new generation will doubtless continue to appreciate.

So, how was it that van Gogh's style underwent such a dramatic transformation in such a short span of years? There is no single answer to this question. Many things had happened to him following the death of his father and the painting of *The Potato Eaters* in 1885. There had been further, and rapid, consolidation of van Gogh's freedom from the obsessive relationship to his religious beliefs that had so scarred his experience in the late 1870s; this was the continuation of a process that had started with his decision to become a painter. A painting called *Still Life with Open Bible*, like *The Potato Eaters* also from 1885, is often heralded as a significant marker. Still in sombre colours, it includes a Bible open at Isaiah 53 and a copy of Emile Zola's *La Joie de Vivre*. Often it is taken by historians to signify van Gogh's radical rejection of the Christian religion following the death of his father. Whilst in measure this might be true, I am more convinced by the view that the open Bible suggests van Gogh's continuing identification with one of its greatest themes: namely, that of the suffering of God's chosen servant. It is possible to see this picture as a symbol of van Gogh's rehabilitation to secular literature, without necessarily reading into it an absolute rejection of the Christian Bible; indeed, biblical themes continue to be far too prevalent in his work for that argument to be sustained.

The rediscovery of secular literature, probably never fully lost, was certainly an important factor in the continuing stimulation of van Gogh's creative imagination. Scholars have enjoyed a field-day trawling various authors in search of possible connections and sources. Certainly Michelet and Zola are well to the fore; but I have taken particular delight in listening for resonances with the poetry of Walt Whitman, which we know van Gogh himself also read with great pleasure. Often, it seems, Whitman writes poetry in the very colours with which van Gogh paints. In a poem titled 'Pictures' Whitman slowly leads the reader through his imaginary gallery. At one point he writes:

> And that is a picture intended for Death — it is very
>   beautiful — (what else is so beautiful as Death?)
> There is represented the Day, full of effulgence — full of
>   seminal lust and love — full of action, life, strength,
>   aspiration,
> And there the Night, with mystic beauty, full of love also,
>   and full of greater life — the Night, showing where the
>   stars are;[16]

I am not suggesting that we should think of van Gogh's oils as depicting specific poetic images, from Whitman or anywhere else; but there is no doubting the similarity of their respective thought-fields. In the same poem that has such a powerful evocation of 'the Night', just a few lines earlier, we find this:

> There five men, a group of sworn friends, stalwart, bearded,
>   determined, work their way together through all the
>   troubles and impediments of the world.[17]

Wrong number of men, but so evocative of van Gogh's unrealized vision for a residential artistic community. Another poem, 'Night on the Prairies', would serve excellently as a libretto for the sky in *The Starry Night* — should one ever be needed:

> I was thinking the day most splendid till I saw what the
>   not-day exhibited,
> I was thinking this globe enough till there sprang out so
>   noiseless around me myriads of other globes.
>
> Now while the great thought of space and eternity fill me I
>   will measure myself by them,
> And now touch'd with the lives of other globes arrived as
>   far along as those of the earth,
> Or waiting to arrive, or pass'd on farther than those of the
>   earth,
> I henceforth no more ignore them than I ignore my own life,
> Or the lives of the earth arrived as far as mine, or waiting to
>   arrive.
>
> O I see now that life cannot exhibit all to me, as the day
>   cannot,
> I see that I am to wait for what will be exhibited by death.[18]

In van Gogh's picture, painted only a year before his death, the cypress also stands, ominous, intimating an alternative route toward the final exhibition.

Van Gogh, as we have already noted, found in the work of the sower a connecting point between life and death, burial and the new life for which the Christian symbol is resurrection. Whitman's short poem 'As I Watch'd the Ploughman Ploughing' reads:

> As I watch'd the ploughman ploughing,
> Or the sower sowing in the fields, or the harvester
>   harvesting,

> I saw there too, O life and death, your analogies;
> (Life, life is the tillage, and Death is the harvest according.)[19]

And earlier I promised a reference to the 'droop'd' star. It appears in the opening lines of *Memories of President Lincoln* and merits reading for its abundance of echoes from a van Gogh-like world. It begins:

> When lilacs last in the dooryard bloom'd,
> And the great star early droop'd in the western sky in the
>   night,
> I mourn, and yet shall mourn with ever-returning spring.[20]

It is not surprising then that we should find van Gogh enthusing to his sister, Willemien, about his discovery of Walt Whitman. In a letter of 1888, he wrote:

> Have you read the American poems by Whitman? I am sure Theo has them, and I strongly advise you to read them, because to begin with they are really fine, and the English speak about them a good deal. He sees in the future, and even in the present, a world of healthy, carnal love, strong and frank — of friendship — of work — under the great starlit vault of heaven a something which after all one can only call God — and eternity in its place above the world.[21]

It may well be that van Gogh never read the specific lines of Whitman I have quoted here. Rather, they stand as testimony to the particular exhilaration I experience when I discover connections of this kind, between different fields of knowledge and interest. Theology, it seems to me, happens around the making of connections such as these.

Returning to van Gogh's story through the years following *The Potato Eaters*, his newfound freedom soon took him to Paris, and it is there that a visible revolution in his style really began to take shape. There are numerous examples which can be used, but I was specially struck by two canvases, both titled *Montmartre: Quarry, the Mills* and both dated Autumn 1886, which I first saw hanging side by side in the Van Gogh Museum in Amsterdam. At the time, it seemed to me that they symbolized with peculiar clarity the hinge around which this monumental change of style was taking place. What I take to be the first, if only by a matter of weeks, carries many of the tones familiar in his earlier work; the sky, for example, is reminiscent of skies in his earliest oils from his days in Nuenen. There are suggestions of increased boldness in the uses of the broad brush, and his palette has radically changed; the sky and the stones from the quarry vibrate with the resonance of newly discovered colour.

These paintings, however, do not stand alone. Around this time there are any number of paintings of windmills, flowers, fish and birds — boots, even — that explore his newfound freedom in form and colour. This is also the time when self-portraits become a favoured medium for personal exploration: forty-one in all, including seven in 1886 and nineteen in the following year. Through the self-portrait, van Gogh discovered himself and his style — simultaneously. The portraits demand detailed examination in their own right; sufficient here to note the way they epitomize his discovery of a colourful palette and the bold, almost reckless, use of a broad brush. The famous self-portrait of 1888 shows a mirror-image of the artist at his easel holding a full palette of colours that had, by then, become his hallmark.

From here van Gogh's personal story becomes increasingly dark, and the detail is too complicated to narrate adequately in this chapter. The move to Arles in February 1888 saw another upward step in the acceleration of van Gogh's already prolific output. These are the months that give birth to immense and radiant canvases of blossoms and wheat fields. His move to the 'Yellow House' harbours the dream of a community of artists living together in creative harmony. The famous *Sunflower* series was initially designed to decorate a room in which Paul Gauguin would come to live and work with him. Gauguin's stay, however, turned out to be brief and itself the cause of immense distress. His departure in December 1888 was precipitated by the first of van Gogh's serious mental crises, the one in which, tragically, he mutilated his own ear. This was the beginning of a number of spells at a hospital 30 km. from Arles in the small town of Saint-Rémy-de-Provence. Whenever his mental condition allowed it, van Gogh worked hard to paint his way out of hospital. There are many scenes associated with the hospital-grounds and the surrounding countryside, and it was here during the summer of 1889, in St Rémy, that van Gogh painted his second picture titled *The Starry Night*.

What an extraordinary context out of which to produce such beauty. The years 1885 to 1889 had seen him spiral deeper and deeper into mental darkness. Repeatedly, fresh symbols had emerged in his painting — wheat fields, flowering orchards, sunflowers, cypress and olive trees, sun, moon and stars — and each, with a kind of obsessive attraction, helped to lure him back out of the darkness into patches of relative light. Never through any of this time was it possible for the darkness entirely to overshadow the colour.

We shall now look at one more painting before we attempt to broaden our theological reflection on this remarkable output of paintings.

Wheat Field with Crows (July 1890)

By the turn of the year 1890 van Gogh was experiencing increasingly frequent bouts of ill health. A few days before the end of 1889, in the middle of one of his 'attacks', he tried to poison himself by swallowing paint and some oil from his lamp. The matter was so serious that his physician ordered the removal of his paints, and for a time he was allowed only to draw.

Once the immediate crisis was over, he was able to continue painting for the next four months, with increasingly frenzied energy. By May, Theo had arranged for him to move to the town of Auvers-sur-Oise, from where he was able to make regular visits to Dr. Gachet in Paris, who became both medical consultant and his close companion through the final months. June and July were times of unparalleled productivity. In the single month of July, before his fatal attack on the 27th day, he painted more than one hundred square metres of canvas, layering them with colour in patterns and forms of the most exquisite beauty. Just how much weight should be attached to the commercial valuation of art is a matter of debate, but it can hardly miss notice that those one hundred square metres of canvas currently have a market value extending to hundreds of millions of pounds. The irony is compounded by the fact that so much of the intellectual debate about his work, then and since, has hinged around an evaluation of his madness.

The July canvases are wide-ranging in content — boats and cows, trees and gardens — but the theme that seemed to draw him at that time, as if into the mouth of a yawning tunnel, was a fascination with fields of wheat. At least sixteen of the twenty-five July oils feature wheat or corn in one guise or another; and amongst them was *Wheat Field with Crows* (Plate 12). It is another painting that has attracted enormous attention in the years since van Gogh's death. It is one of three huge wheat field images from the closing weeks of this life, each top-heavy with a dark and foreboding sky. For many years *Wheat Field with Crows* drew added attention, because historians thought it to be van Gogh's very final effort as a painter of oil on canvas. We now know this not to be the case; but *Wheat Field with Crows* still presents a hauntingly significant image.

It takes time and energy — as well as skill — to cover a canvas of this size with thick layers of paint, and we can almost feel the continuing discharge of energy emanating from its uneven surface. Thinking it to be his final work, it was not difficult for historians to wax lyrical on what they saw as its tormented forms. The sky is not merely dark, but agonizingly convoluted. The reds and yellows of the field seem to sweep us away, over the horizon, drawn with the crows into the eye of a gathering storm. It would have been an appropriate memorial to leave this image for posterity as a final work, and it would have provided a tidy end to an otherwise chaotic life. Current estimates, however, date the picture between 7th and 10th July, and after *Wheat Fields with Crows* there were still other calmer and more carefully crafted images to follow, before the decisive bullet.

Wheat Fields with Crows, however, is not as unambiguously the product of mental torment as at first it might seem. Just possibly, there could be meaning in this seeming madness, locked into its disturbing — but probably hopeful — colours of darkness. It would be wrong to forget that throughout his years as a painter, the blazing yellow of ripe corn had invariably stood as a symbol of new life and the Christian hope of resurrection; and even a blaze like this one could not reverse the habit of a lifetime. The birds, whilst often interpreted as ominous of death, might for van Gogh equally signify a wistful return to the north, to his home region, echoes of which appear in almost all his later paintings. And what of the three tracks in the field? It is important to point out that they are all dead ends: two disappear off the picture, and one vanishes abruptly into an inferno of wheat. But the fact that the central path disappears into the blaze of yellow need not necessarily be understood as an expression of van Gogh's mounting despair, of a sense that there was now nowhere to go. Instead, it might just be a symbol of his imminent immersion into God. After all, images of the journey of faith had been part of his vision ever since his early enthusiasm for Bunyan's *The Pilgrim's Progress*. The crows are actually heading for two somewhat anomalous patches of brightness, which evoke memories of the two great spirals in *The Starry Night*; might these refer to Vincent and his brother Theo, one day forever to be secure in the heavens? Of such speculations there is no end, but concerning their broad drift we can have some measured confidence.

All of which takes us back to reflect again on van Gogh's illness, his 'attacks', increasingly driving him to self-harm and eventual suicide. How did his illness relate to these final paintings? This is another of the questions that has generated an immense literature, and researchers offer plausible arguments to support a wide range of answers. There are several different avenues along which the evidence can be explored. There is a small, but significant, amount of professional medical evidence; this originates with the written comments of Dr. Gachet, but also builds on more modern understandings of the chemistry of mental illness. There is literary evidence from van Gogh's own letters spanning all the years through which his condition(s) developed. And, not least, there is the evidence of the paintings themselves.

Always, there is a lurking question about van Gogh's religious disposition. For some critics of his work, almost any allusion to God in van Gogh's letters signals the onset of mental illness; others find what they read to be his lasting religious convictions, and they interpret them as spiritual resources without which he would not have survived as long as he did.

Concerning the illness itself, I am most drawn to those interpretations that see it as double-edged. One dimension, the one that accounts for the 'attacks' — not evidently present before the incident with his ear in 1886 — is well explained by a diagnosis of some form of epilepsy. Epilepsy was mentioned by Dr. Gachet as well as by Dr. Rey and Dr. Peyron, who had attended him on various occasions since his first admission to the asylum at Arles. In today's language some suggest a more precise diagnosis of 'temporal lobe epilepsy'. This, we are told, would account for a number of otherwise incompatible factors. It would explain the fact that he did not retain a clear memory of what happened during his attacks; he could not, for example, give a coherent account of the incident that ended with damage to his ear. Combined with its almost inevitable accompaniment, reactive depression, it would also explain the growing tendency to self-harm; and it would in some measure explain the extraordinary resources of energy on which van Gogh was able to draw in the better times.

What it does not explain, of course, is the manner of his eventual suicide. All the evidence now suggests that this was neither a frenzied nor an unconscious act, as was indeed the case when he tried to eat some of his paints. On the contrary, his suicide was a calm and calculated act. On 27th July van Gogh set out into the fields, probably very near to the spot from which *Wheat Fields with Crows* had been painted a few days before; and there he shot himself with a loaded revolver. The first shot did not kill him; but, rather than make a second shot, he made his way back to the house — presumably in considerable pain — and took to his bed, where later he was found, wounded and seriously ill. The testimony of those who attended him through the hours until his death on the 29th suggest that he was calm, collected and fully aware of what he had done. Some suggest, therefore, that the suicide belongs with a second diagnosis: namely, that of a chronic clinical depression which had steadily taken its toll on his life over a number of years. Such depressions frequently have an hereditary factor, and it is not insignificant that his brother Cor had also ended his life in this way.

It is possible, therefore, that van Gogh's living and dying are best explained through a variety of complementary factors: a prolonged disposition towards clinical depression, a debilitating form of epilepsy, only becoming evident in his mid-thirties, and — not inconsistent with either of the former — a passionate and persistent belief in the Christian God of resurrection. My own view is that these three together make remarkably good sense of his pictures, and make it inappropriate and utterly unjust to speak of his life work naïvely as the product of madness.

Those who were around at the time of his death show little consistency in their interpretations of events. A local priest confirmed van Gogh's dismal analysis of the state of the church, denying him burial on the grounds of suicide. Fortunately a colleague in a nearby parish took

⌐re compassionate stance. Paul Gauguin, still very much thinking ₁mself the injured party following the event with van Gogh's ear, did more than anyone to keep the rumour of madness running with what was then unstoppable energy. Another friend, Emile Bernard, was more sympathetically moved by the events leading to van Gogh's death. Reflecting later on the event of van Gogh's funeral in a letter to the art critic Albert Aurier, he wrote:

> On the walls of the room where the body lay all his canvases were nailed, forming a sort of halo around him, and rendering his death all the more painful to the artists who were present by the splendour of the genius which radiated from them. On the coffin a simple white linen, masses of flowers, the sunflowers which he loved so much, yellow dahlias, yellow flowers everywhere. It was his favourite colour, as you will remember, a symbol of light he dreamt in hearts as well as in painting.[22]

This letter focuses on what is surely one of the most important keys to van Gogh's entire artistic output. For it was yellow, always yellow, the colour of God's love, which took centre stage in each of the paintings we have considered: *The Potato Eaters*, *The Starry Night* and, lastly, *Wheat Fields with Crows*.

Van Gogh as a Christian person

What can we say, then, about van Gogh's own journey as a Christian person? Was it, as some art historians would have us believe, all over when he made the decision to become a painter? Or did his Christian believing genuinely mature with the years, serving him at different times in different, but appropriate, ways?

The full answer will, of course, never be known; but van Gogh did leave many clues in his letters which, taken in tandem with his pictures, reveal for us a great deal. It was in the letter to Theo from Arles whilst working on the earlier *The Starry Night* that he wrote:

> That does not prevent me from having a terrible need of — shall I say the word? — of religion. Then I go out at night to paint the stars, and I

am always dreaming of a picture like this with a group of living figures of our comrades.[23]

In it we gain some sense of how his friendships, his art and his religion dovetail tightly one with another. It is the word 'need' which those who are not familiar with religious experience read so negatively. What they do not understand is that needs are not necessarily identical with weaknesses; if there are real needs, then it makes sense that they should really be met.

Some time later, the painting completed, he wrote again to Theo concerning a changing motif in his pictures, saying 'it is not a return to the romantic or religious ideas, no.'[24] Again, however, it would be wrong to read this as a rejection of religion as such; its meaning was focused on the romantic in art and concerns his and his comrades' continuing struggle to discover the best possible form of expression.

It is true that van Gogh was not at all interested in 'religious paintings', in the sense of paintings that depict explicitly 'religious' scenes. The exceptions that proved his rule were Rembrandt and Delacroix, the latter of whom he used as the inspiration for a brief series of biblical paintings, a 'Pieta' and a 'Good Samaritan', in the last few months of his life. His distaste for religious painting, however, was no indicator of his distaste for religion more generally. Rather, van Gogh — in very much the same vein as this present book — looked for the religious everywhere, and especially in the so-called secular. He found, as others have, more religious depth in many apparently 'non-religious' paintings than he did in those which blatantly, and often very naïvely, sought literally to represent the mystery of faith.

There is, of course, no shortage of symbolic references to the great biblical motifs in van Gogh's work. Everywhere in the later years there are olive groves, never letting us stray too far from the suffering of Jesus in the Garden of Gethsemane. There are sowers and reapers, and there is that brilliant yellow radiance bursting from sun, moon, stars and corn alike — symbolic expressions of the elusive mystery which is at the core of all authentic religion.

Back in 1882, in correspondence with Theo, van Gogh had actually written about his desire to express a feeling of '*quelque chose là-haut*', or

.ething above'. It was not uncommon for him to switch languages
.id-sentence in search of *le mot juste*. In the same letter, he cites Victor
Hugo's words, *'Les religions passent, mais Dieu demeur'* ('Religions pass
but God remains'). He then goes on to quote Gavarni before adding his
own reflection:

> . . . 'il s'agit de saisir ce qui ne passe pas, dans ce qui passe' [what mat-
> ters is to grasp what does not pass away in what passes away].
> One of the things 'qui ne passeront pas' [which will not pass away] is
> the 'quelque chose là-haut' [something above] and the belief in God,
> too, though the forms may change — a change which is just as neces-
> sary as the renewal of the leaves in spring.[25]

Just a little earlier he had written:

> When one is in a sombre mood, how good it is to walk on the barren
> beach and look at the grayish-green sea with the long white streaks of
> the waves. But if one feels the need of something grand, something infi-
> nite, something that makes one feel aware of God, one need not go far
> to find it. I think I see something deeper, more infinite, more eternal
> than the ocean in the expression of the eyes of a little baby when it
> wakes in the morning, and coos or laughs because it sees the sun shining
> on its cradle. If there is a rayon d'en haut [ray from above] perhaps one
> can find it there.[26]

This is not the testimony of someone who has lost his grip on the
Christian understanding of incarnation. This last quotation connects his
later experience back into his days in the Borinage, and forward into his
years as a painter of sun-scapes. The 'renewal of the leaves in spring'
became one of the signatures of his mature work; it is bracketed by the
work of sower and reaper, and is an expression of confidence in the life-
giving power of God's love.

All this is very much consistent with his use of the quotation from
Victor Hugo. What van Gogh left behind when he became a painter was
not his profound belief in God, but his deep aversion to the kind of

moralizing that he specifically associated with the religion of his family and their circle of acquaintances. As he wrote to Theo, back in his Etten days:

> To believe in God (that does not mean that you should believe all the sermons of the clergymen and the arguments and Jesuitism of the 'bégueules dévotes collet monté' [bigoted, genteel prudes], far from it); to me, to believe in God is to feel that there is a God, not dead or stuffed but alive, urging us toward aimer encore [to love more] with irresistible force — that is my opinion.[27]

When his own obsessive attempts as an evangelist ran cold, he rediscovered as a painter forms of Christian believing much more deeply true to his life experience, and infinitely more compatible with his intelligent and informed understanding of the contemporary world. Hugo, Michelet and Zola came back into their own, therefore, free to feed both his artistic and religious imagination.

It is almost inevitable that someone wrestling with such a profound commitment to the spiritual journey, especially one overlaid with the effects of such appalling illnesses, would litter his writings with comments open to ambiguous interpretation. In a single letter, written whilst in St Rémy, he managed to speak of his illness as tending 'to take an absurd religious turn' and, only a little later, to explain how 'religious thoughts sometimes greatly consoled' him.[28] We need to remember that none of his letters were written for publication anyway; they were simply part of a deeply personal exploration with his brother and a few other very close friends.

Van Gogh's mature religion expressed itself in two ways: in a search for human love — sadly, never fully realized on the scale for which he yearned in his dreams — and in his painting, which now he has passed to us as part of our lasting spiritual heritage. In his art, where he succeeded as magnificently as he failed in his human relationships, van Gogh laid trails of spiritual insight and wisdom, which it can still be our joy to uncover. His commitment to Christ was never really in question; but from the time when he painted Zola's novel alongside a Bible open at Isaiah 53, the Christ in whom he found consolation became ever more

ently the suffering Christ of the Garden, of the *via dolorosa*.
..ughout his life he harboured a nagging fear of 'success' — whatever
..would he make of the way his work is now revered? — and, as he became
more and more the victim of failing health, it was Christ broken in crucifixion that became his effective comfort.

Van Gogh despised what he called 'cleverness' in art and compared it
to 'self-righteousness' in religion. His own art, conformed more evidently
to the image of Christ, was bought at the price of much personal suffering
and was fired by the unpredictable genius of inspiration. To van Rappard,
he once wrote: 'art is something which, although produced by human
hands, is not created by these hands alone, but something which wells up
from a deeper source in our souls . . . .'[29] And to his brother, he wrote:
'the painted portraits have a life of their own, coming straight from the
painter's soul, which the machine cannot reach.'[30] These are not the
words of a madman, but a person of genuine spiritual substance, a person
who knew himself deeply, his strengths and weaknesses, and whose symbolic expression of that understanding in painted forms can be trusted.
Even in the final days of his life, we can still recognize intimations of a
depth in God, which held him firm even through the contradictory act of
his suicide.

As a last word in this section, it is appropriate to return to the words
of a sermon that van Gogh had preached back in 1876; it is the only full
sermon that remains in existence, and it is based on *The Pilgrim's
Progress*. The journeying motif is immediately reminiscent of the path-
ways in *Wheat Field with Crows*, and its final lines about human suffering
can now be heard with added pathos:

> Our life is a pilgrim's progress. I once saw a very beautiful picture: it
> was a landscape at evening. In the distance on the right-hand side a row
> of hills appeared blue in the evening mist. Above those hills the splen-
> dour of the sunset, the grey clouds with their linings of silver and gold
> and purple. The landscape is a plain or heath covered with grass and its
> yellow leaves, for it was in autumn. Through the landscape a road leads
> to a high mountain far, far away, on the top of that mountain is a city
> whereon the setting sun casts its glory. On the road walks a pilgrim,
> staff in hand. He has been walking for a good long while already and he

is very tired. And now he meets a woman, or figure in black, that makes
one think of St Paul's word: As being sorrowful yet always rejoicing.
That Angel of God has been placed there to encourage pilgrims and to
answer their questions and the pilgrim asks her: "Does the road go
uphill then all the way?"

And the answer is: "Yes to the very end."

And he asks again: "And will the journey take all day long?"

And the answer is: "From morn to night my friend."

And the pilgrim goes on sorrowful yet always rejoicing — sorrowful because it is so far off and the road so long. Hopeful as he looks up
to the eternal city far away, resplendent in the evening glow and he
thinks of the two old sayings that he heard long ago — the one is:

"Much strife must be striven
Much suffering must be suffered
Much prayer must be prayed
And then the end will be peace."

And the other is:

"The water comes up to the lips
But higher comes it not."[31]

Connections into our journeys of faith

It is hardly necessary further to spell out connections between van Gogh's
spiritual experience and its potential significance for our own journeys of
faith; much has already been implicit in the preceding pages. We will,
however, attempt to draw together some strands from this chapter around
three specific areas for reflection.

The first continues with the theme of van Gogh's and Christ's experience of suffering, and is a reflection on its connection with human
creativity. It is often said, perhaps sometimes rather glibly, that there is a
high price to pay for creativity; and it has been observed that many of the
artists — literary and musical as well as visual — we know best seem to
have led peculiarly tortured and unhappy lives. It is an observation that
can easily be overplayed and, equally, we can all think of examples to the
contrary. It remains true, however, that much we consider to be 'great' in
art also grows out of great suffering. The twentieth century epitomized
this theologically in a variety of ways; some of the best theological
insights of the century were the product of agonizing reflections on the

Jewish Holocaust, the threat of nuclear catastrophe and the impact of environmental damage on our planet. This focus on suffering, of course, is completely consistent with Christianity's most distinctive insight; namely, that God is uniquely present in and through God's own commitment to suffering love.

From his earliest days as an adult Christian, van Gogh had modelled himself on this Christ. Most clearly, this took the form of immersing himself in the life of peasant communities, first in his home region and then further afield. Even during the late 1870s, when his concern was passionately evangelistic, there was never a time when easy triumphalism over-rode his commitment to costly solidarity with those he found to be in pain. A letter to Theo from The Hague puts it in the wider context of his understanding of human love:

> I have already spoken a few words about the love for humanity which some people possess, for instance, Mme François in the book by Zola. However, I haven't any benevolent plans or projects for trying to help everybody, but I am not ashamed to say (though I know quite well that the word benevolence is in bad repute) that for my part I have always felt and will feel the need to love some fellow creature. Preferably, I don't know why, an unhappy, forsaken or lonely creature.
>
> Once I nursed for six weeks or two months a poor miserable miner who had been burned. I shared my food for a whole winter with a poor old man, and heaven knows what else . . .[32]

The hunger for giving and receiving human love, expressed in this letter as deep solidarity with a man in extreme distress, took its own toll on van Gogh's life. For whatever reason, his inability to form a much longed-for relationship in marriage left him lastingly frustrated; and his quests to discover fulfilment through sexual union took him into a succession of destructive relationships, which also did little to improve his standing amongst family and friends. It would be an injustice, however, to understate the depth of his commitment to those with whom he became involved, or the real quality of his evident caring.

My own view is that we can see the same compassionate qualities that fired his response to the sick miner surfacing again and again in his later years. The common factor is always his relentless commitment to hopefulness, a stolid belief in the cycle of sowing and reaping, of death and God's resurrecting life. There is much that we can learn from this commitment. It is at the heart of all good human living, and it is the *sine qua non* of good human dying. My guess is that it is, amongst other things, the product of a long and focused 'effort of attention' to the reality of the human condition. When tested in the fire, as van Gogh's hopefulness was tested on a scale known only to a few, his confident testimony becomes like healing balm for our own lives, able to strengthen our spirits and 'lighten our darkness'.

This takes us directly into my second reflection, which focuses specifically on van Gogh's experience of mental illness. For all we might like it not to be so, and for all the money and energy which goes into changing public opinion, the diagnosis of 'mental illness' remains a poisoned stigma on a sick person's life. There have been changes in British attitudes in recent years, it is true; the availability of public resources and the quality of care are unrecognizable compared with a matter of decades ago; but the fear associated with visits to a psychiatric clinic — either as a patient or as a caring companion — remains an indicator of just how deeply the poison has taken hold.

Van Gogh took the full brunt of this fear, both during his life and in the way that his reputation was manipulated following his death. My own judgment is that he faced this onslaught bravely in life, and that the inheritance he has left on canvas still has energy to eat away at public opinion more than a century later. As the twentieth century Existentialist writers were quick to show us, the border-line between sanity and madness is a very fine one. Most of us have dealings along the boundary at some time during our lives, and it is not always clear which side of the border is which. That such glorious painting can be fashioned in the border territory — where van Gogh spent so much of his life — is for me deeply moving and a source of enormous inspiration. It makes me want to challenge ever more forcibly the hidden, and sometimes not-so-hidden, assumptions of the society we live in, and it strengthens my own commitment to solidarity with those who, even if only for a time, experience the fearful mental disturbance which van Gogh knew only too well. As the last century has provided fresh images of Christ, enabling us to locate him ever more clearly in life's darkest moments, Christ the bearer of mental as well as physical pain is an image which we do well to foster.

My third, and final, reflection takes us back to the striking way in which *The Starry Night* was adopted by a whole generation of theologians more than half a century ago. Theirs was a painful time, with much intense suffering and heart-searching; like van Gogh, they discovered that the church as they knew it did not have the resources to sustain them in their time of need. The devastation of two World Wars and, since that time, vastly increased knowledge about the appalling conditions in which so great a proportion of the human population lives has exposed with clarity the desperate poverty of too much of the church's message. The response of Paul Tillich and others around the middle of the last century was, like van Gogh's, critical yet not without hope. They did not endorse the cry of their contemporaries, 'God is dead'; rather, they declared the church to be dying and desperately in need of God's renewal in love. No one should be complacent that enough has changed since those days. We have overseen a progressive decline in the size and significance of the churches in the western world. Claims that a turnabout has taken or is taking place are probably premature, more a symptom of despair than of genuine hope. It seems to me that, when and if a turnabout comes, it will not be measured by numbers professing their allegiance, but in the quality of the church's overall commitment to suffering love. This alone, almost despite itself, can release the floodgate of God's resurrecting life, and open up for us this extraordinary glimpse into the colours of darkness. This is what, in later life, van Gogh saw incarnate in his fields of wheat and in the night sky, as earlier he had seen it in the earthy lifestyle of peasants, their world defined by the shapes and colours of potatoes.

There is much to be learned here for our journey of faith. We must be challenged over and over again lest we relax into comfort and complacency about the church as we have it. Victor Hugo hit the nail on the head with his line, 'Religions pass but God remains' — and this includes Christianity (emphasizing the '-ity' rather than the 'Christian') no less than any other. Like van Gogh, we continue to be proud of Christ and seek to honour him in every possible way. Van Gogh reminds us, however, that God's vitality embodied in the person of Christ is not limited by the walls of the church, and we do well to listen and look for his signs outside as well as inside its boundaries.

Selected (and annotated) Bibliography

There is an enormous literature available to the English language reader exploring the life and works of van Gogh. In addition to books in some way used in the text of this chapter, therefore, it is only possible to offer a limited range of other resources. The catalogue still current at the Van Gogh Museum in Amsterdam is Ronald de Leeuw, *Van Gogh at the Van Gogh Museum* (Zwolle: Waanders Publishers, 1994).

There are a wide range of monographs, which vary in quality of reproduction and quality of research. For completeness and amazingly good value, little can beat Inigo Walther and Rainer Metzger, *Vincent van Gogh: the Complete Paintings,* One Volume Edition (Cologne: Benedikt Taschen, 1977).

Other important monographs include Melissa McQuillan, *Van Gogh* (London: Thames and Hudson, 1989); and Franco Vedovollo, *Vincent: The Works of Vincent van Gogh*, trans. Arnoldo Mondadori (New York: Smithmark, 1990).

For the analysis of an individual picture, there is an engaging study of *The Potato Eaters:* Louis van Tilborgh (ed.), *The Potato Eaters by Vincent van Gogh* (Zwolle: Cahier Vincent 5, Waanders Publishers, 1993).

Quotations from van Gogh's letters are all taken from *The Complete Letters of Vincent van Gogh*, 3 vols. (London: Thames and Hudson, 1958). There is, however, a useful edited collection of letters: Mark Roskill, *The Letters of Vincent van Gogh* (London: Flamingo, 1983).

Words and pictures come together in a beautifully produced volume, Bruce Bernard (ed.), *Vincent by Himself* (Boston, New York and London: Little, Brown and Company, 1985).

On wide-ranging issues associated with questions about symbolism in his paintings, and the particular orientation of van Gogh's religious convictions, see H. R. Graetz, *The Symbolic Language of Vincent van Gogh* (London: Thames and Hudson, 1963); Tsukusa Kõdera, *Vincent van Gogh: Christianity Versus Nature* (Amsterdam and Philadelphia: John Benjamins, 1990); and Kathleen Powers Erickson, *At Eternity's Gate: the Spiritual Vision of Vincent van Gogh* (Grand Rapids and Cambridge: Eerdmans, 1998).

Detailed studies of the relationship of his work to that of earlier artists, and importantly Millet, are also many. See, for example, Louis van Tilborough, *Van Gogh and Millet* (Zwolle: Waanders Publishers, 1989).

On the study of colour, such a significant theme in the work of van Gogh as well as more generally, I can thoroughly recommend John Gage, *Colour and Culture: Practice and Meaning from Antiquity to Abstraction* (London: Thames and Hudson, 1995); Trevor Lamb and Janine Bourriau (eds.), *Colour: Art & Science* (Cambridge: Cambridge University Press, 1995); and Edith Anderson Feisner, *Colour: How to Use Colour in Art and Design* (London: Laurence King, 2000).

There are some useful essays, one specifically on van Gogh's use of colour, in John Walker, *Van Gogh Studies: Five Critical Essays* (London: JAW Publications, 1981).

Connections into the theology of Paul Tillich and his contemporaries include James Luther Adams (ed.), *The Thought of Paul Tillich* (London: Harper Row, 1985); Paul Tillich, 'Existentialist Aspects of Modern Art,' in Carl Michalson (ed.), *Christianity and the Existentialists* (New York: Charles Scribner's Sons, 1956); Paul Tillich, *Theology of Culture* (New York and Oxford: Oxford University Press, 1959); and Wilhelm & Marion Pauck, *Paul Tillich: His Life and Thought*, vol. 1 (London: Collins, 1977), especially pp. 75-79.

Quotations from the work of Walt Whitman are taken from Walt Whitman, *The Complete Poems* (London: Penguin Books, London, 1975).

Notes

This chapter is primarily the work of Richard Kidd.

[1] Letter T110 (Amsterdam, 18 September 1877), *The Complete Letters of Vincent van Gogh*, 3 vols. (London: Thames and Hudson, 1958), vol. 1, pp. 140-41.

[2] Letter T79 (Isleworth, October 1876), *Complete Letters*, vol. 1, p. 73.

[3] Letter W1 (Paris, Summer or Autumn 1887), *Complete Letters*, vol. 3, p. 427.

[4] Letter T405 (Nuenen, May 1885), *Complete Letters*, vol. 2, p. 372.

[5] Letter T405 (Nuenen, May 1885), *Complete Letters*, vol. 2, p. 372.

[6] Tsukasa Kōdera , *Vincent van Gogh: Christianity versus Nature* (Amsterdam/Philadelphia: John Benjamins Publishing Company, 1990); see especially pp. 13-26.

[7] Kathleen Powers Erickson, *At Eternity's Gate: the Spiritual Vision of Vincent van Gogh* (Grand Rapids and Cambridge: Eerdmans, 1998), p. 179.

[8] Letter T404 (Nuenen, 30 April 1885), *Complete Letters*, vol. 2, p. 371.

[9] Letter T404 (Nuenen, 30 April 1885), *Complete Letters*, vol. 2, p. 370.

[10] Letter R51a (Utrecht, 24 May 1885) *Complete Letters*, vol. 3, p410.

[11] Letter R57 (September 1885), *Complete Letters*, vol. 3, pp. 418ff.

[12] Letter T533 (Arles, 8 September 1888), *Complete Letters*, vol. 3, p. 28.

[13] Letter T543 (Arles, September 1888), *Complete Letters*, vol. 3, p. 56.

[14] Catalogue written for the exhibition 'Masterpieces of Religious Art', held in connection with the Second Assembly of the World Council of Churches at the Art Institute of Chicago, 15 July to 15 August 1954; quoted in H. R. Graetz, *The Symbolic Language of Vincent van Gogh* (London: Thames and Hudson, 1963), p. 212.

[15] Quoted in James Luther Adams (ed.), *The Thought of Paul Tillich* (London: Harper Row, 1985), opposite p. 1.

[16] 'Pictures' in *Walt Whitman, The Complete Poems* (London: Penguin Books, 1975), p. 665, lines 12-14.

[17] Ibid., line 9.

[18] 'Night on the Prairies' in *Walt Whitman, The Complete Poems*, p. 465, lines 9-17.

[19] 'As I Watch'd the Ploughman Ploughing' in *Walt Whitman, The Complete Poems*, p. 467, lines 1-4.

[20] 'Memories of President Lincoln' in *Walt Whitman, The Complete Poems*, p. 351, lines 1-3.

[21] Letter W8 (Arles, September/October 1888), *Complete Letters*, vol. 3, p. 445.

[22] Quoted in Kathleen Powers Erickson, *At Eternity's Gate: the Spiritual Vision of Vincent van Gogh*, p. 182.

[23] Letter T543 (Arles, September 1888), *Complete Letters*, vol. 3, p. 56.

[24] Letter T595 (St Rémy, 19 June 1889), *Complete Letters*, vol. 3, p. 183.

[25] Letter T253 (The Hague, December 1882), *Complete Letters*, vol. 1, p. 513.

[26] Letter T242 (The Hague, November 1882), *Complete Letters*, vol. 1, p. 483.

[27] Letter T161 (Etten, 23 November 1881), *Complete Letters*, vol. 1, p. 274.

[28] Letter T605 (St Rémy, 10 September 1889), *Complete Letters*, vol. 3, p. 208.

[29] Letter R43 (Nuenen, April 1884), *Complete Letters*, vol. 3, pp. 399-400.

[30] Letter T439 (Antwerp, December 1885), *Complete Letters*, vol. 2, p. 459.

[31] Sermon, printed between letters dated 31 December 1876 and 21 January 1877, *Complete Letters*, vol. 1, pp. 90-91.

[32] Letter T219 (The Hague, July 1882), *Complete Letters*, vol. 1, p. 420.

GENERAL INDEX